PARADI
ON FII

In a time of universal deceit – telling the truth is a revolutionary act.

George Orwell

PARADISE ON FIRE

*Syed Ali Geelani and the Struggle
for Freedom in Kashmir*

Abdul Hakeem

Revival

Paradise on Fire: Syed Ali Geelani and the Struggle for Freedom in Kashmir

Published in England by
Revival Publications
Markfield Conference Centre
Ratby Lane, Markfield
Leicestershire LE67 9SY
United Kingdom

Distributed by
Kube Publishing Ltd.
Tel: +44 (0)1530 249230
Fax: +44 (0)1530 249656
Email: publications@islamic-foundation.com

Cataloguing-in-Publication Data
is available from the British Library

ISBN 978-0-95367-684-2 *paperback*
ISBN 978-0-95367-685-9 *casebound*

10 9 8 7 6 5 4 3 2 1

Cover design: Fatima Jamadar
Book design: Naiem Qaddoura
Typesetting: Abu Abida

Printed by IMAK Ofset, Turkey

CONTENTS

LIST OF IMAGES

FOREWORD

When a man is denied the right to live the life he believes in, he has no choice but to become an outlaw. — Nelson Mandela

PEACE IS A universal human yearning. Every society and every people need peace in order to flourish and to develop their resources, both individually and nationally. Nor is peace the mere absence of war. For peace of heart, mind and society can only exist when accompanied by the weighty presence of justice.

More than fifteen million people of the State of Jammu and Kashmir (J&K) have been denied justice for the past six decades. Kashmiris exist in a permanent state of violent occupation by Indian forces. An occupation that, at this time, has 800,000 troops, controlling a region of breathtaking natural beauty. The violence of these troops has turned a place of mountains, valleys and rivers, once known as 'Paradise on Earth', into the largest open air prison in the world. A civilian pressure cooker that would be instantly recognizable to the people of the Gaza Strip. In Kashmir, non-violent protests for water, electricity and the freedom to travel, are met with the bullets of the occupying troops. And accompanied by the threat of imprisonment. Meanwhile, the international community looks on, shakes its head, expressing 'concern', issuing 'reports' and effectively doing nothing.

The Indian research scholar Abdul Hakim has produced a comprehensive study of the nature of the Kashmir struggle for freedom in providing a biography of its most vibrant voice, Syed Ali Shah Geelani, showing his vision and determination. For the past two decades, Syed Geelani has been the primary symbol of the Kashmiri people's efforts towards self-determination. Like other great figures of our age, men who have committed themselves to fighting apartheid and occupation, Nelson Mandela and Shaykh Raed Salah of Palestine (to name but two), Geelani is no stranger to incarceration. His galvanising calls for a widespread non-violent resistance, including strikes, have seen him imprisoned for sixteen years in a variety of regional gulags.

This book, then, is the story of one man's self-sacrifice told through the struggle of an entire people. *Paradise on Fire* is a call to the conscience of humanity. I pray that people from every part of the world will respond to this call and join the Kashmiri people in their non-violent resistance to oppression and occupation.

Free Kashmir, free Palestine!

Lauren Booth
London
October 2013

PREFACE

WALTER SISULU, the long-time comrade of Nelson Mandela, and for twenty years his prison mate, urged Mandela on his 57th birthday (18 July 1975) to write his memoirs: 'such a story, told truly and fairly, would serve to remind people of what we had fought and were still fighting for' and be 'a source of inspiration for young freedom fighters.'[1] That prompt explains my motivation for narrating Syed Ali Geelani's contribution to the Kashmiri freedom struggle. *The Economist* (29 December 2010) referred to Geelani as the 'highest-profile' Kashmiri leader and 'elderly icon', and doubted 'that anyone among a handful of potential successors could command as much local respect'.

The *Arab News* (17 August 2010) declared him 'the undisputed leader of the insurgency' and confirmed that 'India has consistently tried to court him but he has refused to take the bait.' Geelani has spent over sixteen of his eighty-three years of life in prison, and written (in Urdu) about thirty books. The second edition of his autobiography *Wular Kinaray* (*On the bank of Lake Wular*) was released in July 2012. 'Its first edition was completely sold out within a week. Those who were keen to read it included [...] civil and military elites of every shade of opinion' (review in *Greater Kashmir*, 30 July 2011). However, the story of his self-sacrificing contributions to freedom and justice in Kashmir has not been communicated plainly to the wider audience that can be reached by writing in English.

I have known Geelani for about twenty years and had dozens of meetings with him. Of course, he is not my only source. I have sought information from a variety of public and private sources, especially those close to Geelani. For reasons of confidentiality and security, I have withheld the dates and venues of personal interviews and other detail about some of my sources. This book is the outcome of decades of closely following events in Kashmir, and some four years of reflection and further enquiry during the writing. I have strived to present Geelani 'as he is', without seeking to build him up as a hero or a vilian.

I have done my best to cover briefly the major events of Geelani's political life. My narrative does not follow a strictly chronological line; it is, instead, arranged around broad topics that are crucial to understanding Geelani and the Kashmiri freedom movement over the last quarter century. While he is not present on every page, Geelani's own views are cited or referred to throughout the book.

Geelani took on the might of India and almost single-handedly put the Jammu & Kashmir (J&K) dispute on the international stage. His personality can be summed up in Nelson Mandela's words: 'time and again, I have seen men and women risk and give their lives for an idea. I have seen men standing up to attacks and torture without breaking, showing strength and resilience that defies the imagination.'[2] Geelani has dedicated a lifetime to advocacy of justice and piety; that is why this book cannot just be an individual's life story, it has to present the major ideas that he has lived and sacrificed for.

Under the Indian Independence Act of 1947, J&K was free to accede to India or Pakistan. Its Hindu ruler, Maharaja Hari Singh, wanted to stay independent but eventually signed over key powers to the Indian government in return for military aid and a promised referendum. The promised referendum never happened. Kashmir has been the flashpoint for two of the three India–Pakistan wars: in 1947–48 and 1965. In 1999, India fought a short, bitter battle with Pakistan-backed militants who had moved into the Kargil area.

Over the course of their struggle, many Kashmiri 'pro-freedom leaders' have sold out in one way or another and earned the approbation of the Indian establishment as 'moderates'. Geelani on the other hand has *always* been called an 'extremist'. When the 'Quit Kashmir' movement was launched in the summer of 2010, the entire 'moderate leadership' looked like quislings next to 'extremist' Geelani.

The late Barry Goldwater, Republican Senator for Arizona, said: 'Extremism in the pursuit of liberty is no vice. Moderation in the pursuit of justice is no virtue.'[3] Geelani's life-long mission has been to compel India to fulfil its explicit commitment, to the international community and to the people of J&K, to allow Kashmiris to determine their future. Like all freedom fighters struggling under occupation, he has had to endure immense personal suffering, including torture, intimidation, assassination attempts and frequent incarcerations.

'To openly stress that Kashmir is disputed and hence needs to be settled is to stand accused of being anti-national', wrote Rahul Bedi (*The Pioneer*, 1 June 1996). Similarly, Oxford scholar Sarmila Bose argued: 'The Kashmir conflict not only inflicts unspeakable suffering on all its people, it affects the well-being of the rest of India. It weakens India's constitutional structure, pollutes the political system, drains the economy, misplaces security forces, destabilizes regional and international relations, and destroys India's moral position in the world community.' (*The Telegraph*, 5 April 1996)

I happily disclose that I am an Indian Muslim; I grew up in a highly secular environment, studied and worked with Hindus, and count some of them among best friends. I can vouch for their decency and sense of justice in general. I love my country dearly and do not wish it to be counted among the most brutal regimes in the world. As a civilized country, it should gracefully and honestly fulfil all its commitments made in the past to both Kashmiris and its own citizens – particularly minorities.

I show in this book that Indian minorities in general and Muslims in particular are suffering equally, if not more, at the hands of the same Indian rulers who are brutalizing and slaughtering Kashmiris. According to prominent Indian journalist Siddhartha Vardarajan, 'most large scale incidents of communal violence [against Muslims] have occurred only because the ruling party has either willed them or allowed them to happen'.[4] The chapter devoted to Kashmir's neighbors Afghanistan, Pakistan and Muslims in India touches upon the sufferings of these peoples as a result of the Western/Indian 'war on terror'. It may be of some comfort to Kashmiris to know that they are not standing alone in the line of Indian fire.

The renowned political commentator, A. G. Noorani wrote (*Economic & Political Weekly*, 6 August 1994): 'politicians in power and journalists close to them do suggest that it is unpatriotic to criticize the government's policies or the misdeeds of the security forces.' In a recent article, Pritish Nandy said of India: 'We are a nation in desperate search of villains.'[5] That is why I have opted to write under a pseudonym. If I did not, the Indian government would detain me for sedition; the intelligence agencies label me a 'Pakistani agent'; the police harass and the security forces torture me; the media would demonize me and the judiciary convict me. Also the society would, by and large, isolate me and my entire family.

I must state the obvious that these components of Indian establishment, individually or collectively, are not naïve. They will not do any of the above to me for writing this book. They will instead implicate me for some state-orchestrated violence or any other trumped up charge. In future, I will gladly reveal my identity if ever India behaves constitutionally and practises secular democracy.

To borrow from American filmmaker and activitist Michael Moore (*Financial Times*, 16 September 2011): 'I love this country but loving it doesn't mean silence or turning your head the other way when you see things are going wrong.' Indian Muslims are patriots. They have no secessionist aspirations. Nor do they have more violent tendencies than any other ethnic group. When Pakistan came into being, they chose to stay in plural India, to live side-by-side with their Hindu fellow citizens. They continue to live in and love their homeland despite the many atrocities committed over the last sixty-six years. On any objective assessment, the biggest threat to India's security and stability is not posed by Muslims but Maoists; and a handful of what a senior Indian National Congress leader called 'saffron terrorists'.

The vast majority of Indian Muslims have never been terrorists and will never carry out terrorist activities: doing so is against their religious teachings. It was not Muslims who killed Gandhi, or Indira, or Rajiv, or Karkare. Yes, for the first time in independent India, a brave and honest police officer Hemant Karkare was trying to pin down saffron terrorists. He was conveniently eliminated by those he was about to unmask! Ram Puniyani's *Malegaon to Ajmer* gives ample details.[6] India needs many Karkares and Puniyanis to liberate itself from the clutches of the real terrorists.

Fascist Indians regularly threaten India's Muslims with grave consequences if Kashmir is separated from India. But in reality, Muslims have been slaughtered throughout the country since 1947 while Kashmir has remained very much a part of India. Sarmila Bose (*The Telegraph*, 5 April 1996): 'The political exit of any part of Kashmir will not cause the rest of India to fall apart. Rather its forcible inclusion insults India's professed political values, obstructs the economic prosperity of the whole region and disgraces Indians in terms of morality, humanity and civilization. India should own up to its shameful record in Kashmir and start to set things right. It is the only way forward and it is the only decent thing to do.'

Throughout the book I have indicated parallels between the Kashmiri freedom struggle and two other great freedom movements in the last part of the twentieth century, South Africa and Bosnia. Like Kashmir, both these countries experienced widespread bloodshed but, in the end, there was nowhere to go except the negotiation table. In both cases, the freedom movement won. The sooner India negotiates with Geelani and his party, the better it will be for Kashmir and the whole South Asian region.

Indian sociologist and writer Ashish Nandy observed (*Hindustan Times*, 6 August 2011): 'During the last century [the] most atrocious cruelty has been committed *not* in the name of religion (though we might like to believe that) but in the name of reason and aesthetics. And secular states have killed more people than non-secular states.' Geelani is a deeply religious man, about whom Dr. Javid Iqbal wrote: 'Take it or not, it has to be understood that his politics is Islam-centric' (*Greater Kashmir*, 8 August 2011). That is why it is appropriate to present many aspects of Geelani's struggle in the light of the Qur'an and the Hadith of Prophet Muhammad, God pray over him and grant him peace.

The US and its allies – both Muslim and non-Muslim – are commiting crimes against humanity in general and Muslims in particular. On the other side, there are (among Muslims and non-Muslims) forces of truth and compassion, of which Geelani is a part. Muslims are weak and divided at the moment but picking up strength in scattered pockets here and there. I refer in places to topics not directly connected to Geelani or Kashmir but relevant to how the US sustains its hegemony and how it impacts Geelani and Kashmir. Kashmiris are most unlikely to achieve their right of self-determination until truly independent Muslims (not compliant US allies), regionally and globally, regain a certain power threshold.

1

THE DISPUTE

TARUN VIJAY is a Rashtriya Swyamsevak Sangh (RSS) ideologue and an MP representing the Bhartiya Janata Party (BJP). A former editor of India's leading English daily *The Times of India*, he pronounced in his editorial of 31 May 2008 that 'people who remember their past have a future.' Led by Geelani, Kashmiris have proven beyond doubt that they remember their past.

1.1 Map of Jammu and Kashmir

Jammu and Kashmir (J&K) occupies some 222,870 square kilometres in the strategic, extreme northwest of the Subcontinent next to Afghanistan (northwest), the Sinkiang-Uighur region of China (north), Tibet (east), the Indian states of Himachal and Punjab (south), and the Pakistani provinces of Frontier and Punjab (west). No census has been carried out in J&K since 1981; its population is estimated at 12.54 million, with Muslims the largest group. The Kashmir valley itself is not very long – about 170 kilometres from Banihal in the south to Kupwara in the north, and about 80 kilometres from Gulmarg in the west to Kangan in the east. The Jhelum river flows through the valley, first northward, then bending south-west before crossing through the Uri gap into Pakistan-administered Kashmir (PaK). The Jhelum makes the Valley extremely fertile; the main urban centres are situated on its banks.

The Valley is densely populated, with semi-urban clusters of mostly wooden houses. It is not completely flat – there are a series of outcrops called *karaves*, the largest being the one on which Srinagar airport is built. The *karaves* are cut by gullies, in parts uncultivable and thickly wooded – terrain perfectly suited for guerrilla warfare. This topographical advantage was highlighted by Syed Salahuddin – Supreme Commander of Hizbul Mujahideen (HM), the largest Kashmiri armed group fighting Indian occupation forces – when I asked him how long militants could stand up to the Indian military.

Rinchan, a Buddhist ruler of Kashmir embraced Islam in 1320 at the hand of Syed Bulbul Shah. Persian scholar and missionary, Sayyid Ali Hamadani also played a pivotal role in spreading Islamic values. Islam consolidated its hold during Shah Mir's reign (1339–44). Independent Sultans ruled till 1586 followed by Mughals (1586–1753); and Afghans (1753–1819).

The era of Afghan rule was harsh and oppressive, with burdensome taxation and frequent Shia–Sunni riots. Thereafter, Kashmir became one of the roughly 584 princely states in India under the direct or indirect control of the British Empire. Gulab Singh was the ruler of an erstwhile Sikh kingdom. The British rewarded his neutrality during the first Anglo–Sikh war, by literally selling him the Kashmir Valley for Rs. 7.5 million. Thus, the Dogra dynasty was established on the betrayal of India's freedom movement against British occupation. Salahuddin explained this further in an interview to an Indian news portal:[2]

> In 1819 Maharaja Ranjit Singh conquered Kashmir, but his disorganized empire fell to the British in 1846 when they took control of Punjab. Kashmir was then sold to the self-titled Maharaja Ghulab Singh of Jammu for Rs 7.5 million under the Treaty of Amritsar.

> Ghulab Singh also brought Ladakh, Zanskar, Gilgit and Baltistan under his control. A succession of [Hindu] Maharajas followed, marked by several uprisings by the Kashmiri people, of whom a large percentage was now Muslim. In 1889 Maharaja Pratap Singh lost administrative authority [over] Kashmir due to the worsening management of the frontier region. The British restored full powers to Dogra rule only in 1921.

Tavleen Singh, an honest and courageous Indian journalist, observed in her landmark book *Kashmir: A Tragedy of Errors* (1995), p.xiv:

> Dogra rule was hated because Muslims, who constituted the majority of the population, were discriminated against in every way. [...] Kashmiri Muslims with extremely low literacy levels were mainly landless peasants and craftsmen with almost no hope of bettering their lives.

Formal annulment of the Ottoman caliphate in 1924 led to popular agitations across the Islamic world. In India while the Hindu-dominated Indian National Congress (for its political reasons) supported the Khilafah movement, the 'J&K government banned it.'[3] Sir Albion Bannerji, appointed in 1929 to a senior post in the Council of the State of J&K, quit before his two years were up, commenting: 'There is no touch between the government and the [largely Muslim] people, no suitable opportunity for representing grievances and the administrative machinery itself requires over-hauling from top to bottom.... It has at present no sympathy with the people's wants and grievances.'[4]

The brutal Dogra autocracy triggered a revolt in 1931, which was ruthlessly crushed with 22 Muslims killed. Another eruption in 1946 against the Hindu ruler Maharaja Hari Singh led to the formation of a Muslim government-in-exile in August 1947. At an annual session of the National Conference in Sopore, India's first Prime Minister Jawaharlal Nehru was invited as a guest speaker. Addressing Kashmiri Muslims he conceded: '[the] Dogra government forced you to lead a subhuman existence.'[5]

Until Partition in 1947, Kashmir retained its historic links with Central Asia: the mail passed through normally; Russian Muslims came down through Gilgit to go on the pilgrimage to Makkah. Weakened after 1947, these ancient links are now 'extinct' (*Frontline*, 23 March 2012). Gandhi, speaking at Wah on 5 August 1947, affirmed that the will of the Kashmiri people was the supreme law in J&K, and that this was acknowledged by the Maharaja and Maharani themselves. He had read the so-called 'Treaty of Amritsar,' which was in reality a deed of sale; he fully expected it to be defunct in August 1947. Gandhi believed that sheer common sense made it obvious that the will of the Kashmiris should decide the fate of J&K, and the sooner it was done, the better. (cited in *The Indian Express*, 23 August 2000)

Under the terms of Partition, all princely states under British rule had to accede to India or Pakistan, except that to do the latter (a) the majority population of the territory had to be Muslim and (b) its borders contiguous with the territory that would become Pakistan. It happens that (as noted in prominent Indian magazine, *The Outlook* (9 July 1997)): 'Most people of Jammu and Kashmir were Muslims, the ruler was Hindu. Its transport links were mainly with the areas that would become Pakistan, the rivers which transported its timber flowed in the same direction [...] the case to include it in Pakistan was hard to rebut.' For all that, the Indian governments argue that the 1947 Indian Independence Act did not envisage the division of princely states on the basis of majority subjects' religion.

The wishes of the majority Muslim Kashmiris were ignored by the Hindu ruler of J&K who hit back hard at protests. According to Geelani,[6] 'In just a few weeks, in late 1947, Dogra forces and Hindu chauvinists in Jammu killed some five lakh Muslims.' Muslims in the Poonch district rose up against the Hindu rulers. In his book *Kashmir: The Unwritten History*, Christopher Snedden, an Australian author and academic specializing in South Asian studies, 'dismisses India's claim that Pakhtoon tribesmen [from the Frontier province] stoked the Kashmir conflict in October 1947.' He adds that 'there is the secret correspondence between Jawaharlal Nehru and Sardar Patel making it clear that they were aware of what was going on [i.e. it was a local uprising].'[7]

When Muslims from the Frontier region came to help Kashmiri Muslims, the Maharaja fled his capital, Srinagar, and called in Indian government troops, accepting the condition that he sign the instrument of accession to India. Aware that such a decision made under duress would be of questionable legal weight, the Indian government clearly agreed that the accession was provisional and subject to 'reference to the people'.

Captain Dewan Singh was the Assistant of Maharaja Hari Singh. In a 2 June 1994 report in the Indian daily, *The Telegraph*, Captain Singh described the momentous event on the eve of 26 October 1947. The seventy-five-year-old Assistant of the then ruler said the atmosphere was choked with tension as he waited in Jammu palace outside the room where the Maharaja signed the instruments of accession with India. He recalled: the last viceroy of British India Louis Mountbatten had advised Maharaja Hari Singh to join Pakistan in the tense days leading to Indian independence. Being a Muslim majority region, Lord Mountbatten reasoned, it made sense for Hari Singh to opt for Pakistan. But Kashmir's ruler was staunchly pro-India. He was to meet Lord Mountbatten the following day for further consultations. But he cried off, pleading ill health, says Dewan Singh. And the meeting, which would definitely have changed the Subcontinent's history, never took place.

The accession of Kashmir to India is analogous to the annexation of Texas by the USA. When Mexico separated from the Spanish

Empire and became an independent republic, Texas was an integral part of it. Later, Texas rebelled, declared independence from Mexico and had its new status recognized by the USA and the major powers of Europe. Threatened by incursions from Mexico, the Texas governement asked the US to annex it in 1844, a 'request' approved by the US Congress in March 1845 and followed by the deployment of American troops to the boundary of Texas. The government of Mexico at the time protested strongly and suspended diplomatic relations. This history (along with other factors discussed later in this book) makes continued US support for Indian occupation of J&K more likely.

Since Muslims from the Frontier had taken a part of the J&K state (the part now known as PaK), India brought the issue to the United Nations (UN) in January 1948. India accused Pakistan of sending 'armed raiders' and urged the UN to compel Pakistan to withdraw. According to Salahuddin: 'The British government at that time [of Partition] played a very bad role. Kashmir is the unfinished agenda of 1947. Even today there is no legal succession document and that is why India lost its case in the United Nations.'[8]

After UN intervention, armed hostilities halted at the Ceasefire Line or Line of Control (LoC). India assured the UN that, following the withdrawal of 'raiders', it would hold a plebiscite. Pakistan challenged Kashmir's accession, accusing India of using 'fraud and violence' in this process, and offered a plebiscite under UN supervision to settle the dispute.

On 21 April 1948, the UN Security Council (UNSC) passed a resolution ordering (a) ceasefire, (b) withdrawal of outside forces from J&K and (c) a plebiscite under the control of an administrator nominated by the UN Secretary-General. A UN Commission for India and Pakistan (UNCIP) was formed to work out the mechanism for plebiscite. After a (never explained) delay of 76 days, UNCIP members arrived in the Subcontinent on 7 July 1948 despite the UNSC instruction 'to proceed at once' and enter into intensive negotiations with both governments at the highest level towards formulating an agreement to a ceasefire and synchronise withdrawal of all regular Pakistani forces and the bulk of Indian forces (constituting a truce between the two sides) and reaffirmation that 'future status of the State shall be determined in accordance with the will of the people'. Thereafter:

On 13 August UNCIP adopted a Resolution, which is a draft agreement committing the Pakistan and India governments that the 'future status of the State of Jammu and Kashmir shall be determined in accordance with the will of the people.'[9]

On 20 August, Prime Minister Nehru wrote to UNCIP Chairman stating that his government 'have decided to accept the Resolution.' On the basis of India's understanding (stated in the letter) of several key terms of the Resolution, Pakistani Foreign Minister Zafrullah Khan sought 'elucidations' from UNCIP regarding its proposals and the explanations it had given to India. He expressed reservations about ambiguity on the specifics of the plebiscite. UNCIP decided to return to Geneva to prepare an interim report for UNSC.

On 11 December, UNCIP supplemented its August 13 Resolution with provisions regarding conduct and conditions of the proposed plebiscite, which both India and Pakistan accepted in communications dated, respectively, 23 and 25 December. The proposals as thus agreed to by both governments were embodied later in the UNCIP Resolution of 5 January 1949.

The peace settlement envisaged three stages: ceasefire, truce (synchronized withdrawals of forces), and plebiscite.

Joseph Korbel, a member of the UNCIP, was quoted in *Muslim India* (#188, August 1998):

> The Security Council nominated a prominent Australian jurist and member of the High Court of Justice, Sir Owen Dixon, as the United Nations Representative. The reaction in India and Kashmir was not calculated to inspire him with self-confidence....

> Sir Owen Dixon arrived in the Sub-Continent on May 27, 1950.... He visited the capitals of both countries, traveled extensively in Kashmir, and on July 20 opened a four-day conference in New Delhi with the Prime Minister of India,

Jawaharlal Nehru, and the Prime Minister of Pakistan, Liaquat Ali Khan. He did not leave for the record any document about the day to day activities, but every scrap of information available and his subsequent report to the Security Council marks him as a great man, a keen observer with a penetrating analytical mind and a state of justice....

The resolution of the Security Council had called on both parties to prepare and execute the demilitarization of Kashmir within five months.... This was followed by a request to both sides to demilitarize the territory to a minimum of forces (Azad, state troops, Indian army, and local militia) consistent with law and order. The Prime Minister of Pakistan agreed to take the first step to withdraw the Pakistan army. But Sir Owen's gratification was short-lived. The plan for demilitarization was rejected by India.

(*Danger in Kashmir* (Princeton University Press, 1954), 362)

With all avenues for a negotiated settlement exhausted, Sir Owen Dixon left the Subcontinent on 23 August 1950.

Our double-speak continued. Nehru said in a Report to the All India Congress Committee, on 6 July 1951 (cited in *Muslim India*, #196 (April 1999)): 'Kashmir is not a commodity or sale to be bartered. It has individual existence and its people must be the final arbiters of their future.' Then again, as quoted by Geelani in his book *The Oppressed Nation*, Nehru told the Indian Parliament on 7 August 1952: 'the promise we have made with the people of Jammu & Kashmir is not only with them but also with the people of Pakistan and the whole world and we shall fulfil it in any case. If the people of Jammu and Kashmir decide to part company with us, we shall be pained no doubt, but we shall accept their decision and shall not prevent them by use of force.'[10]

Kashmiris are not uniquely the victims of the UN's failure to resolve international disputes effectively and impartially. Many well-informed writers and statesmen have remarked this failure and tried to come to terms with its causes. The reluctance of the major powers (most often the US) to implement international law fairly and impartially, unless it suits their 'interests', is most painful for the victims of political injustice. (See for example: Col. Nanda;[11] Nelson Mandela;[12] former Singapore Prime Minister Lee Kuan Yew;[13] most poignantly, former Bosnian President Alija Izetbegovic[14]).

Dr Ghulam Nabi Fai is the President of the Kashmiri American Council. In June 2011, he had complained that 'the United Nations is invidiously selective about the application of the principles of human rights and democracy'.[15] The FBI arrested Fai in mid-July 2011 on the charge of working for the Pakistani government. The mainstream media and government in India rejoiced. However, *The Washington Post* (20 July 2011) explained Fai's arrest as a response to the detention of CIA agents in Pakistan. It commented: 'Dr Fai is a genuine Kashmiri leader and a responsible US citizen. He should not become a casualty of the intelligence agencies' turf war.'

Praveen Swami, writing in *The Hindu* (21 July 2011), confirms Fai as an important, legitimate ambassador of the Kashmir cause: 'His arrest is the result of India's diplomatic efforts and conspiracies.... His only crime is that he is a freedom-loving man.' Addressing a seminar in December 2011, Geelani likewise defended Fai as a legitimate lobbyist for the Kashmiri people, 'pleading the genuine cause which is supported by the resolutions of the United Nations.'[16]

Nevertheless, Fai was sentenced (30 March 2012) to two years imprisonment. In handing down the sentence, Judge Liam O'Grady told Fai that the sentence was 'necessary, even though you have done some very moving things on behalf of the Kashmir people and though your cause is a wonderful cause.'[17] Geelani described this verdict as 'a contemptible attempt to appease India'.[18]

Before the US adopted an openly biased stand in favour of India, former president Bill Clinton considered Kashmir 'the most dangerous place on Earth'.[19] This disputed territory has triggered three wars between India and Pakistan in the past. Now, these neighbours possess nuclear arms with the long-range missiles to deliver them. A Brookings Institution report notes that 'the nuclear tests of 1998 and declaration of nuclear power by both states persuaded many outsiders that South Asia, especially Kashmir, had become a nuclear flashpoint.'[20]

After grabbing the state illegally, our bias against its citizens was growing. In a 1953 letter to Minister for Communications, Jagjivan Ram, then Education Minister Maulana Azad writes: 'As many as 53 persons from Jammu and Kashmir apply for a clerical post and only one is appointed. The rest are from outside the state. This baffles me. Obviously those in charge of recruitments are not sensitive to the fact that such instances complicate our stand on the question of Kashmir,' (*The Sunday Guardian*, 21 February 2013).

On 31 March 1955, Prime Minister Nehru stated (once more) on the floor of Indian Parliament that 'Kashmir is not a thing to be bandied about between India and Pakistan but it has a soul of its own and an individuality of its own. Nothing can be done without the goodwill and consent of the people of Kashmir.'[21] Sadly, this too remained an empty promise. We (the people of India) grabbed J&K against the will of its people. Then we gave it a special status under our Constitution pending final settlement. For example, citizens of India are not *ipso facto* citizens of J&K, cannot (even after years of residence) settle there permanently or hold property or vote in elections to the J&K at state or local levels.

A woman citizen of J&K loses her property and other rights if she marries a non-state subject. Article 360 of the Indian Constitution permitting a declaration of financial emergency does not extend to J&K; nor does Article 365 authorizing the President to issue directions to the state government, in exercise of the executive powers of the Union. Article 352 likewise has only limited application.

Such legal niceties indicate that J&K is not an ordinary Indian state; how then is it 'an integral part of India'? The Hindu nationalist party BJP and its affiliates continually question the wisdom of granting special status to J&K under the Indian Constitution. Amitab Matoo, a Kashmiri Pandit who once taught at New Delhi's prestigious Jawaharlal Nehru University, responded: (*The Times of India*, 13 June 2000) 'Jammu and Kashmir's uniqueness is obvious for a variety of historical reasons recognized even by the Supreme Court.'

The government for its part has acknowledged the unresolved

nature of the Kashmir dispute resolution several times – in the Tashkent Agreement after the 1965 war with Pakistan, and again in the Shimla Agreement after the 1971 war with Pakistan. The 1971 war was orchestrated by the Indian government, by illegally supporting Bengali separatists, to split Pakistan. Geelani believes that 'the main cause for the separation of East Pakistan was also Kashmir.'

The early 1950s were politically chaotic in Kashmir. A school-teacher named Sheikh Abdullah was made leader of Kashmiri Muslims. When, later on, he questioned the sanctity of the accession to India, he was thrown into prison. The Indian government then installed another hand-picked politician, Bakshi Ghulam Ahmad, who would head the Kashmir government from 1953 to 1963 and establish a government-backed militia called the 'Peace Brigade'. According to Kashmiri academic Wajahat Ahmad:

> Kashmiris who were found listening to Pakistan Radio were brutalised by the 'Peace Brigade'. The hoodlums drew monthly government salaries of around 30 Indian Rupees for a job which involved looting, beatings, torture and burning the property of dissenters. During the 1950s and 1960s, leaders and activists of major pro-Pakistan and pro-plebiscite parties... were either banished to Pakistan-controlled-Kashmir or imprisoned under draconian laws.... The Enemy Ordinance Act denied the accused the right to access a defence counsel and entailed death sentences or life imprisonment for convicts.... Many forcibly exiled dissenters were never to reunite with their families and died in Pakistan or in Pakistan-administered Kashmir.[22]

C. Rajagopalachari, always the statesman and realist, wrote (*Swarajya*, 25 September 1965): 'It would be as foolish a thing as any foolish thing a nation can do, if we proceed on the assumption that we can hold any people down by sheer force [...] the political decision concerning Kashmir, or any part of it, should be on the basis of self-determination.'

Shortly after Nehru's death, Indira Gandhi became Prime

Minister in January 1966. Veteran Congress leader Jaya Prakash Narayan sent her a long, 'strictly confidential' letter on 23 June 1966. It was first published in Bhola Chatterjee's *Conflict in JP's Politics*. The gist of his argument was:

> We profess democracy, but rule by force in Kashmir, unless we have auto-suggested ourselves into believing that the two general elections under Bakshi Sahib expressed the will of the people, or that the Sadiq government is based on popular support except for a small minority of pro-Pakistan traitors. We profess secularism, but let Hindu nationalism stampede us into trying to establish it by repression. Though some of them might, for their own reasons, give us their support ... that problem exists not because Pakistan wants to grab Kashmir, but because there is deep and widespread political discontent among the people.[23]

After Sheikh Abdullah was released from prison, he signed the 'Kashmir Accord' in 1975 in which he renounced his demand for a plebiscite. In return, the Indian government promised to restore nominal autonomy to Kashmir within the Indian Union and reinstated Sheikh Abdullah as Chief Minister. The Accord was challenged by Jammu Kashmir People's League, Awami Action Committee and Jama'at-i-Islami. Sheikh Abdullah's government promulgated the draconian Public Safety Act (PSA) in 1978, which allowed 'preventive detention' of peaceful dissenters on completely fabricated charges.

State managed 'elections' continued to be held in Kashmir with direct and active intervention by Indian armed forces and other sections of the administration. When the 1987 elections were announced, the leaders of eleven pro-freedom parties devised a strategy to prevent the split of their vote bank. They formed the Muslim United Front (MUF) to contest elections against the pro-India secular parties. Though Maulana Abbas Ansari was chosen its leader, Geelani played a prominent role in its formation. What happened next is well articulated by Tavleen Singh in her book *Kashmir: A Tragedy of Errors* (p. 101):

With the birth of the MUF it quickly became clear that the National Conference-Congress alliance was going to be given a run for its money. Farooq [Abdullah] panicked. This is the most likely explanation for his reaction. There was never any serious chance that the secular alliance could be defeated but he seems to have decided to make victory doubly sure.

The plan appears to have had the concurrence of Delhi and most Kashmiris still remember how, once the counting started and it began to look like the MUF would win at least ten seats in the Valley, Farooq's reaction was to immediately fly down to Delhi [...]

The rigging was blatant. In the constituency of Handwara, for instance, Abdul Ghani Lone's traditional bastion, as soon as counting began on 26 March, Lone's counting agents were thrown out of the counting station by the police.

The rigged election was the beginning of the end. When I was next sent to Kashmir some months afterwards nearly everyone I met said that most of the youths who had acted as election agents and worked for the MUF candidates were now determined to fight for their rights differently. They had no choice but to pick up the gun, was the message I was given.

A record-breaking electoral fraud meant that the MUF which was expected to win more than 20 of the 43 electoral constituencies could win only 4; despite receiving a high vote share of 31 per cent. The above account by an outstanding Indian journalist puts the record straight that mass uprising in Kashmir began when all peaceful options had been exhausted; and not because our infamous neighbor wanted to create trouble.

Indeed, Geelani has often been accused of legitimizing Kashmir's accession to India by participating in elections. But, the late Hizbul Mujahidden (HM) commander Abdul Majeed Dar explained: 'If the MUF had won the election, then we would have declared independence on the floor of the Assembly. We said this openly during the campaign. There were pro-Pakistan songs at our rallies.' Or, as Geelani himself puts it: 'If we have to clean a dirty well, we need to dive into it.' His participation in various elections was part of a long-term freedom strategy and *not* his acceptance of Kashmir as an 'integral part' of India.

After the eruption of insurgency, Prem Shankar Jha had written (*The Sunday Observer*, 14 April 1990): 'The harsh truth is that there are only two ways in which Kashmir can remain a part of India. The first is if most of its Muslim population is driven out, the second is with the consent of its Muslim population. All those who blithely speak of taking "a hard line" in Kashmir are either incredibly stupid or incredibly brutal. For, the hard line will escalate violence until New Delhi is forced to adopt a scorched-earth policy.' For the hardliners, there may be no either/or, no political balancing to be done – they can be both incredibly stupid and incredibly brutal.

Just a month before Jha's meaningful assessment, V. M. Tarkunde articulated the crux of the Kashmir dispute in his editorial in *The Radical Humanist* (March 1990):

> One of the biggest mistakes committed by Jawahar Lal Nehru was to back out of the plebiscite proposal on the wholly irrelevant ground that Pakistan in the meantime had accepted arms and entered into a military pact with the United States. The offer of plebiscite was not in the nature of a concession made by India to Pakistan, but was recognition of the right of self-determination of the people of Jammu and Kashmir.
>
> The denial of the right of self determination by India on irrelevant ground led naturally to a plebiscite movement in Kashmir. It [later] became a secessionist movement and was further strengthened by the subsequent policy of the Government of India which showed that the Government had no confidence in the people of Kashmir. This was evident from the fact that every election in Jammu and Kashmir, except the one in 1977, was rigged at the instance of the

Indian Government. This convinced the people of Kashmir that India did not want them to have the democratic right of self government.

The situation was made worse by the frequent communal riots, which took place in India and in which the minority community [Muslims] suffered the most. This naturally strengthened the anti-Indian feeling of Kashmiri Muslims.

Former Indian Defense Minister George Fernandes admitted in *The Other Side* (March 1992): 'no matter how you look at it, in Kashmir it is the revolt of the masses against a State that has been insensitive to their hopes and aspirations and has consciously and deliberately tried to suppress them into becoming an underclass....' In the socialist model that India pursued from Independence until the early 1990s, government was a major employer. But despite Maulana Azad's timely warning to Jagjivan Ram in 1953 (cited above), nothing changed for Kashmiris. When the mass uprising erupted, the spread of central government employees in Kashmir on 1 January 1989 was something like this:[24]

Officers

Hindus	1,613	83.66%
Muslims	133	6.89%
Sikhs	161	8.35%
Others	21	1.10%

Clerical and non-gazetted staff

Hindus	4,043	79.27%
Muslims	662	12.98%
Sikhs	320	6.28%
Others	75	1.47%

Lal Kishen Advani, the former Home Minister of India personally supervised the demolition of the Babri Mosque on 6 December 1992. Three years after commiting this barbarity he was quoted (*The Hindustan Times*, 23 June 1995) as saying about 'the Kashmir problem': 'Suppressing insurgency should be the prime task of the Governments and the political solution would follow the suit.' Tavleen Singh commented (*India Today*, 22 November 2000): 'Since Advani took charge of the Home Ministry his approach has been military rather than political. This approach has not worked and it is time to consider what else can be done and how.'

Years roll by, but the Indian governments had not learnt any lesson. Nothing had changed on the ground for Kashmiri Muslims. 'Out of a total of 48 District and Session Judges as many as 23 belong to non-Muslim communities ... Out of 47 Sub-Judges only 18 are Muslims and 29 non-Muslims, the Sub-Judges serve as Chief Judicial Magistrates ... At the level of *Munsifs* [Sub-judges], the position (is) still worse ... Out of 52 *Munsifs* 29 are non-Muslims and only 23 belong to [the] majority [Muslim] community....' (*Greater Kashmir*, 23 June 2001).

As Edward Gargan pointed out in 'Valley of Violence and Silence' (*New York Times*, 22 November 1992), there would have been no need to worry about the Pakistanis if the Kashmiris' grievances had met with sympathy and support among the masses of India. But, throughout the last six decades of India's occupation of Kashmir, the Indians masses have largely ignored or actively supported the injustices and atrocities visited upon the Kashmiris.

If the major powers had acted, in the face of India's intransigence, in a responsible and just manner, the South Asian region need not have become a nuclear flashpoint. But they never did. In June 1993 the Subcommittee on Asia and the Pacific of the US House of Representatives, commenting on the public claims by Delhi that the Kashmir insurgency is 'caused by Pakistani meddling', said: 'the evidence does not support this thesis....' Despite that, it went on to concede, 'The Subcommittee is inclined to believe that the U.N. resolutions calling for a plebiscite in Kashmir have been overtaken by history.'[25]

In Tavleen Singh's view, Kashmir has been the primary source of trouble between India and Pakistan. Absent that trouble, 'reduced defence would have brought the prosperity and development that the subcontinent desperately lacks.'[26] Geelani too has said repeatedly over half-a-century, that the scarce financial resources poured by both India and Pakistan into defence sector should be diverted to healthcare, education and infrastructure development.

Yet, Tavleen Singh rationalized India's interest in Kashmir in these terms: 'Kashmir is special to India because it is seen as the most important proof of Indian secularism.'[27] Proving 'secularism' with military force has brought severe hardship and misery to the people of the Subcontinent. Geelani firmly believes that a lasting solution is not possible without genuine, substantive and meaningful talks designed to achieve concrete results within a predetermined timeframe. The talks must involve the true representatives of Kashmiris and the governments of both India and Pakistan: 'people of this region have a shared destiny. The choice is either swim or sink together.' In Tavleen Singh's view 'everyone has a role to play but the key lies in India's hand.'[28]

Over the past decade or so, Geelani has taken full control of the freedom movement. Asked what the solution to this political problem is, he said:

> India had said that it will ask the people of Jammu and Kashmir about their future. The people must be asked. Now, the Indian leaders say they have asked the people. How? Through the state elections? I am a witness to all these political elections. In 1952, elections were just held for two seats, [the] rest were fixed. In 1957, Sheikh Abdullah was in jail. Ghulam Muhammad Bakhshi had replaced him. His men rounded up all opposition members and [had] their nominations rejected. India calls this election? Till 1957 India used to say that the people's wishes will be respected, and then said in 1957 that the assembly had accepted Kashmir's accession. Even Sheikh Abdullah, on 11 April 1964, rejected this saying the assembly was not a true representative and cannot decide the future of Kashmir. Those who do not have the right to be elected cannot decide on accession.[29]

The UNSC Resolution no. 122 of 24 January 1957 rejected that declaration by the J&K assembly. It reaffirmed that the future of J&K is yet to be determined in accordance with earlier UN Resolutions. As late as September 1994, well after the outbreak of the armed struggle, UN Secretary-General Kofi Annan referred to the J&K dispute as 'one of the oldest unresolved conflicts still on the UN agenda.' Writing in *The Hindustan Times* (15 July 1999), Indian scholar Bharat Karnad summarized the situation like this: 'The fact is that most of the world considers the LoC as nothing more than a cease-fire line pending a final solution. This is political and ground reality and it is this status that has the sanction of international law. The most obvious manifestation of which is the continuing presence of the United Nations Military Observer Group in India and Pakistan (UNMOGIP).... India has unilaterally decided that its functioning is invalid, post Shimla Accord – which position, incidentally, is not agreed to by Pakistan nor supported by any major country.'

Geelani believes that post-plebiscite, Kashmir's relations with Pakistan should be determined in the light of Article 257 of the Pakistan Constitution, which states: 'When the people of the State of Jammu & Kashmir decide to accede to Pakistan, the relationship between Pakistan and that State shall be determined in accordance with the wishes of the people of that State.' As for the formulas and road-maps being floated to maintain the status quo, Geelani is clear that 'Hurriyat [grouping of pro-freedom political parties] rejects all the road-maps including [former Pakistani dictator] Musharraf's four-point formula. No interim solution can lead to settlement of Kashmir issue.' He also rejects the idea of dividing J&K on communcal lines: 'Bangladesh was created under this policy and now the same is being done here. I want to make it clear that people of Kashmir won't allow conspirators to succeed in their nefarious designs.' (*Greater Kashmir,* 27 August 2007)

Ebbing and flowing, the Kashmiri independence struggle has claimed over 100,000 lives since the mass uprising in 1989. Both India and Pakistan now have nuclear weapons. Because Kashmir is the flint against which either could strike a nuclear spark, fatalities of this magnitude could become mere footnotes. Pakistani analyst

Tahir Amin[30] views three dimensions to this issue: (a) gross human rights violations; (b) right of self-determination under the UN resolutions and (c) the security threat in a region that is home to one-fifth of humanity. Indian commentator Asghar Ali Engineer asked an interesting question in the *Economic and Political Weekly* (1 July 2000): 'Did Kashmir betray us [India] or did we betray it?'

At this point a clarification is necessary to correct a misconception common in South Asia that Indian-controlled Kashmir is a more precious piece of real estate than the Pakistani-controlled part. From a strictly economic perspective, perhaps. But, strategically, the northern part of Kashmir has provided Pakistan contiguity with China and Central Asia, and denied India valuable access to Afghanistan and Central Asia. Kashmir is currently 43% administered by India, 37% by Pakistan, and 20% by China. The political analyst Luv Puri, a Fulbright scholar and holder of a European Commission Award for Human Rights and Democracy, confirmed in a 2011 interview with *Al Jazeera* that, it is 'a misconception that the Pakistani side of J&K is economically backward. In fact, it is economically better off.'[31] Christopher Snedden further confirms that in PAK 'the literacy rate is high, almost 90 percent'![32]

2

A LIFELINE OF RESISTANCE

SYED ALI SHAH GEELANI was born in the small hamlet of Khonus on the border of Sopore in north Kashmir on 29 September 1929. His mother was Bakhta Begum. His father Syed Peer Shah Geelani used to work as a seasonal coolie earning Rs 10 monthly. He was uneducated but wanted his children to become educated. 'We were three brothers and two sisters. My parents lost their first son soon after he was born. Otherwise we would have been six,' Geelani recalls. Geelani married twice. His first marriage was in 1953. He remarried in 1970 after the death of his first wife. Geelani has seven children, five girls and two boys.

Geelani's student life appears to have been a roller coaster, as his political life would prove to be. He began education at the primary school in Botengo, a four-kilometre walk. His teacher was Pandit Nitayanad. Students gave him one kilo of rice and eggs by way of fee. Master Nitayanand despite being a Hindu used to teach Islamic studies, among other subjects – he knew Urdu, Arabic, Persian and other languages. 'We were so poor that we couldn't afford to buy the books. We used to depend upon the books of our classmates. I secured third position in primary school. There was no Middle School or High School near our village. I had to join a High School in Sopore to pursue my studies further.'[1]

Sopore was even further away; Geelani would now take a longer walk to school every day. When his elder sister got married in Dooru he started staying at her house in order to get to the school, still over six miles away, on time. He remained at Sopore High School until seventh grade. Thereafter, Muhammad Din Fok, a visitor from Lahore, promised to take him to Lahore and get him admitted to a good educational institute. But, as Geelani recalls, 'instead of sending me to some school he sent me to his elder daughter's house at Muzang as a domestic help. I stayed there for one year and I just kept on weeping as I was in shock.' After his family's intervention, he managed to get back to Sopore. Some time later his elder brother Meerak Shah took him again to Lahore and he was able to continue his studies there. 'First I tried to memorize the Qur'an, but couldn't complete it.' Then he was admitted to the Oriental Night College where he completed *Adib 'alim* – a course in theology.

On his return to J&K, Geelani needed a job. He got in touch with Maulana Masoodi, then General Secretary of the National Conference, who managed the *Khidmat* newspaper at Mujahid Manzil, Srinagar. Geelani was asked to work as a reporter on the paper, his first full-fledged job. In 1946 Sheikh Abdullah raised the 'Quit Kashmir' slogan, and the Dogra government cracked down on Mujahid Manzil. Geelani was obliged to go back to Sopore. In 1947, he returned to Srinagar and enrolled in the University of Kashmir for the course of *Adib-i fazil*, which he completed, then took the degree in *Munshi fazil*, Urdu and Persian Honors. He continued studying under the guidance of Maulana Masoodi.

Maulana Masoodi advised him to join the J&K police, but he refused. He then secured a teaching appointment for Geelani in Pather Masjid Primary School. A year later he was transferred to Rainawari High School, where Qari Saiffudin, an associate of Jama'at-i-Islami was also teaching. Saiffudin introduced Geelani to the Jama'at. The Jamaat was launched in J&K by Maulvi Ghulam Ahmed and Syed Saaduddin in 1946. From Rainawari, Geelani was transferred to Raghunath Mandir Middle School, Kani Kadal, where he stayed for a year before returning to Srinagar for three years.

Geelani was deeply impressed by Maulana Masoodi – by the very simple way he lived, and by his scholarship. 'He taught me

like his son,' recalled Geelani. Many Jama'at activists who came
to Mujahid Manzil met Geelani. Some National Conference (NC)
members complained to Maulana Masoodi that Mujahid Manzil
had become 'a den of Pakistanis'. Maulana Masoodi then helped
Geelani to get work nearer to his native village, at Bomai Middle
School. However, as Geelani could not continue his studies there,
and he soon left that position for Intermediate College Sopore
where he would teach for nearly six years. 'This period was very
crucial for me,' Geelani says, 'as it gave me exposure. I used to address congregations in masjids. During those days I was reading the
literature of Jama'at-i-Islami and I used to convey it to my students
in my lectures. After six years I was transferred to Dangerpora High
school.'[2] Throughout this period, the Jama'at 'steadily built up its
strength through a host of social and cultural activities such as running schools or institutions for religious instruction…. Over time,
it built up strong pockets of influence across the state, especially in
downtown Srinagar and the apple-growing area of Sopur,' writes
Joshi in *The Lost Rebellion: Kashmir in the Nineties* (1999, 11). Geelani
was much inspired by Jama'at ideology and principles and became
a basic member in 1952 in Bomai.

From Dangerpora Geelani used to come to Sopore and address
Friday congregations there. The late Abdul Gani Malik (J&K Chief
Minister, Bakshi Ghulaam Muhammad's local MLA) disapproved
Geelani's speeches about the resolution of the Kashmir issue and
Islam, and secretly urged him to join his party and get a ministerial
position. Geelani refused. He was then transferred further to Nadihal Bandipora but did not take up the post. He took a long leave
and then resigned in 1959 to go into politics full time. He was made
Area Head of the Jama'at in Sopore. He says: 'After I joined Jama'at
fully, I was made District Head of Kupwara and Baramulla. I was
arrested for the first time on August 28, 1962. I remained behind
bars for 13 months on the charge of raising [the] Kashmir issue. In
1964 I was made General Secretary of Jama'at.'

Abul A'la Mawdudi founded the pan-Islamic movement Jama'at-
i-Islami in Lahore on 26 August 1941 with the aims of explaining
Islam to non-Muslims and establishing Islamic order in the Muslim

societies of South Asia. Geelani dedicated his life to the realization of this aim. Beside Mawdudi, Geelani's vision was deeply influenced by Imam Ibn Taymiyyah (the great Syrian theologian and activist). He also read intensively the poetry of Mohammad Iqbal. (In childhood he used to read the novels of Munshi Prem Chand.) The politics and philosophy of Egypt's Muslim Brotherhood also influenced Geelani's idealogical and political outlook. In March 2011 the Brotherhood was at the forefront of the movement that ousted the thirty-year tyranny of Hosni Mubarak – the equivalent in Egypt of Kashmir's Abdullahs. Many Brotherhood leaders greatly admire Geelani and his contribution to Kashmir's freedom struggle.

The collusion between the Hindu ruler of Kashmir and the Indian government in 1948 had sparked a sharp reaction among Kashmiri Muslims. Sensing this, Indian politicians kept a low profile, planning to gradually shift power from Hindu puppets to Muslim puppets. With local sensitivities in mind, the Dogra ruler was replaced with Sheikh Muhammad Abdullah on 5 March 1948. Abdullah had called his political party the Muslim Conference but, following his imprisonment from 8 August 1953 to 8 April 1964, he renamed it as the National Conference.

Like no other Indian state, J&K initially retained its own flag. According to Ghulam Mohiuddin Sofi (former political secretary of late Maulana Masoodi and the first MP from Kashmir) the Indian tricolor was hoisted for the first time in 1953 at what is now Municipal Park in Kashmir Valley. Before that Sheikh Abdullah used to hoist Kashmir's state flag on 15 August, India's Independence Day. In 1953 both flags were put up, with the Kashmiri one flying a foot higher. The practice of 'hoisting only tricolor became a regular feature after Ghulam Muhammad Sadiq took over from Bakshi as Chief Minister of the state,' Sofi added (*Greater Kashmir*, 27 August 2007).

The customs barriers (normally found at the boundary between sovereign states) between Kashmir and the rest of India were lifted after the puppet government of Sheikh Abdullah was replaced by the puppet government of Bakshi Ghulam Mohammed. In classic colonial ways 'free trade' was then imposed on Kashmir:

the government in New Delhi has gradually taken full control of Kashmir's hydro resources. In early January 1965, Articles 356 and 357 of the Indian constitution were extended to Kashmir, enabling direct rule without the consent of the local state legislature. Later in the same month, the formal launch in Kashmir of the Indian National Congress was announced. Another symbol of Kashmir's special status, the title of 'Prime Minister' was abolished as of 10 April 1965. Shekhar Gupta, the Editor-in-Chief of *The Indian Express*, summed up the process in these words (6 August, 2000): 'We had consistently and calculatedly diluted the autonomy promised to Kashmir under the Instrument of Accession and Article 370.'

While ordinary Kashmiris went about their daily chores, Geelani and the Jama'at kept a watchful eye on the increasingly sinister implicatons of the changing political framework of relations with India. Nelson Mandela has remarked that 'fear of prison is a tremendous hindrance to a liberation struggle'.[3] Geelani's struggle was not hindered by any such fear. He was imprisoned in 1962 for the first time for his active pro-freedom role. After his release, the Jama'at appointed him as its General Secretary. He was again arrested in 1965, this time spending twenty-two months behind bars. Since then, he has spent a significant part of his life in Indian and Kashmiri prisons. These detentions were imposed only for the 'crime' of demanding implementation of numerous UN Security Council Resolutions relating to Kashmir. The Indian authorities and the international community project Mirwaiz Umar Farooq as their preferred alternative to Geelani. Umar Farooq has never once been imprisoned; rather, he is free to jet-set across the globe. By contrast, Geelani is not permitted to travel abroad even for cancer treatment (see Chapter 13).

As the public face of the Jama'at, Geelani has been heavily criticized in the Indian media for his ideological views. The Jama'at itself is also subject to a smear campaign. The most common allegation is that it preaches violence. Though the Jama'at speaks out against injustice and oppression, Clause 5.4 of its constitution clearly states: 'Jama'at will not indulge in clandestine activities for achieving its goals.' Indeed, way back in September 1948, its Central Executive

Council, the highest decision-making body, passed a resolution stating: 'for the achievement of its goals, Jama'at does not consider the use of such means that are against truth and integrity or means that lead to chaos and anarchy. [It] relies on democratic means i.e. mental and character building and thus changing the public opinion through preaching and counseling.'[4] Geelani clarified in *Oppressed Nation* (2001, 14) 'Jamaat-e-Islami does not champion the Kashmir cause for the sake of patriotism, nationality, race, language, or regionalism but for establishing the truth and justice.'

Addressing a public meeting at a mosque in Makkah in 1963, Jama'at founder Sayyid Mawdudi emphasized: 'My last advice to all the Islamic activists the world over is not to attempt revolutions through underground activities or armed struggles. This is an indication of impatience and will result in worse consequences. True revolution always stems on the back of mass public support. Spread the message of Islam; undertake large scale mentoring and bear all challenges in this effort with patience and perseverance. Such a gradual revolution will be long lasting [and one] that will not be uprooted by opposing powers. If a revolution is attempted in [a] rush, it will die down swiftly in the same manner as it is achieved.'[5] As a result, Jama'at's ideology is lauded even by its detractors. In 1964 Sheikh Abdullah conceded: 'They are doing a laudable job of character-building, which is the need of the hour.'[6]

The Jama'at in Kashmir started taking part in the Panchayat (local council) elections in 1969 through 1987. During this period, it also contested all the elections held for state and national assembly. In 1971 Geelani was nominated to contest the parliamentary election for the first time from Baramulla, and would have won but for rampant rigging. In the state assembly election in 1972, Geelani won against the Congress candidate by a significant margin of votes. Along with other Jama'at members, Geelani staged a walkout on the very first day of the Assembly to protest against the Governor not allowing his address in Urdu, the official language. 'We always used to oppose the bills brought to legalize liquor. On many occasions I was forcibly evicted from the Assembly,' Geelani recalled in a May 2012 interview with *Greater Kashmir*. Geelani retained this seat in the state assembly in the 1977 elections. However, he lost the national assembly election in 1983 to the National Conference candidate. Geelani was later made Parliamentary Affairs Chief of Jama'at.

Yoginder Sikand is an Indian author and political commentator who has done extensive research on Jamaat and Geelani and is considered an authority on Kashmir's socio-political architecture. In his view: 'Jamaat cultivated an essentially lower-middle class constituency, consisting of traders, students and lower level government employees, many of whom were disillusioned with the politics of secular groups, such as the National Conference and the Congress as well as with the perceived other-worldliness, ritualism and limited personal piety associated with the cults of the Sufi shrines. [Jama'at's] network of schools provided a mix of modern and Islamic disciplines. Its social work programmes, such as setting up village-level *bait-ul mals* [micro-finance institutions] for the collection and distribution of *zakat* [mandatory charity] funds, as well as its focus on publishing large amounts of literature, won it a growing support-base. So did its consistent championing of the issue of plebiscite for the Kashmir people for determining their own future.' (*The Economic & Political Weekly*, 20 January 2001)

Syed Salahuddin is the Supreme Commander of the largest armed group in Kashmir, Hizbul Mujahideen (HM). He credits Geelani with reinvigorating the Kashmir issue after the infamous 1975 accord signed between Indira Gandhi and Sheikh Abdullah. Geelani spoke publicly in favour of Kashmir's accession to Pakistan at a time when few Kashmiri politicians dared to do that. However, Geelani was simply echoing the pro-Pak sentiments of the Kashmiri masses. As Tavleen Singh recalls: 'I remember going to Srinagar in August 1989 shortly after our Independence Day that had been mourned with a blackout and Pakistani Independence Day was celebrated with firecrackers and parades.'[7]

From its inception, the J&K Jama'at maintained an identity distinct and separate from the Indian Jama'at. Sheikh Abdullah, after being released from jail in 1964 asked the then chief of the Indian Jama'at, the late Maulana Abul Lais, if the J&K Jamaat was part of his organization. The answer was: 'They are different from us in the context of administration as well as constitution.' Sheikh Abdullah smiled and said: 'You have solved our problem.'[8]

For an entire generation of Kashmiris, Sheikh Abdullah was an icon, but his secular approach conflicted with that of the Jama'at (he was 'greatly influenced by Jawaharlal Nehru' as Tavleen Singh has remarked[9]). Geelani's assessment is straightforward: 'Jamaat had no personal differences or conflicts with the late Sheikh Abdullah. He was the dominant personality on the political horizon of Kashmir. He would recite Qur'an in public, but his practice was diamectrically opposite. He had always adopted authoritarianism in every phase of his political life. Abdullah never showed a democratic temperament. He came to power after 1947, which was the worst period of authoritarianism. The Superintendent of Police Ghulam Qadir Ganderbali was a ruthless interrogator. He was the product of this very dark period of Sheikh Abdullah's rule. Ganderbali used hot irons on the bodies of his political opponents and stuffed hot boiled potatoes in their mouths.'[10] The prominent Indian economist and writer Ankleshwar Aiyar confirms this assessment (*The Hindustan Times*, 19 August 2008): 'The rot began with Sheikh Abdullah in 1951: he rejected the nomination papers of almost all opponents, and so won 73 of the 75 seats unopposed! Nehru was complicit in this sabotage of democracy.' In 1975, Jama'at contested (and lost) another rigged election against Sheikh Abdullah at Ganderbal. In his opening address to fellow legislators at the constituent assembly; Abdullah said: 'You are no doubt aware of the scope of our present constitutional ties with India. We are proud to have our bonds with India, the goodwill of those people and government is available to us in unstinted and abundant measure.'[11] After the elections, Sheikh Abdullah took his revenge on the Jama'at: he imposed a state of emergency in J&K and closed hundreds of Jama'at-run schools – more than 600 teachers were thrown out of work.

After the 1975 elections, 'corruption, nepotism and unemployment were rampant. The state government assumed powers to detain persons up to two years without recourse to law. Press censorship emerged. [Sheikh Abdullah] wanted his ministers to take an oath of personal loyalty to him. His deputy Mirza Afzal Beg refused. He was expelled from the National Conference. Abdullah's rule became despotic and dictatorial.... J&K state was in a mess. The elite became richer; the poor poorer. No development took place. There was an utter neglect of the people. A disgruntled populace was the right material to seed insurgency.'[12]

Geelani attributed this overall degeneration of Muslims in their wordly affairs to the secular approach championed by (among others) Sheikh Abdullah. He wrote: 'This un-Islamic philosophy of separation of politics and religion has become deep rooted amongst our people to such an extent that notices have been put up in mosques forbidding political speeches there. Mosques which are centres of Islamic civilization, where our Prophet preached and spread the teachings of Islam; where training was imparted to soldiers and *mujahideen*; from where governors and ministers were appointed and from where perfect guidance was provided for every walk of life have now become only the places of worship and sermons. Muslims have been prevented from seeking any guidance from the mosques to face the problems of the world as Muslims.'[13]

According to *The Sunday Mail* (12 June 1994), the pre-accession Prime Minister of Kashmir, Mehar Chand Mahajan, gave the credit for India's occupation of Kashmir to Sheikh Abdullah: 'It was at his instance and pressure that India agreed to send its army to Srinagar to confront the raiders.' Nor was this a momentary lapse on the part of Sheikh Abudllah; rather, it was a clearly formulated agenda. As early as October 1948, he had told an Eid gathering: 'The pledge I gave to Pandit Nehru last year that Kashmir will be part of India, has now become an eternal bond. This bond of unity between India and Kashmir, this kinship of heart and soul, this ever-growing and ever-strengthening link between the two great peoples can never be broken.'[14]

Evidently, Sheikh Abdullah chose to throw his lot behind Nehru's commitment to secularism and engineered the state's accession to India. Then, as Geelani has complained: 'The irony is that the protagonists of secularism, socialism and atheistic democracy have always prevented the believers of Islamic system, by force, from rendering any service to their ideology.'

The rule of the National Conference (NC) party from 1947 to 1953 was a painful chapter in Kashmir's history. Anyone who dared talk about freedom was tortured and/or exiled. About NC, Geelani recalls: 'They have never been well wishers of Kashmiris. Had they been sincere, they wouldn't have assumed power in 1975 which they got in charity after burying the demand of plebiscite. Those who raised voice against this betrayal were subjected to inhuman and brutal torture. Ghulam Muhammad Bulla of Sopore was tortured to death in Srinagar Central Jail. It was the first custodial killing in the Valley,' (*Greater Kashmir,* 7 December 2010).

Pakistan protested the 1975 Accord at the UN, as did China. Even hardline secular Kashmiri leaders Abdul Ghani Lone and Muzaffar Baig believed that the 'accord had been nothing short of a sellout'. After the death of Sheikh Abdullah, the reality came home to Kashmiris, many of whom celebrated the anniversary of his death as a day of deliverance and that of his birth as a day of mourning. Manoj Joshi records that: 'There was a near-total strike in Srinagar and other towns of the valley, and effigies of the late "Lion of Kashmir" (as Sheikh Abdullah was fondly called) were burnt. That night there was a blackout as people refused to turn on the lights.'[15] Moreover, for all his abject surrender to India, Sheikh Abdullah was hardly respected even among Indian occupiers. For instance, Nanda branded him 'the most disloyal Chief Minister of Jammu & Kashmir'.[16]

As expected, Kashmiri Pandits loyal to the Indian government mouthed loyalty to its surrogates in Kashmir. 'There is no leader in the Valley today with either the popularity or legitimacy of Sheikh Abdullah' wrote intellectual Kashmiri Pandit Amitabh Mattoo in *The Times of India* (3 December 1999). Just how popular Sheikh Abdullah was is evident from the fact that his grave is guarded by armed police. 'Kashmir will never be at peace with itself as long as the grave of Sheikh Mohammed Abdullah needs to be protected with guns,' opined a security official who asks to be unnamed.

Sheikh Abdullah left behind an equally corrupt and callous

political successor in his son, Farooq Abdullah. Geelani said: 'After assuming power in 1983, Farooq proved to be a clown and did not show any seriousness or maturity on any matter. It was Farooq Abdullah who signed the orders to hang *shaheed* Maqbool Bhat in 1984. It was the same Bhat with whom Farooq Abdullah had taken an oath to fight for the freedom of Kashmir. When Farooq Abdullah saw [the] ground sinking under his feet in 1987, he shamelessly rigged elections to change the public verdict. So long as Farooq Abdullah-like traitors are here, India will not give weight to democratic ways' (*Greater Kashmir*, 7 December 2010).

Confirming the above assessment of Geelani, Balraj Puri defined Farooq's character in *The Economic and Political Weekly* (19 August 2000):

> Perhaps Farooq Abdullah would have served the interest of the country better if he was not over-burdened with the anxiety to prove his loyalty. He never missed an opportunity to proclaim his loyalty not only to the country but also to every party that came to power at the centre. He has been shifting his allegiance from the Congress to the Janata Dal and to the BJP as they succeeded one after another as the ruling party in New Delhi. In fact anticipating the victory of the NDA (BJP-led alliance) in the 1999 Lok Sabha poll, he joined its leaders, uninvited, when they released its manifesto, in the drafting of which he had no hand and which he and his partymen had not even read.

> Further to prove his *bona fides*, he specially flew to Mumbai to attend the birthday celebrations of the Shiv Sena leader and Maharashtra chief minister Manohar Joshi. He received an Amity award at an RSS-sponsored function last year where he spoke of its patriotic virtues. This strategy might have helped Farooq to remain in power but it has been the major cause of alienation of the [Kashmiri] people for the last decade and a half.

When Geelani's young daughter Suraiya Jabeen passed away in April 2001, Prime Minister Vajpayee faxed a condolence message from Tehran, while his Deputy, L. K. Advani, spoke to Geelani on the phone. But Farooq Abdullah was incapable of such elementary courtesy. Geelani, rightly, holds the National Conference and the Sheikh family directly responsible for the bloodshed and sufferings of Kashmiris. 'Had NC and [the] Sheikh Family not betrayed the nation, had they not turned the Muslim Conference into the National Conference in 1938 or ratified the accession in 1947, the situation would have been different today and we wouldn't have to receive the bullet-riddled bodies of our loved ones. The Kashmir issue is the consequence of the deceptive politics of the Sheikh Family and NC.' (Ibid.)

Besides corruption and misgovernance, Farooq Abdullah is also hated for his deception and blatantly self-serving lies. For example, he declared at the World Conference on Human Rights in Vienna on 16 June 1993: 'We have Hindus, Muslims, Christians and Buddhists and everyone enjoys equal rights of freedoms under our Constitution.' In Geelani's view, Farooq Abdullah's 'stabbing' of the Kashmiri people was sustained by his participation in subsequent 'managed' elections: 'After the sacrifices of thousands of people, he participated in the 1996 elections and created the Special Task Force (STF), a group of brutal killers unleashed on Kashmiris. Again in 2008, when thousands of people were on the streets, NC joined the election bandwagon, damaging the cause for which Kashmiris have sacrificed.' (Ibid.)

Moreover, wrote Sandhya Jain in *The Pioneer* (27 February 2000): 'Dr. Abdullah is perhaps the only eminent Muslim who has claimed Lord Rama as his heritage; he also conducted himself with decorum at the Tirupati Shrine.' Post uprising, according to *Greater Kashmir* (29 January 2000), 'Dr. Abdullah's role has now been restricted to rubber stamp administrative head of the state.' One might well ask when his role was more than this? Indeed, the Abdullah family has served Indian interests to such perfection that 'New Delhi has never over the past 50 years allowed an alternative to the National Conference to grow' (*The Pioneer*, 1 February 2000).

India used the Abdullahs for political and economic advantage together with cultural assimilation of the local population. On

2 December 2007 Geelani addressed a seminar titled 'Cultural aggression and how to combat it' organized by the Dukhtaran-i Millat (Daughters of the Nation). He blamed the NC (in opposition at the time), for 'abolishing Islamic teachings' from the curriculum in Kashmir. He urged the student community and the teachers to unite against the 'cultural aggression' launched by the J&K and New Delhi governments. He held the NC responsible for the exclusion of Islamic teachings from Kashmiri schools when it came to power in 1947.

NC reproached Geelani for contesting elections at the time when the Plebiscite Front led by Sheikh Abdullah was fighting for freedom from India. He explained that he had done so 'with the only intention to fight so-called Indian socialism and secularism. I fought the elections to try and establish Islamic government in Kashmir and save our people who were being oppressed and exploited in the name of Kashmiri nationalism.' Geelani attended the India Today Conclave in New Delhi in March 2011 along with Farooq Abdullah. There he repeated his explanation for contesting elections, adding that the Indian National Congress had also contested elections in 1935, under British rule, while campaigning for freedom for that rule – and had not been blamed for that.

Geelani holds the NC responsible for accepting 'fake accession documents signed by Maharaja Hari Singh in 1947 which triggered unending agony for Kashmiri people.' He asks why the NC 'signed an accord in 1975 when they were demanding plebiscite in 1953. NC had two-thirds majority in 1977 elections. The late Abdul Gani Lone tried to pass a resolution to take the state [back] to the pre-1953 position. But NC members opposed the resolution.' The official position of Kashmiris, before 1953, was that J&K was a disputed state awaiting a plebiscite to settle its final status. Yet, in 1953, the NC 'officially' accepted J&K as a part of the Indian Union without explicit mandate from the Kashmiri people. 'Kashmir would have been different sans Sheikh dynasty's treachery and their art of black-mailing sentiments of people', wrote Kashmiri political analyst Hassan Zainagiree (*Greater Kashmir*, 28 January 2008).

Prominent Indian economist and writer Swaminathan S

Anklesaria Aiyar echoes Geelani's view in an article in *The Hindustan Times* (19 August 2008): 'Many Indians say that Kashmir legally became an integral part of India when the Maharaja of the state signed the instrument of accession. Alas, such legalisms become irrelevant when ground realities change. Indian kings and princes, including the Mughals, acceded to the British Raj. The documents they signed became irrelevant when Indians launched an independence movement. The British insisted for a long time that India was an integral part of their Empire, the jewel in its crown, and would never be given up. Imperialist blimps remained in denial for decades. I fear we are in similar denial on Kashmir.'

In Geelani's view education in Kashmir is being used as a tool of cultural aggression. He warned Kashmiris not to 'expect that under occupation your religion, relationships, and lives will remain safe. [...] If we believe we are an occupied nation then nobody can damage our culture.'[17] It was of the utmost importance 'to continue fighting Indian occupation itself.'

2.1 Syed Geelani leading the 18 August 2008 march to the UN Office in Srinagar.

Teachers at every level of education have to be ready to make sacrifices when they are threatened with dismissal for refusing to oblige the authorities' demand that they and their students attend state-sponsored cultural events. Geelani urged the people to start Islamic education in established and future schools and emphasized the need to introduce Arabic, Urdu and English languages as compulsory subjects.

After Farooq Abdullah reached his 'sell by' date, he was replaced in 2008 by his son Omar Abdullah as J&K's new Chief Minister. Omar is the third generation Abdullah to be installed by New Delhi as their viceroy in J&K. His mother is a British Christian. His wife is a Hindu. His sister is married to a Hindu. This is why it is widely believed in Kashmir that over half of his family may not even be Muslim.

Immediately after assuming office, Omar launched attacks on the pro-freedom leadership in general and Geelani in particular. He also resorted to boilerplate appeals for Kashmiris to 'engage in dialogue' with the Indian government. Geelani replied, as he usually does, that there could be no formal talks until India accepts that the status of Kashmir is in dispute. He added (*Greater Kashmir,* 7 December 2010): 'We would continue to present our viewpoint before the Indian people and would have no hesitation in meeting any non-official Indian.' Omar repeated his father's patently false claim that Geelani is 'isolated' among Kashmiris with only a handful of 'misguided youth' as his followers. Kashmiris proved the falsehood of this claim when over a million of them showed up in Srinagar in response to his call in the summer of 2008.

The seizure of political power is never the end of occupation forces but only a means to secure control of economic resources. This has been witnessed in other parts of the Muslim world too. *The Economic & Political Weekly* (24 August 1991) highlights the economic exploitation of Kashmiris:

> In the midst of winter, Srinagar was without power for three days in the week, while power from Salal was being supplied to the northern grid, to meet the needs of Delhi [...] Step by step, all the key power projects in the state were taken over by the [Indian government owned] National Hydel Power Corporation (NHPC). Again, it is during periods of central rule, or when puppet governments were in place, like the

one of G. M. Shah, that the decisions to hand over various projects to the central [Indian] organizations were taken.

The 400 kv transmission line was handed over to NHPC during the period of G. M. Shah, while Jagmohan's two spells of governor's rule were very beneficial in extending Delhi's control. The Sawalkot and Baghlihar projects on the Chenab were handed over to NHPC during his first spell in 1986, and in 1990 the 200 kv line project was handed over to NHPC [...] [which] will control not only the generation but also the distribution system, particularly in the Valley, the implications of which can well be imagined.

Other exports from Kashmir are those of fruits, mainly apples, handicrafts, carpets and shawls. The trade in apples is controlled at Delhi's Azadpur mandi [market] by Punjabi [Hindu] traders. The auction in this market is clandestine, lending itself to price fixing by the traders. Knowledgeable observers estimate that the growers in the valley get only about 20 per cent of the auction price.

Investment in Kashmir by Delhi and the pan-Indian bourgeoisie has been basically in two fields: roads and communications for military purposes [...] and in power generation and transmission, so as to better exploit Kashmir's natural resources of water and forests. Capital investment for industry has been virtually non-existent....

Overall, Kashmir is important as a market for Indian manufacturers, and not as an area for the investment of the Indian big bourgeoisie's capital. Other than rice, most items of mass consumption are imported. Kashmir's imports are about four times its exports. The excess of imports over exports has to be made up through payments from other income: from tourism, and from its earnings in handicrafts and agriculture.

A major expenditure over the years in Kashmir has been on the highway linking Jammu and Srinagar. This highway has been built and maintained at great cost. As in the case of the railways that the British built after the 1857 uprisings, the highway in Kashmir was built for military reasons, to enable the Indian armed forces to sustain a substantial presence in the Kashmir valley.

According to a May 2008 article in *Greater Kashmir*, the NHPC generates 2400 MW of power, of which more than 1600 MW is generated in J&K. The 390 megawatt Dul Hasti hydel project is not the only facility which J&K failed to get from the government of India. In 2000, New Delhi forced the State government to hand over seven power projects to NHPC. They include: 240 MW Uri II, 330 MW Kishanganga, 120 MW Seva II, 1000 MW Bursar, 1020 MW Pakaldul, 44 MW Chitak and 45 MW Nemo-Buzgo. While the NHPC is getting power from 690 MW Salal Power Station at 65 paisa per unit and from the 480 MW Uri I at Rs 1.50 per unit, J&K has to purchase the same power, generated from its own water resources, at up to Rs 13 per unit. The traitorous elite of J&K are selling out local resources, while ordinary Kashmiris are then obliged to buy them back at more than ten times the price at which they are sold.

The economic exploitation has been so glaring that even Farooq Abdullah was compelled to admit (*Greater Kashmir*, 4 May 2008): 'all the benefits of the mega projects of the state including Baghlihar are taken away by New-Delhi.' As a result, J&K has been able to add just 1.26 MWs of energy to its power kitty during the 11th five-year plan period as against the planned 1800 MWs. By contrast, NHPC, over the same period, added a whopping 510 MWs of energy to its kitty from new power projects in J&K. Throughout this time (the 11th five-year plan ended in March 2012) J&K has supposedly been ruled by a democratically elected government. Omar Abdullah admitted in the Legislative Assembly on 13 March 2012 that the NHPC is not inclined to return power projects to the state as it earns 50 percent of its profits from J&K. These are some of the realities against which the struggle for meaningful self-determination has been waged for so long by Kashmiris under Geelani's leadership.

Geelani is the first Kashmiri to be appointed to the Executive Council of the Makkah-based World Muslim League (WML). His election (2000) was a great morale booster. He is the third Asian

Muslim after Maulana Abul A'la Mawdudi (the Jama'at's founder) and Maulana Abul Hasan Ali Nadwi of Nadwat al-Ulama to receive this honour. It brings him a larger forum and wider audience, albeit non-political. WML, founded in 1962, is an international Islamic NGO that operates across the Islamic world, enjoys observer status at the OIC (Organization of the Islamic Conference), and Grade-A observer status at the UN, with consultative status at the Economic and Social Council. It is also a member of the UN Educational, Scientific, and Cultural Organization (UNESCO) and the UN International Children's Emergency Fund (UNICEF).

The 62-member WML has representation from almost all countries with significant Muslim populations. The eight-member Executive Council, its highest policymaking body, is committed to 'safeguarding the interests of Muslims and teachings of Islam'. According to *Hindustan Times* (13 March 2001), 'Jamaat's Pakistani counterpart and other fundamentalist groups had actively canvassed for Geelani's election. On its part the League bestowed the honour on him in recognition of his role in the Kashmiri struggle and as a mark of the Muslim world's solidarity with the struggle of Kashmiris.' Geelani's election was announced days before India's Foreign minister Jaswant Singh visited Saudi Arabia.

Hassan Zainagiree, a Kashmiri political analyst, praised Geelani (*Greater Kashmir*, 28 January 2008) for his integrity and consistency over a lifetime of resistance – unlike so many others who betrayed their people and their earlier promises as soon as the going got tough, who exchanged loyalty to the cause for personal celebrity and '5-star luxuries': 'While all others, in one way or the other, softened, diluted or changed their earlier stands on Kashmir (including those who took to the gun and then baptized politics), Geelani remained loyal to the blood of the martyrs.'

Geelani is now 83 and has suffered mightily at the hands of Indian security forces. Aside from the long years in prison (which, as will be detailed below, he used as best he could to study and write), his life and that of his family have been under continual threat. Harassment at meetings where he has been speaking has been more or less constant. On 17 occasions between October 1995 and June

2000, Geelani and members of his family were directly targeted by Indian security forces and/or the renegade militia armed and supported by them: the harrowing incidents include bomb blasts, rocket and grenade attacks directed at his home (which has been severely damaged several times), and attempts to intimidate by sustained gunfire. It is important to remember that other All Party Hurriyat Conference (APHC) leaders have also been the victims of such attacks.

Many believe that Geelani's time is up and that, once he is gone, the freedom movement he nurtured for over fifty years will die away. His poor health, his age and his inevitable death should be viewed, however, in the context of what happened at the historic battle of Uhud. When many Muslim fighters lost their lives, when defeat at the hands of the idolaters seemed imminent, and when rumours were spread among them that their leader, the Prophet, had been killed, some did indeed panic or flee. But many others stood firm and fought on because that for which they were fighting cannot suffer death and defeat. Those who panicked are admonished in the Qur'an (3: 144): 'Muhammad is but a messenger before whom other messengers passed away. If, then, he dies or is slain, will you turn on your heels? He who turns on his heels will not harm God in any way.'

The rule of *sabr* (patience and perseverance) is a golden feature of Islam. It holds for all those who go on striving for the highest values including the value of freedom from injustice, oppression and exploitation. Geelani's life exemplifies *sabr* in our time and our region of the world.

NEIGHBOURING PEOPLES

OVER THE LAST TWENTY YEARS, two major developments have occurred in Geelani's neighborhood: China has emerged as an economic and political power capable of challenging US hegemony; and Pakistan is the first Muslim state to become a nuclear power. Both developments have pushed successive US regimes to bring the South Asian region under their influence. The focus of Geelani's life over the last half century has been to bring morality to Muslim societies in general and Kashmir in particular. He has not been concerned only with the issue of Kashmir. On the contrary, he has spoken long and loud against the sufferings of Palestinians, Afghans and Iraqis among others.

Geelani considered Pakistan as 'the fortress of Islam' and Afghanistan 'its most important and strongest wall'.[1] He also felt that 'during the last fifty years Indian Muslims have suffered a lot'.[2] This chapter looks at the geostrategic situation in the South Asian region, how it affects the Kashmiri freedom struggle, and Geelani's views on three of his closest neighbours, namely Afghanistan, Pakistan, and Muslim Indians.

AFGHANISTAN

In retaliation for the 9/11 attacks on US soil, US/NATO forces began bombing Afghanistan on 7 October 2001. Concurrently, the

US launched a worldwide 'war on terror' against Muslims engaged in movements for freedom and self-determination, including Kashmir's. Various Kashmiri pro-freedom leaders caved in under the 'changed scenario', but not Geelani. He said: 'Some people have been saying that things have changed after September 11 and we need a new approach. But for me nothing has changed. In Kashmir the strength of the Indian Army has not changed. The custodial killings, rapes and arrests have not stopped. In this context we need to continue our struggle.'[3] Geelani analyzed the background of the 9/11 attacks and presented his views:

> Sometimes, as a result of earthquakes, floods, accidents and epidemics many more human lives are lost. But on such occasions, a human being can do nothing except express his helplessness against nature. But this incident [9//11] is extremely tragic and heart-rending because it is a deliberate human act. When a person goes down from the exalted position of humanity, he feels no hesitation in perpetrating worst form of brutality and barbarity. This is why human beings are given so much importance in all religious and moral codes so that they learn to behave ethically and treat others in a brotherly, friendly and tolerant manner.

> Today's civilized world and champions of democracy should be asked about their contribution to the building and development of humanity, preservation of human dignity and protection of human rights! Being equipped with power and wealth, how do they treat weaker persons and nations? They should also be asked to remember highly destructive consequences in Hiroshima and Nagasaki. Have they not expelled the inhabitants of Palestine from their land under Balfour Declaration and flattened their houses with bulldozers? Have they not created an ocean of over four million Palestinian refugees who are wandering like gypsies? Have they not brought a nation from different parts of the world and armed them to [the] teeth before settling them on occupied land snatched from Palestinians?

UN was created in 1945 so that world peace could be guaranteed and all disputes and conflicts could be settled through mutual dialogue and collective decision making. It was meant to minimize probabilities of war if not completely eliminate them. The former President Clinton while addressing the 1998 UN General Assembly himself admitted that since UN inception, over twenty million people have been killed. Is there a justification for such a great loss of human life when a world institution has been created to bring about peace by settling disputes?

Who had been playing with millions of human lives in Vietnam for 12 years? What treatment is being meted out to people demanding independence in Chechenya? Who is responsible for shedding [the] blood of 1.5 million human lives in Afghanistan? Was the UN not responsible for stopping the tyranny of [the] Soviet Union? What breakthroughs have been achieved by present civilization in Rwanda, Eritrea, Somalia and Bosnia? In Bosnia, honour and chastity of 20,000 women was openly violated. While conducting genocide, Serbs did not refrain from demonstrating their inhuman and inconceivably brutal acts. Iraq has been a victim of siege and torture for the past twelve years.

The country [India] which gained independence from British rule, has completely forgotten its own days of slavery and freedom struggle. It suddenly became a tyrant imperialist force and turned J&K, one of the most beautiful regions in the world into an ocean of blood. Has any civilized nation ever asked India why it is suppressing this weak nation of Kashmir and not fulfilling the promises it made on the floor of the UN?

Back to 9/11, behind which some human beings were at work. When human beings degenerate and become desperate, they are sources of more destruction and devastation than earthquakes, floods and epidemics [put together]. Therefore, it becomes the primary responsibility of those who value human life and welfare to pay greater attention to human development and establish a system based on superior human and moral values. They should be reminded that all human beings are progeny of one parent and they have all been created by the One powerful Creator.

As human beings, we are brothers of each other and cannot be separated on the basis of caste, colour, race, language, region or profession. Our human relationship is of greatest importance and we must preserve this at any cost. This aspect has been given the primary status in Islam but is completely ignored in today's civilized world. The Qur'an states: *O mankind, We created you from a single (pair) of male and female, and made you into nations and tribes so that you know each other. Surely, the most honoured among you in the eyes of God is the most righteous among you. And God has full knowledge and is well aware (al-Hujurat* 49: 13).

In Islam, human life is recognized as most respectful and inviolable. Killing one person (unjustly) is considered the killing of entire humanity and saving one human life equals saving the whole humanity. Survival and safety of human beings is possible only when we have love and respect for others. Anyone whose heart is not filled with a sense of love and sympathy for those killed in this attack does not deserve to be called a human.

The government of USA and its President have put the entire blame of this incident on Osama bin Laden and his organization, Al-Qaeda. Osama is presently living in exile in Afghanistan under the Taliban. This is why, with him, the Taliban are also labeled a terrorist government. The question arises – what is the basis on which America has accused Osama and Taliban for this crime. Justice demands that all witnesses, evidences and proofs should be collected and the entire case should be handled by the International Court. As a result of this fair process, every possible step should be taken to punish the guilty. The US President's unambiguous and unilateral declaration that 'you are either with us or with terrorists' is against their own precepts that no one should be declared guilty unless accorded an opportunity to be heard.

To appease India, America may ask Pakistan to disband the freedom struggle in independent portion of Jammu and Kashmir as it has vital economic and strategic interests in India. It may declare the armed struggle as an obstacle to solving the Kashmir problem and may promise a solution through negotiations. But can such a promise be tenable given millions of such promises made to solve the Palestine occupation? Isn't US making use of all its means and resources to arm and strengthen Israel? Isn't Israel butchering and crushing the hapless and defenceless Palestinians on the back of US support? Moreover, if at all a solution is brought about with the cooperation and intervention of the US, will it be compatible with the great and unparalleled sacrifices of the overwhelming majority of the people of Jammu & Kashmir? Entertaining such expectations on the basis of historical US policies is like living in a fool's paradise. By exploiting the fear of terrorism, US is bent upon executing its policy of destroying Islam and the Islamic nations with the active cooperation of its allies. And it calls India its 'natural ally'. It is imperative to examine the effects and consequences of these plans and foil them effectively. The US claim that its war is not against Muslims and Islam cannot be accepted in the light of facts and evidence.

Afghanistan has great historical importance. Though it is a small and poor country from a material point of view, from the Islamic and religious perspective, it can be placed on top of the Islamic world. Pakistan is the fortress of Islam and Afghanistan is its façade. In my view, immediately after this incident [i.e. 9/11], an emergency meeting of the OIC should have been convened demanding thorough and independent investigation and punishing the guilty. But the state of the Muslim *ummah* [global Muslim community] is so deplorably incoherent that a joint session of OIC could not be held until after two weeks! They are compelled to follow the dictates of Western powers in spite of possessing immense material, manpower, oil, mineral and strategic geographical location. The fundamental reason for all this is that Muslim governments are not backed by their own people. Reason: they are not serving their population but serving their own self-interests and those of the West. This is why they are economically weak and are dependent on former colonial powers and institutions created by them like the World Bank, International Monetary Fund, Asian and African Development Banks etc.

From the ideological point of view, the Muslim leadership is mentally and practically cut off from the enlightening and beneficial system of Islam. They are enamoured [of] deceptive and un-Islamic ideologies. In most Muslim countries, governments are ruling with complete disregard for the feelings and aspirations of their people [and reliant] merely on the state's coercive apparatus and muscle power [fully supported by the US and European powers]. There exists no harmony or compassion between the state and its subjects. The country's resources and wealth are either being misused or not being put to their best use. Absolutely no attention is being paid to develop human capital through effective training and value-based Islamic education.

Instead of protecting and promoting religious and cultural heritage, means of communication are being used to destroy it. These contradictions have thrown the entire *ummah* into great crisis and distress. This state has rendered the whole *ummah* weightless and ineffective at global level. Instead of solving others' problems, they are unable to solve their own. The situation created by the 'war on terror' in the aftermath of the bloody incidents of 11 September has further exposed the disturbed and confused state of mind and body of the Muslim *ummah*.

Against this backdrop, the President of Pakistan described its cooperation with US as compulsion. In the absence of such cooperation by him, India would have fully exploited this by offering its full assistance to the US, provoking it to declare Pakistan as a 'terrorist state' and perhaps even attacking Pakistan's nuclear assets. These fears may not be entirely untrue, but history offers such occasions to nations only rarely to assess their moral, technological and social strength. Interestingly, throughout the Islamic world, Pakistan has the distinction of being the only nuclear power. Due to this unique position, Pakistan had an opportunity to play a leading role in this crisis. Pakistan would have been justified in strongly condemning terrorism and declaring such elements as the worst enemy of humanity. Concurrently, it could have told the US fearlessly that blaming any individual, organization or country of a crime without any proof is a travesty of justice and Pakistan as a sovereign nation has a right to dissent.

With regard to President Musharraf's speech of 19 September 2001, it is imperative to clarify that the Treaty of Hudaibiya [which the Prophet Muhammad entered into with the idolaters of Makkah] does not apply to the present case. In that case, on one side were the infidels of Makkah and on the other side was the Head of the Islamic State himself, the Prophet (pbuh). The anxiety of his Companions on the terms of the Treaty was justified as they viewed that they were entering into this agreement from a position of weakness. Since the Prophet was doing all this directly under the guidance of God, he wanted the implementation of this agreement with full confidence and surety. By declaring this as a great victory for Muslims, God later removed the fear and doubt of the Companions.

This agreement was not against any Muslim state; rather, the fundamental objective of this agreement was safety and protection of Islam and Muslims. This was so important that when the rumour of the assassination of his top companion [Usman] reached them, all of the Muslims were prepared to wage *Jihad* against the infidels of Makkah at the risk of their lives. This option was provided to Muslims within the scope of the Treaty of Hudaibiya. Unlike

Pakistan, the Muslim soldiers of 1400 years ago had only one sword each as they had left their homes not with the intent of war; they were hundreds of miles away from their base; they were surrounded by the infidels of Makkah and all the factors appeared against them. In spite of all this, they showed exemplary loyalty to their leader Prophet Muhammad and respect for the blood of their Muslim brother Usman.[4]

A large number of residents along the areas of the Durand Line that divides Afghanistan and Pakistan are extremely religious and therefore fiercely independent. In Geelani's view, this fort of Islam has been significantly weakened as a result of Pakistan's cooperation in the 'war on terror'. In late 2001, Geelani made some suggestions to deal with these crises for the benefit of humanity in general and Islam in particular:

1. Unless US and its allies in the 'war against terrorism' present clear and credible proof against Osama bin Laden or the Taliban and an impartial international judiciary accepts such a proof, no cooperation should be offered to them.

2. Pakistan must not allow its territory, airspace and army bases to be used by the US against Afghanistan. Even if the allegations against Osama Bin Laden are fully established, there is no justification for committing aggression against the whole nation. This should be strongly resisted.

3. US should be prevented from providing arms and financial assistance to the Northern Alliance and installing a puppet regime in Afghanistan. Our brotherly country Iran should be advised against taking any step which harms Afghanistan and should be reminded of giving priority to the supreme interest of the *ummah* as a whole.

4. Pakistani protesters agitating against their country's cooperation with the US should avoid violence. Their

protest should be persistent, forceful but peaceful at the same time. Similarly, the government of Pakistan should not use force in suppressing its people's discontent with its policies.

5. If the US invades Afghanistan, it should be called terrorism and condemned and protested worldwide in the same manner as protests were held against 9/11. Muslims should be at the forefront of such protests. Individual terrorism should not be countered with state terrorism.[5]

The US invasion of Afghanistan happened (as Geelani feared it would) and opened the door to a lasting rapprochment between American and Indian policies (and attitudes) to Afghanistan, Kashmir, Pakistan and Muslims generally. Speaking at a global forum in New Delhi in April 2008, former US Pacific Commander-in-Chief (Retd) Admiral Dennis C. Blair said that India and America should together pursue their common interests in areas such as maritime security, peacekeeping operations, counter-insurgency and counter-terrorist training. He also said (*The Tribune*, 21April 2008): 'India in Jammu and Kashmir and the United States in Afghanistan and Iraq are facing fundamentalist Islamic terrorists who probably get trained at some of the same centres.' The tacit reference is to Pakistan and Kashmir.

In early 2003, US Defence Secretary Donald Rumsfeld claimed that with most of Afghanistan secured, the American forces' mission would switch to stabilization and reconstruction.[6] After eight years of this assertion, a March 2011 UN report confirmed that the number of civilians killed in Afghanistan had increased 15 per cent over the previous year. Evidently, the occupying US/NATO forces are losing the war to the Afghan resistance. By Feburary 2011, Secretary of State Hillary Clinton was also beginning to utter the formulae that precede admissions of military failure (*The Guardian*, 28 March 2011): 'Now, I know that reconciling with an adversary that can be as brutal as the Taliban sounds distasteful, even unimaginable. And diplomacy would be easy if we only had to talk to our friends. But that is not how one makes peace.'

Expectedly, the sole superpower is trying to save itself from an open humiliation. After twelve years of Afghan resistance, in his 12 February 2013 State of the Union address, Obama brazenly toned down the objective of this illegal war. He claimed: 'America will complete its mission in Afghanistan and achieve our objective of defeating the *core* of al-Qaeda' (*Times of India*, 13 February 2013). *Forty-plus* powerful Western nations, led by the sole superpower are out to defeat just 'the core' i.e. a few hundred Muslims (spending twelve years and trillions of tax-payers' dollars)? However Geelani believes that the US/NATO cannot accomplish even this insignificant and laughable objective!

Of course, the invaders and their allies would not wish to run away empty-handed. Mineral wealth estimated at US$ 1 to 3 trillion lies unexplored across the Hindu Kush. There's enough uranium, lithium, copper and iron ore to potentially turn Afghanistan into a commodities powerhouse. The world's biggest iron ore deposits (at least 1.8bn tons) are located in central Afghanistan. Bids to explore and exploit were invited in August 2011. According to media reports, all fifteen bidding companies are from India – including giants Tata Steel and Jindals, India's third-largest private steel company.

Anti-Islamic sentiments however camouflaged are discernable among some of America's military, political and religious circles. They are amplified by people like Rod Parsley, the pastor of a profitable Ohio mega-church. In his book, *Silent No More*, Parsley claims the United States was ordained by God to defeat Islam. In the chapter titled 'The Deception of Allah' he writes: 'I cannot tell you how important it is that we understand the true nature of Islam, that we see it for what it really is. In fact, I will tell you this: I do not believe our country can truly fulfill its divine purpose until we understand our historical conflict with Islam. I know that this statement sounds extreme, but I do not shrink from its implications. The fact is that America was founded, in part, with the intention of seeing this false religion [Islam] destroyed.'

In February 2008, Parsley endorsed John McCain's candidacy for President. Joining Parsley on stage in Cincinnati, Ohio, McCain returned the compliment: 'I am very honoured today to have one of the truly great leaders in America, a moral compass, a spiritual guide, Pastor Rod Parsley. Thank you for your leadership and your guidance.' Against this background, it is agonizing to see the leaders of Muslim states standing shoulder-to-shoulder with the US in their war on Muslims. McCain visited Kashmir in August 2011, though Chief Minister Omar Abdullah admitted that he did not know why (*Greater Kashmir*, 17 August 2011). McCain's visit is intended as a threat – like Afghanistan, Kashmir is in the line of American fire.

Syed Salahuddin affirmed to me that after 9/11, the base camp of militants in Muzaffarabad had 'calmed' down. Geelani had foreseen in 2001 that 'if the US succeeds in installing its puppet regime in Afghanistan, it will never have friendly relations with Pakistan. US, India and Russia will always use such a regime against Pakistan.'[7] Geelani was right. Others are catching on. For example, Indrani Bagchi, writing in *Times of India* (5 February 2013) notes that 'India and the US have now established deep contacts on their activities in Afghanistan' – 'activities' is judiciously vague, but everyone knows what is meant.

PAKISTAN

As Pakistan is a principal party to the Kashmir dispute, an overview of its stand on Kashmir is necessary. We can limit the discussion to the period after 1989, and after the mass uprising against occupation. Pakistan came into being on 14 August 1947, coincidentally the 27th night of Ramadan in the Hijri year 1366, an auspicious beginning duly noted at the time, and celebrated. The mood in India was not positive towards Pakistan. Geelani complained that 'there were people who refused to admit the existence of two nations in India.'[8]

Within a few weeks of Pakistan's creation, veteran politician Ram Manohar Lohia claimed that 'Pakistan will have to go in one of three ways. Either [the] population of Pakistan will overthrow [the] League government and establish [a] secular state and reunite with India; secondly, [the] new leaders of Pakistan may realize [the] folly of [the] two-nation theory and change their ways and enter into agreements with us and start from being a confederation and once again become a single India; thirdly, war. Pakistan will disappear within the next five years.' (Speech on 18 October 1947, cited in *Frontline*, 12 March 2012.)

The British had left the lands that they had occupied and robbed for centuries, but they left behind well-trained, local surrogates to ensure that, behind the appearance, the reality was business much as before. The ruling elite in Pakistan (and other former colonies) acted in the interest of the former colonial power rather than of their own people. Arundhati Roy believes that 'Pakistan was never allowed to administer its own affairs, ever since it became a country. That country has not been allowed to develop democratic institutions. At least India was allowed to, and now it is kind of hollowing them out, but Pakistan was never allowed.'[9]

Geelani observed, with obvious regret, that 'Pakistan was created to root out nationalism and patriotism but the irony is that the poison of [that] same nationalism and patriotism divided Pakistan into two.'[10] After losing East Pakistan, Pakistan was a shattered nation in December 1971. With nearly '94,000 Prisoners of War (PoWs) in her camps, with 50,139 square miles of territory in Punjab, Kutch and Sind in her control, and with Pakistan on its knees, India let slip the opportunity to impose, if necessary, an unambiguous settlement of the Kashmir problem. The glaring fact of Shimla Agreement in 1972 is that Pakistan had outmaneuvered India from a hopeless position.' That is the assessment of Pankaj Vohra, the political editor of *Hindustan Times*.

For public consumption all civilian and military rulers of Pakistan like to express support for the Kashmiri freedom movement. The late Prime Minister Benazir Bhutto expressed a determination to internationalize the Kashmir issue while keeping the door open to bilateral negotiations with India. In a July 1994 interview with Nihal Singh, editor of the Dubai-based *Khaleej Times*, she said: 'We don't want the bilateral talks to become a pretext for crushing the Kashmiris.' She stressed the need for 'tangible progress' on the

Kashmir issue during the discussions. But the Indian media were quick to note any drift in Pakistani handling of the Kashmir dispute. *The Pioneer* (7 June 1994) commented: 'International opinion is solidifying around the view that Pakistan is not as interested in the welfare of the people of Kashmir as in using HR [Human Rights] as a stick to beat India with.'

For all her fine words, when in office Benazir did nothing concrete to solve the Kashmir issue. But it must be admitted that she was good at fine words. In a 1994 interview with *The Sunday Times*, when asked if it was 'really worth coming into conflict with India over the matter because India will never let Kashmir go and whether it is not a no-win situation,' she replied: 'I don't see it as a no-win situation. Because I don't believe that history is the story of might winning against right.'

The Qur'an (4: 135) enjoins the believers to 'speak truth, even if the matter relates to one's own people'. Although most of Geelani's criticism is directed at India, he has not shrunk from taking the Pakistani leadership to task. He is indignant that Pakistan's 'strategy is to shake hands with the people who play with our lives, rape our daughters, arrest our people, kill them and discard their bodies.'[11] He has also criticized the Pakistani media for not reporting violations of human rights in Indian-occupied Kashmir for fear of undermining the so called 'peace process'.

Geelani always regretted Pakistan's failings as a Muslim nation: 'Experience of the last 53 years proves that the policy of preventing the emergence of Islamic revolution in the country and the tilt in favour of Western countries, specially the US, has greatly harmed Pakistan. As a result of this very policy, Pakistan was split into two pieces. The same policy sustained and promoted regional, linguistic and provincial prejudices in the country. The same policy made Pakistan incapable of taking suitable steps with regard to J&K in spite of having a just and lawful stand. Presently, the same policy is causing economic crisis, internal disturbances and unrest.'[12]

India made the most of the 9/11 attacks for its own geostrategic objectives. In a telephone conversation on 8 June 2002 with US Secretary of State Colin Powell (reported next day in *The Financial*

Times), Indian Foreign Minister Jaswant Singh welcomed a pledge that General Pervez Musharraf gave to the US, and he asked the US to ensure that the suspension of cross-border infiltration in Kashmir was made 'permanent' and 'irreversible'. He went on to outline the larger goal: 'This is a step forward and in the right direction,' adding: 'an irreversible end to infiltration requires that the infrastructure of support to cross-border terrorism [read Islamic institutions] within Pakistan be dismantled.'

India makes allegations of 'cross-border terrorism' to (a) undermine the fact that the Kashmiri freedom movement is homegrown and (b) take a shot at its arch foe Pakistan in order to brand it a 'failed state'. When 'Pakistan suggested the involvement of the UN Military Observer Group along the LoC to verify India's allegations regarding its involvement in cross-border terrorism, India rejected the suggestion outright,' wrote retired Indian army officer Col. Ravi Nanda.[13]

Geelani told the *The Indian Express* (6 November 1999): 'India should recognize that it will never capture the hearts and minds of the Kashmiri people and should disengage from Kashmir. Otherwise, Kashmir will remain a dangerous canker in India's body politic with incalculable consequences.... We have to choose between an India which is suppressing and humiliating Kashmiris with its military power and a Pakistan that has been supporting our movement at every step. The Indian might is crushing our bodies, soul and egos. At such a time, even a word of sympathy from Pakistan is soothing.'

Hindu hardliners often criticize Geelani for seeking Pakistani help. But seeking support from cross-border sympathizers is normal, predictable behaviour. For example, in Malaysia a section of its Hindu population was attacked by some ill-informed Muslims. P. Uttayakumar, a founder member of the Malaysian ethnic group Hindu Rights Action Front, explained in a January 2008 interview to Press Trust of India in Kuala Lumpur that after exhausting all legal avenues and channels, 'We are going international. Now I want to go to my mother country [India] to ask for help. What else can we do? Where else do we go?'

Geelani's pro-Pak stand has also been scurrilously exploited by the Indian media and security agencies to accuse him of funnelling aid from the Pakistan government to his own and his family's pockets. India's federal investigative agency, the Central Bureau of Investigation (CBI), registered a formal charge against Geelani in April 1997 of accepting money from abroad in contravention of the Foreign Contributions Registration Act. The First Information Report (FIR) accused him of receiving two million Saudi riyals (over US$ 500,000) and two million US dollars from the Kashmiri American Council. 'The FIR says Geelani used a part of the money to purchase property worth Rs. 8.7 million in Altaf's (Geelani's eldest son-in-law) name; two palatial houses in Srinagar, an orchard in Doru Village in Sopore, and two double-storey houses at Dangarpora (Sopore) and at Pirbagh in Badgam' (*The Week*, 11 May 1997).

Praveen Swami points out in *Frontline* (September 1997) that 'there has been little to prove this charge, which is obviously a spin provided by the authorities to discredit militancy and its leaders.' The issue subsided only after Geelani gave details to the CBI. For example, the house in which he lives with his family at Hyderpora in Srinagar is donated to a trust by him. Such accusations are a tried and tested weapon of oppressive regimes. Nelson Mandela recalled: 'Government propagandists repeatedly claimed that the leaders of the [freedom] campaign were living it up in comfort while the masses were languishing in jail. This allegation was far from the truth, but it achieved a certain currency.'[14]

Having personally witnessed how Geelani and his family live, and indeed struggle for the basic necessities of life, I can affirm that the allegations of profiteering from the Kashmiri cause are utterly false.

Musharraf visited New Delhi in 2004 in an effort to secure support from Kashmiri and Indian leaders for his 'Kashmir solution'. Geelani led a five-member delegation of the Tehrek-e-Hurriyat. He was the first to get an audience with Musharraf, which lasted 90 minutes. He told Musharraf that confidence-building measures were meaningless unless the human rights violations and killings in J&K stopped. He rejected any suggestion that Kashmiris were tired because of Indian atrocities and would accept a quick solution even if it were unjust. He assured Musharraf that Kashmiris were mentally and physically prepared to oppose the Indian occupation for a long time to come. He gave details of the killings and human rights violations to Musharraf and demanded that India withdraw its security forces and release all freedom fighters languishing in dozens of Indian jails.

3.1 President Musharraf meeting Syed Geelani in New Delhi in 2004.

Geelani also advised Musharraf that aligning with the US would be counterproductive for Pakistan and for Kashmir. Indian security analyst, B. Raman observed that 'Pakistani leaders have never had any qualms over letting themselves be used by the US in a manner designed to serve their interests, provided the payment for such use was adequate.' After Osama Bin Laden's assassination in Pakistan,

Raman wrote on the specific contribution of Pervez Musharraf:

> Musharraf was more sensitive to the US interests and more accommodating to US demands. He readily agreed – without ever dragging his feet – to many of the requests that emanated from the George Bush administration. He transferred senior lieutenant generals and a chief of the ISI because the US viewed them with suspicion as close to the Afghan Taliban. He allowed the US Air Force to use Pakistani bases in Balochistan for mounting rescue operations in Afghanistan, and permitted an immense increase in the US intelligence presence in Pakistani territory.
>
> Musharraf agreed to the US intelligence and investigating officers accompanying joint teams of the ISI and the police when they raided suspected hideouts of Al Qaeda operatives in places such as Faisalabad, Karachi and Rawalpindi. The former Pakistan president facilitated the interrogation of two retired senior Pakistani nuclear scientists by the US. He placed AQ Khan, the so-called father of Pakistan's atomic bomb, under house arrest after the discovery of his proliferation activities by the US. He ordered his intelligence and investigating agencies to informally hand over hundreds of terrorism suspects to the US for rendition and interrogation in the Guantanamo Bay detention centre and other places without following the due process of the law.[15]

Geelani's assessment of Musharraf is that he was 'fearful of India's military and economic power and had no faith in himself or his people'.[16] He regarded the Musharraf regime as hostile to the Kashmiris, while maintaining that the Pakistani masses remained their allies. Milton Bearden, a senior CIA officer and former Pakistan station chief, addressing the Senate Foreign Relations Committee, concluded, in view of Musharraf's background and long association with the US army:

> Musharraf may represent a last good chance to bring the powerful force in the world and our system of values to bear on the course Pakistan will choose for the new millennium

[...] He might be able to guide elements within Pakistan society away from the dangerous, fundamentalist path [read
Islam] [...] to a more reasonable and responsible course
[read pro-US/Israel].[17]

Even this CIA official may have underestimated Musharraf's
readiness to ingratiate himself with the US and its interests. Many
Pakistanis gave him the nickname 'Busharraf'.

*3.2 Brothers in arms – President Musharraf meeting
President George Bush in Islamabad, March 2006.*

Addressing a public meeting at Masjid Hamza in Amerakadal,
Geelani spoke scathingly of the government that had betrayed a
country established in the name of Islam (*Greater Kashmir*, 16 June
2007): 'the deployment of its rulers is decided in Washington instead
of Islamabad. This is a tragedy that has put in jeopardy Pakistan's
own existence.' He warned that 'there remains no guarantee for the
protection of Pakistan's geographical borders after it is delinked
from Islamic ideology.' An article in *The Economist* (2 April 2011)
makes the same point: in Pakistan 'except for Jamaat-e-Islami, parties have nothing to do with ideology. The two main ones are family
assets – the Bhuttos own the PPP, and the Sharifs own the PML(N).'

Over the next few years, non-stop drone attacks and the presence on the ground of US-terrorists like Raymond Davis, proved Geelani right. Even the former Interior Minister Rehman Malik admitted that US 'drone missiles cause collateral damage. A few militants are killed, but the majority of victims are innocent citizens' (*The Indian Express*, 23 April 2011). Bush had ordered a total of forty-five drone strikes in Pakistan; in his (first) four years, Obama has ordered more than 300 and counting. The people of Pakistan are outraged, but their leaders effectively ignore their outrage. Former Pakistan Prime Minister Gilani, having tabled a parliamentary resolution condemning the drone attacks, is quoted as privately telling the Americans (*The Express Tribune*, 13 December 2010): 'We will protest in the National Assembly and then ignore it.'

It is no surprise that in the US, Pakistani politicians are regarded contemptuously as corrupt and ineffective. In a 6 January 2011 interview to Council on Foreign Relations, Stephen Cohen observed: 'Someone in the US State Department was quoted in a WikiLeaks document that if it weren't for nuclear weapons, Pakistan would be the Congo. I would compare it to Nigeria without oil. It wouldn't be a serious state. But the nuclear weapons and the country's organised terrorist machinery do make it quite serious.'[18]

Geelani counseled way back in 2001: 'God forbid, if [Pakistan's] ideological identity is compromised and national and other petty interest take precedence, its distinctive status will be completely lost. Pakistan is the only place of shelter for Islam and the Muslim *Ummah*. It should adopt the policy of fulfilling this fundamental responsibility during every crisis.'[19] The former Bosnian President, Izetbegovic, shared this understanding of where political energy resides among Muslims: 'Only Islam can reawaken the imagination of the Muslim masses and render them capable of being once again active participants in their own history. Western ideas are incapable of this.'[20]

India holds Pakistan responsible for not only Kashmir but also its internal troubles. On 18 February 2007, on the eve of then Pakistan Foreign Minister Khurshid Kasuri's visit to India to carry forward the 'peace process', two powerful bombs went off around midnight in two coaches of the Delhi–Lahore cross-border train. The train had then just reached Diwana near Panipat, eighty kilometres km north of Delhi. The coaches turned into an inferno. A third bomb placed in another coach failed to detonate. The 'peace process' was set back. Investigation revealed that three suitcases filled with detonators, timers, iron pipes containing explosives and bottles filled with petrol and kerosene had been smuggled onto the three coaches.

Sixty-eight people died instantly and many more were injured – all Muslims, and a majority of them Pakistanis. A Special Investigation Team (SIT) of the Haryana Police was sent to different parts of the country to follow leads. According to the 19 July 2010 cover story in *Outlook* magazine, the trail led to Indore, a town in the BJP-ruled state of Madhya Pradesh. Here, according to *Outlook*, 'the SIT managed to locate the Abhinandan Bag Centre in Kothari Market, from where the Kodak brand of suitcase containing the explosives was purchased and the tailor who stitched the covers of the suitcases located.' Although no terrorist outfit claimed responsibility, the Indian government's first reaction was to blame Pakistan for the blast.

Outlook claims that 'within official circles it is widely known that investigations were discreetly stopped when the trail led to Hindu activists [note, not 'terrorists'] in Indore.' 'The commonly given explanation' according to *Outlook* is that, given the Indian government's policy of blaming Pakistan for every terrorist incident in India, 'it would have damaged the country's credibility if, after blaming them [Pakistanis] for the blast, it was proved to be the work of Hindus.' Apparently, it was the office of the then National Security Adviser, M. K. Narayanan, which informally advised the police to go slow and not investigate the Hindu connection!

In an article called 'The spotlight on "Hindu Terror"' (*Hindustan Times*, 27 January 2013), Shishir Gupta and Rajesh Ahuja exposed how 'On Jan. 16, 2009, joint secretary Dr. K. P. Krishnan of the [Indian] finance ministry received a letter from John Fennerty, Deputy Counselor in the US Embassy, informing the government that America on Feb. 2 will move the UN Security Council to add five more names to the designated terrorists list. One of them was prominent Lashkar-i-Tayyibah terror financier Mohammed Arif Qasmani, blamed by the US for [...] the 2007 bombing of Samjhauta Express'! The US has been completely silent on this atrocity since the saffron terrorists confessed to it. Evidently, it has no intention of giving up on the pursuit of those it insists must be blamed even for what they did not do. The Ambassador's letter shows that the UN is a convenient stick for the US to punish its adversaries; that the 'designated terrorists list' is fabricated in the interest of US goals; and that India has become a willing partner in a fake 'war on terror' prosecuted in order to punish Muslims, individuals and nations, innocent and guilty. Pakistan is *a* principal target, if not *the* principal target.

But the Pakistani leadership is indifferent. The outgoing President Zardari suggested putting the Kashmir issue 'on the back burner for a later, wiser generation to handle, and concentrate [instead] on boosting trade' (*Hindustan Times*, 20 November 2011). He converted this into a formal agreement with India during his April 2012 visit to New Delhi. In an article in *Hindustan Times* (15 April 2012), Indian media superstar Karan Thapar termed this 'a radical change in Pakistan's attitude. It's nothing short of a U-turn.'

Addressing a Pakistani youth organization by telephone, Geelani complained: 'one Muslim is cutting the throat of another Muslim. Innocent people offering prayers are being showered with bullets in mosques. Killing the people offering prayers in *imambaras* is considered a feat. Armed groups of Sunnis are killing Shias and armed groups of Shias do the same to Sunnis. Even guests, friends and relatives from our neighbouring countries are not being spared.'[21] According to the Pakistan government's economic survey released ahead of 2011–12 budget, the direct and indirect cost incurred by Pakistan on America's 'war on terror' during the past ten years amounts to about $68 billion, equivalent to almost half of the country's total debt. Against this, the US has provided $13 billion in aid to Pakistan, of which almost $9 billion was military disbursements! This explodes the myth that the US is paying for Pakistan's war efforts.

Addressing a conference in Hyderabad on 22 April 2012, Geelani said: 'The British pitted India and Pakistan against each other by creating the Kashmir issue. The Western world was able to sell its arms and ammunition to these two neighbouring countries due to Kashmir. It is the main reason for animosity between India and Pakistan. Once this issue is resolved in its right historical perspective, the rivalry and animosity between the two nations will automatically come to end and they will live like good neighbours.' (*Greater Kashmir*, 25 April 2012)

MUSLIM INDIANS

According to the most conservative estimates, there are nearly 150 million Muslims in India, about fifteen per cent of India's billion-plus population. They have, for decades, complained of social and economic neglect and oppression. For instance, they account for less than 7% of public service employees, only 5% of railways workers, around 4% of banking employees and there are only 29,000 Muslims or 0.02% in India's 1.3 million-strong military.

Moreover, Muslims are intermittently required to prove their loyalty to the country that they and their forefathers consciously chose as their own, over six decades back. Geelani wrote: 'Indian Muslims were not responsible for the partition of the country. But after 1947 they were given very harsh punishment for this uncommitted sin. All political parties express concern for their plight only at the time of elections. False promises and apologies for politicians' past sins and lapses form part of their election campaign. After the election, they are ignored in every field for five years or until declaration of next election.'[22]

Anjan Basu, a veteran Hindu social analyst and executive editor of the Bengali daily *Pratidin*, observes that '[Muslims] are denied many of their basic rights and freedom in an unjustified way.' And 'Six decades after the partition, Indian Muslims still face deep-seated discrimination' (*Washington Times*, 21 August 2007). Many Hindus believe that Pakistan was created for Muslims and they do not have right to live in India. This is not much incentive for

Kashmiri Muslims to stay with India. More important than the economic deprivation has been the issue of their security. Geelani dedicated a chapter of his book *The Oppressed Nation* to the atrocities committed by successive governments on minorities in general and Muslims in particular. A few excerpts:

> During the Congress [Party's] rule idols were kept in this mosque [Babri masjid] on 27 December 1949. Had Congress been honest with the minorities, the cultural and religious aggression of 27 December 1949 could have been put to an end on 28 December 1949 itself. But the Congress policy, in the words of late Prem Nath Bajaj, is to put into practice and implement what the communal parties [like RSS, BJP and Shiv Sena] say and preach.[23]

> Who are the people who made the whole Sikh population the target of cruelty, violence and barbarism after the assassination of Indira Ghandi in 1984? Killing three to five thousand members of the Sikh community mercilessly in retaliation for the killing of one person does not befit a humane society or government! True, the personality of late Indira Gandhi was very precious. She was the Prime Minister of India and it was the demand of justice to punish her killers. But treating the entire Sikh nation or community as murderers and killing them indiscriminately is the worst example of any Congress rule.[24]

> Similarly, the Congress Prime Minister kept on looking at the scenes of destruction of Babri masjid silently. He could have stopped the *'Karsevaks'* by declaring a curfew and calling in the army. He could very well have dismissed Kalyan Singh's [BJP] government and imposed Presidents Rule in U.P. But he appeared very eager to implement the policies of BJP, Bajrang Dal and Vishwa Hindi Parishad. On 7 December 1992 when Muslims came out on [the] streets to demonstrate their hurt feelings, the Congress Government went into action and heaps of [dead] bodies were stacked. This is the government which prefers secularism, justice and fairplay, equality and protection of fundamental rights as its creed.[25]

Besides large-scale anti-Muslim pogroms, there have been numerous cases of Muslims targeted by the state's terror apparatus. 'Killing unarmed people in cold blood in fake encounters is deeply disturbing. It extinguishes the values that underpin democratic governance, the foremost being the right to life and liberty. The battle against terrorism and bigotry will never be won if human rights are abused. Not in Kashmir or elsewhere in the country' (*The Pioneer*, 27 April 2000). Despite this warning, fake encounters and anti-Muslim riots continue unabated. 'The rest of India is becoming Kashmir in some ways. The militarization, the repression, all of that is spreading to the whole country,' warns the Booker Prize winner Arundhati Roy. In a 2011 interview she said:

> From the moment India became independent, it began a protracted war. That war has been fought since 1947 in Nagaland, Manipur, Mizoram, Kashmir, Hyderabad, Goa, Telangana, of course later the Punjab.... So you see somehow a pattern of an upper-caste Hindu state waging war continuously on the other. When there is a problem, like there was, let's say, in Bombay in 1993 or in Gujarat in 2002, when the aggressors are Hindus, then the security forces are on the side of the people who are doing the killing.[26]

BJP's parent organization, RSS, has played a lead role in almost every anti-Muslim riot in India. (In the Appendix, I present a few excerpts from various Commissions set up by different Indian governments to investigate a number of anti-Muslim riots. They provide an authentic view of RSS/BJP's role in anti-Muslim riots over the last six decades in India.) The Babri mosque was demolished in broad daylight by the BJP on 6 December 1992. 'This criminal act performed by the BJP and its allies inflamed communal passion not only in India but also in Pakistan and Bangladesh,' wrote Col. Nanda.[27]

In the aftermath of the Babri mosque demolition, Mumbai police's communal colours came to the fore. More than a thousand Muslims were slaughtered on the streets of Mumbai during the 1992–3 pogroms. Under huge public outcry, the then ruling

Congress government (both in Mumbai and New Delhi) set up an enquiry commission headed by retired Justice Srikrishna. The enquiry report lays bare the biased role played by thirty-one police officers, including R. D. Tyagi. Then a Joint Commissioner, he shot dead nine persons at the famous Suleiman Usman Bakery at Muhammad Ali Road, labeling them 'Kashmiri terrorists'. Another senior police officer, N. K. Kapse was promoted after a departmental inquiry exonerated him of any guilt in shooting down seven persons at the Hari Masjid area of Rafi Ahmed Kidwai Road. Except for the one policeman who was merely dismissed from service, all the police got off lightly despite being found guilty of complicity in acts of mass murder and arson.

In 2002, the BJP wrote another dark chapter in the history of 'the largest democracy in the world'. Members of an offshoot affiliated to the BJP were travelling on the Sabarmati Express from the Central Indian state of Uttar Pradesh to the Western state of Gujarat. These *karsevaks* (a team of BJP volunteers dedicated to pulling down mosques and terrorizing Muslims) were returning after attending a political ceremony aimed at forcibly constructing a Hindu temple on the very site where the sixteenth century Babri mosque once stood. On 27 Feburary 2002, these *karsevaks* got down at Gujarat's Godhra train station just before 8 a.m. They attacked a Muslim tea-vendor and his young daughter on the railway platform. Some Muslims present at the platform protested. As expected, they were thrashed by these vegetarian 'sons of mother India'. Hardline Hindus call all non-vegetarians [read Muslims] cruel for causing pain to animals. But we will see in the next few pages how peaceful vegetarians treated their fellow humans!

The Godhra train station is located in the predominantly Muslim district of Signal Falia. After word got around of what the *karsevaks* had done, and shortly after the train started rolling out of the station, it is alleged, a few dozen Muslim residents of the area rushed to stop the train. They gathered around the coach carrying some of those criminals. After verbal exchange, Muslims are alleged to have set coach no. S-6 on fire, burning fifty-nine passengers inside. Islam prohibits its followers from such inhumane acts; if some

Muslims indeed committed this crime, then those Muslims should have been tried in a court of law and given severest punishment. A renowned civil activist Jyoti Punwani claims that 'an experiment conducted in June 2002 by the government run Forensic Science Laboratory (FSL) in Ahmadabad showed that the fire could only have been caused by pouring inflammable liquid from inside the coach and then starting the fire in the bogie' (*Tehelka*, 11 October 2008). (It may surprise the BJP, but the FSL is not run by either the Pakistani Intelligence Agency ISI or by Kashmiri 'terrorists'!)

Indian Railways appointed a Commission under Justice U. C. Banerjee to carry out a thorough investigation. The Commission concluded in 2005 that the fire was an accident! 'I stand by my report 200 per cent that it was an accidental fire in a coach of the Sabarmati Express at Godhra station on 27 February 2002, and I will not deviate from that,' Justice Banerjee told the *Press Trust of India* (*Indian Express*, 23 Feburary 2011). According to *Outlook* (23 February 2011), 'he had prepared his inquiry report after extensively going into all aspects and examining 80 witnesses before finalising his conclusion.' The train fire at Godhra 'was caused by an accidental fire, but was falsely attributed to an organised Muslim "conspiracy",' confirmed Praful Bidwai in a *Rediff* piece on 2 June 2012. A number of independent investigations raised questions as to whether the BJP government orchestrated the killings in the train in order subsequently to legitimize genocide against Muslims.

This theory is not far-fetched. BJP is a party that has publicly praised Adolf Hitler. There is historical evidence of how Hitler engineered incidents that eventually led to World War Two. 'Within hours of the tragedy on board the Sabarmati Express, the BJP and its affiliates – the Vishwa Hindu Parishad, The Rashtriya Swayamsevak Sangh and the Bajrang Dal – started preparations for one of the worst acts of genocide in the history of this country,' wrote Ashish Khetan.[28] The day after the train fire in Godhra, Gujarat Chief Minister Narendra Modi issued this chilling warning on state-run television:

> I want to assure the people that Gujarat shall not tolerate such incident. The culprits will get full punishment for

their sins. Not only this, we will set an example [such] that nobody, not even in his dreams, will think of committing a heinous crime like this.[29]

Later that day, Modi repeated the same threat on the floor of the Gujarat assembly. Eminent Indian journalist Siddhartha Vardarajan explained how it translated into reality:

> The next seventy-two hours were to demonstrate exactly what the ruling BJP in Gujarat and New Delhi had in mind. A pogrom of unimaginable proportions was unleashed [against Muslims] with the full sanction of the government. Goons from the RSS, BJP, VHP and Bajrang Dal were given a free hand by the state authorities and police.... Over 600 Muslims had been killed [actually 2000], more than 200,000 had been displaced because their homes had been looted and burnt, and Muslim property worth several thousand crores of rupees [billions of dollars] destroyed, all under the watchful eye of the police and administration.[30]

3.3 The burnt bodies of innocent Muslims roasted by BJP supporters in Gujarat during the 2002 anti-Muslim genocide.

Vardarajan notes that 'one of the most peculiar features of the anti-Muslim violence in Gujarat was the detailed information about

Muslim businesses that the RSS-led mobs had gathered in advance. Presumably it was from officially-conducted surveys of some kind that this data was culled.'[31] No reasonable person can doubt that the torching of the train coach and subsequent massacre were all pre-planned in a sequential manner to terrorize Muslims.

A decade later, a vast majority of the perpetrators of this hate crime, at least in part committed under license of the American-led response to 9/11, remain at large. The failure of the justice system is a cost to the whole nation, but that cost is borne first and foremost by the surviving victims and the Muslims of India as a whole. Harsh Mander, Director of the Center for Equity Studies, confirmed this in an article in *Hindustan Times* (6 March 2011):

> There is something about the violence of mass hate which makes its wounds fester even after many others heal. In villages and towns of Gujarat, survivors have adapted themselves to the everyday reality of second-class citizenship. I estimate that nearly 100,000 people have been permanently ejected and their erstwhile settlements 'cleansed' of Muslim residents. A quarter of these internally displaced people endure in austere relief colonies, established after the carnage by various Muslim organizations. The remainders have moved to the safety of poorly serviced Muslim ghettoes.
>
> Across the state today, I observe what I regard as the 'Dalitisation' of the Gujarati Muslim. Like Dalits [lowest caste Hindus], Muslims in Gujarat today live in segregated settlements, socially devalued and economically ostracized. They are discriminated against in schools and police stations, deprived of basic public services, discouraged in both private and public employment, and excluded from social intercourse such as wedding and birth celebrations. Dalits have lived with these social and economic disabilities for centuries. But the process of pushing Muslims to the same humiliating margins of Gujarati society as Dalits was compressed into the single past decade [since BJP rule began]. This is the enduring legacy of the politics of hatred and division, which has triumphed in Gujarat. We don't know if

and when this will ever change.

Muslims in Gujarat today don't live in the expectation of another imminent orgy of mass violence. But they survive daily discrimination as an incontrovertible element of survival. Markers of Muslim identity are fading from Gujarati public life. In many villages, one of the conditions imposed [by Hindus] on Muslim residents who wished to return was that the call of the *azaan* [Muslim call for prayer] from their mosque should no longer resonate in the village.

3.4 *Ashok Mochi (above) at Sahapur in Ahmedabad on 28 February 2002.*[32]

The legal definition of genocide as articulated in the UN Convention on the Prevention and Punishment of the Crime of Genocide (1948) is very clear:[33]

Genocide means any of the following acts committed with intent to destroy, in whole or in part, a national, ethnic, racial or religious group, as such:

(a)   Killing members of the group;

(b)   Causing serious bodily or mental harm to members of the group;

(c)   Deliberately inflicting on the group conditions of life
      calculated to bring about its physical destruction in
      whole or in part;

(d)   Imposing measures intended to prevent births within
      the group;

(e)   Forcibly transferring children of the group to another
      group.

On at least the first three counts what happened in Gujarat
was genocide, and all those who participated in it and those who
sanctioned it need to be brought to justice. 'Civil society has had
no doubt that it was Chief Minister Narendra Modi who was to
blame for the genocide,' confirmed Ashish Khetan.[34] Instead of
facing an impartial trial (and possible conviction) for mass-murder,
why is Modi being nominated as BJP's Prime Ministerial candidate
for 2014 elections? The reason is simple: 'IPS and IAS officers are
pawns in his games [...] corporate India, big fat cats of the western
world and even "vested interests" in vital ministries in his state and
in New Delhi are backing Modi.'[35] Little surprising then that even
Indian Supreme Court has given him a clean chit!

A BJP-linked incident involving a close assocaite of Geelani will
not be out of place here. Kashmiri lawyer Hisamuddin, a prominent
member of Jama'at, narrated to me how in the 1970s, in his student
days, he visited BJP's Atal Behari Vajpayee at his home in New
Delhi. Vajpayee was then just an MP and therefore easily accessible.
He embraced Hisamuddin and offered him sweets saying: 'I have
specially got these sweets as my Kashmiri son [Hisamuddin] was
coming to meet me.' This gesture so impressed Hisamuddin that
when I met him in the early 1990s, he was eagerly waiting for the
BJP to come to power. He naively believed that a Vajpayee-led BJP
would play fair with Kashmiris and allow the long-awaited plebiscite. Hisamuddin was apparently killed in cold blood by Indian
agents on the morning of 15 September 2004 at his residence in
Srinagar. Vajpayee was then the Prime Minster of India.

In *Oppressed Nation* (p. 3) Geelani quotes Vajpayee as saying: 'You can go to a mosque and offer *namaz* [prayers]. We have no problem. But if you have to choose between Mecca or Islam and India, you must choose India. All the Muslims should have this feeling: we will live and die for this country'. Geelani then explains: 'Mr Vajpayee has clearly stated his planning to assimilate Muslims into the culture, way of life and civilization of the majority [Hindus]. This according to Vajpayee is the only solution to the Hindu–Muslim conflict prevailing in India. Other parties also intend to do the same although their way is different.' Nevertheless, while deeply concerned about the atrocities committed against Muslims in India over the last several decades, Geelani has urged them to refrain from violence or other illegal activies.

Even senior BJP leader and former Foreign Minister Jaswant Singh admitted in a rare 28 March 2011 article:[36]

> Indians [...] are abandoning the sense of fellowship that marked the country's earlier years of struggle. But, without a fundamental sense of solidarity with one's fellow citizens, no parliamentary democracy can function. There is also a growing sense that India has forgotten how to accommodate dissent, that alternative viewpoints are considered entirely irrelevant. As a result, the government views disagreement as a 'disservice', a rebellious challenge that must be crushed.

It is no secret that with the political ascent of the BJP, India's diplomatic and military ties with Israel have increased manifold over the last ten to fifteen years. Rather less well-known is how closely attitudes, procedures and public rhetoric in India mirror the same in Israel's relations with Palestinians and Arabs generally. Hate-crimes on one side are treated as one-off incidents, for example. Thus, as Mumbai advocate and human rights campaigner Mihir Desai points out (*The Outlook*, 19 July 2010): 'For the past 10 years, stories about Hindu right-wing violence have been trickling out. Instead of a systemic investigation, there has been an event-to-event investigation. The larger story has remained under-investigated and under-reported.'

On the other side, guilt is assumed and attributed to the entire community and extended as far as necessary by association – in the case of India, to Pakistan – without any need for evidence or reference to facts. The narrative of an entire community or nation being disposed to violence is sustained by accusations that are repeated again and again, even after they have been proven to be ridiculously false. The accusations have a rhetorical, not a legal, purpose. They serve to intensify public fear and to legitimize the state's response to it, however irrational or ineffective that response may be. For example, Wajhul Qamar Khan was arrested for the 2003 blast on a local train in Mulund, Mumbai. After the well-orchestrated Mumbai massacre of 2008, the Indian government handed over a dossier to Pakistan in which Khan is named among fifty fugitives hiding there. But in May 2011, a *Times of India* reporter located Khan in Thane's Waghle Estate near Mumbai, where he had been living with his mother, wife and children for the last seven years! Similarly, Feroz Rashid Khan, named in India's most wanted list of terrorists allegedly hiding in Pakistan, was found to be in Arthur Road Jail in Mumbai, facing trial in the 1993 serial blasts case.

'There are close to 23 security agencies, 35 state anti-terror cells and special units operating in India on hundreds of cases in which people [mainly Muslims] have been branded as terrorists, only to be found innocent after a trial extending from five years to eternity. By that time, the officer concerned has moved on in his life, with a gallantry medal pinned on his chest for exemplary courage!'[37] After the arrest of many innocent Muslim Indians in Mumbai and U.P. for alleged terrorist attacks, Vicky Nanjappa posted a long list of such incidents on the top Indian news portal *Rediff.com* on 14 February 2008 at 14:18 Indian Standard Time under the headline, 'IISC attack: Have cops found the right man?'

But in respect of such fabricated stories, India is behaving no worse than its 'natural ally', the US. On 3 June 2011, when Ilyas Kashmiri was killed in a US drone strike, he had already been dead for over a year. In September 2009, the CIA claimed that it killed Kashmiri and two other senior Taliban leaders in North Waziristan. But the lure of the limelight was seemingly irresistible even in death, because on 9 October, Kashmiri returned to give an interview to the late Syed Saleem Shahzad of *Asia Times Online*. Similarly, Baitullah Mehsud, the former commander of the Tahrik-i-Taliban Pakistan (TTP), rose from the dead many times. On at least sixteen occasions, Mehsud was in the gunsights when CIA drones loosed their Hellfire missiles. Yet, until August 2009, he proved unable to settle into the afterlife. Another Taliban leader Mullah Sangeen also enjoyed at least two resurrections. In 2007, US-led forces claimed to have killed Mulla Sangeen Zardan, a senior commander of the Haqqani network in Afghanistan. But on 16 August 2011, the Obama administration designated him a 'terrorist' and 'froze' his assets in the US!

3.5 Saffron terrorists burning the Qur'an on the streets of New Delhi in the early 1990s. No action was taken against them for 'creating hate' and 'disturbing the peace'.

There are other commonalities between these two 'largest democracies in the world'. Terry Jones, the American pastor, who courted notoriety by threatening to burn copies of the Qur'an on the anniversary of the 11 September attacks, withdrew his threat under pressure from political leaders. Then, on 20 March 2011, he oversaw the burning of a copy of the Qur'an by another pastor, Wayne Sapp. Muslims everywhere were outraged and protested but, though this atrocity was done by a Christian religious leader, no Muslim in the world labeled it 'Christian terrorism'. In India a decade earlier in the late 1990s, BJP supporters burnt the Qur'an on the streets of the national capital, New Delhi. Unlike Wayne, these saffron terrorists were not marking any anniversary, merely expressing their hate for and intent to inflame Muslims.

Another alarming trend has emerged recently. Hundreds of innocent Muslims have been framed by the security forces for various 'terrorist activities' that they never committed. Bar Associations in several states including Uttar Pradesh and Maharashtra *officially* prevented their members from defending Muslims in the courts. It is possible that some of these RSS-inspired Bar Associations were partners-in-crime and fearful that legal process would prove the Muslims innocent and expose the real terrorists. In the interest of restoring confidence in the judiciary and preserving the social fabric of India, the motives of those Bar Associations should be urgently investigated.

Thane city's advocate Abdul Kalam explains (*Times of India*, 22 April 2011): 'After the communal riots, it has been found that Hindu advocates are reluctant to fight cases of Muslim victims or accused. We don't say that all non-Muslim advocates are biased, but during moments of crisis, many upright advocates have developed cold feet.' If some Muslim lawyers have come forward to defend Muslims, they have been physically intimidated or even killed. One such example is the young lawyer Shahid Kazmi who was defending the accused of earlier Mumbai bomb blasts. At the age of 32, he was killed in broad daylight in Mumbai by some henchmen of 'patriotic' underworld don Chota Rajan.

Qateel Siddiqui, a terror suspect, had not been formally charged even seven months after his arrest. Then, in the first week of June 2012 he was murdered inside his cell in Pune Jail. For Indian Muslims, the situation is becoming impossible – no protection from the police; no recourse to the judiciary; no support from the media.[38]

Yoginder Sikand has argued that 'the increasing resilience of the Islamist elements within the Kashmiri struggle can also be seen, in a crucial sense, as a response to the escalation in anti-Muslim violence in India, and the increasing threat to [the] Muslim community's identity at the hands of chauvinist Hindu groups in league with the Indian state' (*The Economic & Political Weekly*, 20 January 2001). Sensing possible implications, noted Indian film-maker Mahesh Bhatt warned (*Hindustan Times*, 27 April 2008): 'if Gujarat riot victims continue to feel biased against and India bends over backwards to accommodate US interests, then the day is not far when worst forms of terror like suicide bombings could become a reality [in India too].'

'Indian Muslims are Indian by choice. Kashmir has nothing to do with Indian Muslims,' Geelani affirmed in an interview to *Hindustan Times* (9 April 2000). But a determined effort is on to create a fear-psychosis among Indian Muslims that if Kashmir is separated from India terrible consequences will follow. Eminent journalist Hiranmay Karlekar framed that fear in this way (*The Pioneer*, 2 May 1997): 'Given Pakistan's sustained waging of a vicarious low-intensity war in Kashmir, any settlement that appears to take the Valley away from India will be considered a national humiliation in this country. This will unleash a wage of searing anger which the forces of Hindu fanaticism will try to ride to capture power at the centre. They will attack the Government, charging it with betraying the nation, and Indian Muslims, accusing them of being Pakistani's fifth column. This is almost certain to trigger communal slaughter, as bad as the one in 1947, if not worse.'

The fear being stoked by such alarmist scenarios has no rational basis. Karlekar's dark thoughts had already been considered and dismissed by Ashok Mitra (*The Telegraph*, 16 May 1990): 'Not even a miniscule fraction of the population in the Valley is currently in a mood to continue the political connection with the Indian Union. We must, it is said, hold on to Kashmir by hook or crook. If the Valley is lost, Hindu fundamentalism in the country will raise its head; it will begin to spit fire. Seething with dark anger at the dis-possession of Kashmir, it will target the life and property of our one hundred million and odd Muslim compatriots: this is a frightening argument [...] It really amounts to the following: in case Kashmir leaves India, the Hindu fanatics will in retribution try to liquidate the nation's Muslim minorities. As we cannot allow that to happen, so Kashmir has to be retained by us, if necessary by force.' Two years later, Former Foreign Secretary of India R. D. Sathe made another logical argument, qouted in *Muslim India* (#115, July 1992: 307):

> The argument that India's policy of secularism will be jeopardized if the Kashmir valley breaks away from India is spurious. Indian secularism cannot be dependent or measured on the basis of what a very minuscule portion of the vast Muslim minority of India thinks and does. Integration of Kashmir into India was accomplished by doubtful means. In any case if a people wish to break their link with India they must not be denied the choice. But this must be done in a civilized manner. Kashmir's defection would (not) weaken India's policy of secularism.

Geelani has expressed disappointment at the indifferent attitude of Muslim Indians and their lack of activism in supporting the Kashmiri freedom movement. In *The Oppressed Nation* (p. 75) he complained:

> We have a religious bond with Muslims of India. All Muslims are brothers. On account of this relation we have strong complaints towards our brothers. In the period of trials and tribulations through which the people of Jammu & Kashmir in general and Muslims in particular are passing, the Muslims of India have not played the role they were expected on the basis of faith and brotherhood.

> Fifty or sixty lakh Kashmiri Muslims, in spite of being surrounded by Indian forces, always strongly protested, demonstrated and even laid down their lives whenever anti-Muslim and even anti-Sikh riots took place in India. Whenever Muslims were killed and mosques destroyed same was their response. But I am constrained to say with extreme regret and pain that even when mosques, pilgrimage centres, monasteries, shrines, ancient monuments and symbols of Islamic civilization were erased [in Kashmir] the Muslims of India never demonstrated their sense of unity, fraternity and brotherhood with their brothers in Kashmir.

Geelani is so deeply immersed in the Kashmiri freedom movement that he fails to realize what Muslim Indians are going through. Mahtab Alam, a civil rights activist and freelance journalist, sums up well the situation that Muslims face in India: 'To be a Muslim in India today is to be encounterable,[39] to be constantly suspected of being a terrorist, to be illegally detainable and severely torturable, to have the possibility of being killed without being questioned, no matter if one is a believer, agnostic or an atheist. Carrying a Muslim name deserves and qualifies for the above treatment.'[40] A *Tehelka. com* article of 2 February 2013 also complained 'fake encounters prove, [the] state intentionally tags Muslim youths as a potential threat for the country. It creates stereotyping and hatred among fellow citizens.'

4

IMPRISONMENT AND WRITINGS

'A MAN INVOLVED in the [freedom] struggle is a man without a home life. I did not relish being deprived of the company of my children. I missed them a great deal', Nelson Mandela recalls in his memoirs. He often wondered if neglecting the welfare of one's family in order to fight for that of others could be justified. He concludes: 'I do not mean to suggest that the freedom struggle is of a higher moral order than taking care of one's family. It is not; they are merely different.'[1]

On 28 August 1962, at the age of thirty years, Geelani was arrested and imprisoned for the first time, for thirteen months. During this period his father passed away: 'the largest democracy in the world' did not see fit to allow Geelani to attend his father's funeral. Since then, Geelani has spent more than sixteen years of his life in prison and has thus become one of the few public leaders to spend so long a period in prison.

While in prison, on 7 September 1986, Geelani suffered cardiac pain and was rushed to intensive care. Rumors of his death brought his followers and well-wishers on to the streets. To calm them, the government was obliged to deny the rumours through a radio broadcast. When the armed resistance against the continued Indian presence in J&K began in 1989, he along with his colleagues in the MUF resigned their seats in the Legislature to join the public. For that he was imprisoned for the longest single term, a full two years.

A breakdown of Geelani's detention timeline is presented below:*

	Date of Arrest	Imprisoned For
1	28-08-1962	13 months
2	07-05-1965	22 months
3	05-07-1975	04 months
4	07-12-1975	04 months
5	August 1980	04 months
6	06-03-1984	10 months
7	28-01-1985	20 months
8	10-04-1990	24 months
9	22-10-1993	12 months
10	1995	03 months
11	1999	07 months
12	09-06-2002	10 months

The list is incomplete and does not include his virtual house-arrest since 2008. He has not been allowed to move freely within J&K or even attend Friday prayers during this period.

According to Mandela, 'prison is designed to break one's spirit and destroy one's resolve. The challenge for every prisoner, particularly every political prisoner, is how to survive prison intact, how to emerge from prison undiminished, how to conserve and even replenish one's beliefs.'[2] Geelani is living proof that the challenge can be met with patience, perseverance and replenished belief.

Geelani's indomitable spirit inspired millions of Kashmiris to keep up the struggle. Among those who followed his example of leadership are Mohammed Ashraf Sahrai, Miyaan Abdul Qayoom and Aasiya Indrabi, all of whom have been in and out of prisons. Reflecting on his decades of imprisonment, Nelson Mandela observed that 'little can be said in favour of prison, but enforced isolation is conducive to study.'[3] Geelani too made good use of the enforced isolation both to read intensively in Islamic literature, history and poetry and to produce books for the benefit of his followers. His writings cover the on-going freedom movement, his experiences in jail, and his political beliefs.

4.1 Leaving his Hyderpora residence for yet another detention in 2010.

Yoginder Sikand has studied the Kashmiri liberation movement and the writings of Geelani closely: '[His] major writings all date to the 1990s, a period when the J&K Jamaat [JIJK] had immersed itself in the armed struggle, in which Geelani himself played a key role, and for which he was forced to spend several years in various Kashmiri and Indian jails. Not surprisingly, Geelani's writings focus almost solely on the issue of Kashmir's freedom from Indian control. He devotes little attention in his writings to Islamic law, theology and doctrines, for being an ideologue of the JIJK he takes Maududi's voluminous writing on these subjects as authoritative.'[4]

Sikand believes that Geelani's concern is to place the Kashmiri struggle within the Islamist discursive framework, to present his struggle as a jihad, whose initial goal is the merger of Kashmir with Pakistan and, longer term, the establishing of an Islamic polity in the region. His understanding of the struggle is markedly 'less radical' than that 'of [some] Pakistan based militant outfits'. The armed struggle being waged in Kashmir was necessitated by a combination of factors: (a) India's denial to the Kashmiris of their right to self-determination; (b) its brutal suppression resulting in the deaths of many thousand of Kashmiris; and (c) the rapid rise in India of anti-Muslim Hindu chauvinist groups like the BJP and Shiv Sena. He believes that the Indian state has, by its actions, proved its extreme hostility towards the religious and moral rights of Muslims and the tenets and symbols of Islam. 'Wherever such a situation obtains, jihad becomes a binding obligation (*fard*) for all Muslims.'[5]

In declaring the struggle a jihad, Geelani makes it clear that it is directed against the Indian state and its agents, not against Hindus or Indians *per se*. Thus, in an appeal to the Kashmiri militants in April 1992,[6] Geelani stressed that 'the *mujahadeen* have just two enemies: the Indian state and its agents. To waste the power of our youth on targets other than these two is like pouring salt on the wounds of our oppressed people.' On numerous occasions, Geelani has appealed for communal harmony and emphasized that Hindu–Muslim relations in the state have traditionally been cordial. In the past, the Valley has never witnessed bloodshed that has erupted in India periodically, and on a menacingly increasing scale: Kashmir was spared the horrors that afflicted Muslims and Hindus elsewhere at the time of Pakistan's creation.

Furthermore, Geelani's opposition to the Indian state is limited to his prime objective of liberating Kashmir from Indian control. Once that objective is attained, he affirms that the J&K Jama'at would like to see India as free, prosperous and peaceful. Criticizing certain unnamed Kashmiri militant groups for spreading anti-India hatred, he says:

> Emotional slogans such as 'Crush India' are neither realistic nor do they reflect the spirit of Islam.... Islam is based on invitation to prosperity, salvation in the Hereafter, protection of the truth, ending every form of oppression and creating understanding between all children of Adam. [...] Our struggle should be geared to gaining our rights.... The slogan of Islam is not one of destruction but of invitation [to] prosperity, peace and truth.[7]

Geelani vehemently rejects the concept of Kashmiri 'nationhood'. This follows from his religious conviction that Islam and nationalism are incompatible. Thus he questions the very basis of the political agenda of the major rivals of J&K Jamaʿat, the various Kashmiri nationalist groups such as the JKLF. Geelani considers nationalism a 'poisonous' Western concept with which Muslim peoples were deliberately infected so as to divide and therefore weaken them politically, militarily and economically. Muslims should instead identify themselves primarily as belonging to a single, undivided community, cohering on the basis .of 'common belief (*'aqidah*) and faith (*iman*)' and recognizing no differences of colour, race, language, caste, tribe or clan. Territorial nationalism has ruined the Muslims, and has deflected them from the task of 'changing the conditions of the entire human race'.

Geelani distinguishes 'patriotism' (*watan dosti*), which Islam allows, from territorial nationalism or 'nation worship' (*watan parasti*), which Islam clearly forbids. 'Nation worship' – 'my nation, right or wrong' – leads to group prejudice, a quality of the pre-Islamic period of *jahiliyyah*' or Ignorance, and is the source of the strife and bloodshed that characterizes the world today. 'Nationalism is the slogan of the Ignorance, because the nation has usurped from Islam the right to decide the criterion for what is right and what is wrong. Because of this, large states, such as India, prey on smaller, weaker states, causing endless suffering and misery, with millions of people being sacrificed, in the Kashmiri case, "by the priests of Mother India".'[8]

In Geelani's view, the former colonial power, while retreating from Muslim lands under pressure, were still strong enough to leave behind their puppets and keep Muslims divided on linguistic, sectarian or nationalistic lines. The ideology of men like Gamal Nasser and Ataturk was immensely damaging to the *ummah*, politically, morally and economically. Only Islamic movements (like the one Geelani represents) are committed to destroying the idol of territorial nationalism and restoring the dignity and idealism that Muslims enjoyed as Muslims before being cramped by nationalism. Since Geelani views all Muslims as constituting a supranational community, he accepts as 'an undeniable truth' that in Kashmir or India Muslims and Hindus are considered separate peoples. This appears to contradict his frequent appeals to Hindus and Muslims to rebuild the harmonious coexistence that they had enjoyed in Kashmir for centuries. He does appear to be saying that for Islam to be preserved and promoted in Kashmir, it is necessary for it to be separated from India.

Geelani's critique of nationalism as antithetical to Islam is a critique of Kashmiri nationalist groups such as the JKLF. He makes it abundantly clear that the 'Islamic' solution to the Kashmir question is not the establishment of an independent Kashmiri nation state but the incorporation of Kashmir into an already-existing Muslim state, Pakistan, and a necessary step towards the eventual unification of all Muslims. In his 1992 pamphlet *Maslay ka hall* (*The Solution to the Issue*), he made this point explicit:

> when [a] group shares common ideological, cultural and communal relations with a neighboring [Muslim] group as well as a common border.... For such a group to maintain a separate political identity of its own is against the broader interests of the entire Muslim *millat*.

On the same basis he criticizes the alleged Pakistani policy of supporting all pro-freedom groups in Kashmir regardless of their ideology and simply for being 'against India'. He argues that supporting secular nationalism (Kashmir or other) is un-Islamic and a grave threat 'to Pakistan's stability and existence'.[9]

From his analysis of Geelani's major writings, Sikand deduces four points as particularly central to his discursive framework: (1) the struggle in Kashmir is not a national liberation movement but a jihad; (2) the jihad is directed at the Indian state and its agents, and not against Hindus or Indians *per se*, meaning that the *mujahidin* have no intention of intervening in India's internal affairs after the liberation of Kashmir; (3) the jihad aims at freeing Kashmir from Indian control and merging it with Pakistan, as part of a wider project of establishing a united Muslim bloc – an independent

Kashmiri state is ruled out as un-Islamic; and (4) the merger with Pakistan 'is seen as the only just answer to the Kashmir crisis, and an effective means to establish peace and cordial relations between India and Pakistan' (Yoginder Sikand, *Economic and Political Weekly*, 20 January 2001).

In recent discussions, Geelani has chosen to put the debate of 'merger with Pakistan' versus 'independent Kashmir' on hold. He advises Kashmiris to focus on the demand for a plebiscite, and not to jump the gun. Sadly, Geelani's flexibility and pragmatism are never highlighted by the Indian media or anti-Geelani groups in Kashmir.

Like all repressive regimes, India never wanted some of Geelani's prison memoirs to be published and his painful experiences known to the outside world. 'Unfortunately, my diary and the third volume of *Roodad-e-Qafas* narrating events of Agra Central Jail and Jammu Jail were confiscated by [the] Indian security agencies. I met Mr. Vimal Mohan, Commanding Officer of BSF in a condolence meeting at the residence of Mr. Kaleemullah of Nawab Bazar. During the course of our conversation, he made a comment on some pages of my diary. Then I realized that they are being scrutinized thoroughly,' writes Geelani.[10] In another book, *Maqtal say vaapsi* (*On Returning from the Scaffold*), Geelani mentions that he is continually being jailed for his pro-Pakistan views, and for refusing offers from the Indian intelligence to 'play a double role' for them. It also describes how he was mistreated and even tortured in prison.[11] 'I found the solitary confinement the most forbidding aspect of prison life,' recalls Nelson Mandela, 'but the human body has an enormous capacity for adjusting to trying circumstances'.

Mandela also recalls: 'one of the state's most barbarous techniques of applying pressure: imprisoning the wives and children of freedom fighters. Many men in prison were able to handle anything the authorities did to them, but the thought of the state doing the same thing to their families was almost impossible to bear.'[12] Iftekhar Geelani is a Delhi-based journalist and married to Geelani's daughter Anisa. He has worked for a number of Indian and foreign media organizations. On 9 June 2002, he was picked up by Indian intelligence agencies on sedition charges. Anisa's father Geelani was also imprisoned at that time, in Bihar. But the brave daughter of a brave father happily faced this test. Iftekhar was released after eight months as the Indian government failed to prove any charge against him. Geelani's elder son-in-law, Altaf Ahmed, has also been jailed several times.

History records many examples of occupiers imposing suffering in the hope of breaking the will of those who resist occupation. Bal Gangadhar Tilak faced this situation when he faced the repression of the British Raj. As editor of *Kesari*, Tilak published an editorial on 12 May 1908 called 'The Misfortune of the Country'. The British police slapped sedition charges against him under Section 124-A of the Indian Penal Code. He was arrested on 25 May 1908, convicted by jury trial (popularly known as the 'Second Sedition Case') on 17 July 1908 and sentenced to six years' imprisonment. Tilak is now celebrated as a great hero in India! 'History shows that penalties do not deter men when their conscience is aroused.... For men, freedom in their own land is the pinnacle of their ambitions, from which nothing can turn men of conviction aside.'[13]

Geelani announced his intention to address a public meeting at TRC, Srinagar after Friday prayers on 20 April 2012. But on the evening of 19 April, a heavy contingent of police cordoned off his house and informed him that he was not permitted to leave it. Geelani's party spokesman Ayaz Akbar told media on 20 April 2012, such a police action 'without any written order from the administration or court' shows that New Delhi and its puppets in J&K 'have accepted defeat and they cannot fight him politically' and that Geelani is the real representative of the wishes and aspirations of the people of Kashmir (*Greater Kashmir*, 20 April 2012).

Geelani has maintained good contacts with the people throughout his struggle. When not himself in Indian or Kashmiri prisons, he uses every opportunity to visit victims of Indian security forces and to attend the funerals of those killed by them. Before Ikhwanis (discussed in Chapter 8) burnt down his ancestral home in Sopore in October 1993, he used to visit and stay there despite his exhausting commitments.

4.2 Syed Geelani meeting common Kashmiris who are the victims of state terror.

In contrast to Geelani and his family (whom the security forces victimize), many of the separatist leaders in J&K, whom the authorities call 'moderates', have to be protected from the people by those same security forces. Chief Minister Omar Abdullah told the state Assembly on 23 March 2011 the government is spending Rs 2.384 million annually on state security cover for a number of individuals including Mirwaiz Umar Farooq, Prof. Abdul Gani Bhat, Maulvi Abbas Ansari, Aga Syed Hassan Mousvi, Bilal Gani Lone, Hashim Qureshi and Sajjad Gani Lone (Z-category), Salim Geelani (no relation), Zafar Akbar Bhat, Shahid-ul-Islam, Muhammad Yaqoob Vakil (Y-category), Abdul Hassan Mustafa, Moulvi Manzoor Hussain, Masroor Abbas Ansari, Tariq Anwar, Rafiq-ul-Haq and Sheikh Muzaffar. The Chief Minister also confirmed that 'JKLF chief Yaseen Malik, Fazal Haq Qureshi (chairman of PPF), Shabir Ahmad Shah, Nayeem Ahmed Khan and Syed Ali Shah Geelani have refused [the offer of] security from the police' (*Greater Kashmir*, 23 March 2011).

5

KASHMIR'S PANDITS AND ITS INTEGRITY

POST-INDEPENDENT POLITICAL LEADERSHIP in India has come, primarily, from a single family of Kashmiri Hindus popularly known as 'Pandits'. Pandit Jawaharlal Nehru was the first Prime Minister of India, after him his daughter Indira Gandhi, and then her son Rajiv. Now Rajiv's son (the fourth generation of the same family) is being groomed to head the 'largest democracy'! This dynasty traces its ancestry to Kashmir. Despite his emotional public assurances to Kashmiri Muslims, 'Pandit-ji', as Nehru was fondly called, 'used his Kashmiri origin as well as some of his idealism to serve what he considered the wider national interest [of India]' (Balraj Puri, *The Illustrated Weekly of India*, 18 March 1990).

In pursuit of his Islamic belief, Geelani has always been concerned for the Hindu minorities living in J&K. Way back in December 1963, when communal tension simmered in Sopore he rushed there (from Bandipora) and gave a speech urging Muslims to follow the teachings of the Prophet and to do no harm to the minorities. This greatly eased the tension in the town and reassured the Pandits.

Pandits numbered between 150–300,000 of the state's total population – 'a small but disproportionately well-educated and successful minority' (Lewis M. Simons, *National Geographic*, October, 2000). When the mass uprising broke out in 1989, the Indian government moved Pandits out of the Valley in preparation for the unleashing of maximum force to crush the Muslims' aspirations once for all. To execute this plan, Jagmohan (now a prominent member of the BJP) was appointed as Governor.

Jagmohan has an interesting background. He first won the favour of Indira Gandhi during the Emergency Law imposed by her in 1975. 'In April 1976 he was in charge of demolishing an old *basti* [a predominantly Muslim housing district] in the Turkman Gate area of Delhi. He did this with such efficiency that people barely had time to move out before their houses were bulldozed to rubble. Several people [mainly Muslims] were killed in the aftermath; exact figures were never known.'[1] Because they were Muslims, and not worth the count!

The Emergency in 1975 across India was but 'a baby dose of authoritarianism in comparison to what Kashmir has been subjected to. The heavy, oppressive and all-pervasive presence of the armed forces makes even pro-India Kashmiris feel like a colonized people: a sentiment not conducive to producing loyal citizens' (Madhu Kishwar, *The Indian Express*, 13 July 2000). In Tavleen Singh's view, Jagmohan 'suited Mrs Gandhi's Kashmir policy to perfection. In fact, for what she wanted done, she could not have found a better man.' He later incentivised Pandits to leave the Valley, even offering Pandit government servants (of whom there were many) full payment of their salaries wherever they relocated.[2] In effect, the Pandtis were promised a vacation on full pay in exchange for leaving their homes in the Valley.

This relocation was state-sponsored but nevertheless blamed on the pro-freedom leadership in general and Geelani in particular. Tavleen Singh once visited the main market of Geelani's home town Sopore where she was introduced to a Hindu shopkeeper Jai Kishen. He told her: 'Most of the Hindus had left in the dead of night at Jagmohan's behest but that he had not felt the need to go because he did not think he was in any danger from his Muslim neighbours'. What happens if Kashmir gets its freedom, asked Tavleen. He replied: 'Then I will also get it. What is wrong with that?'[3] In an interview to Pakistan's Geo TV, HM Supreme Commander Syed Salahuddin explained a bit more about the role of Hindus in

Kashmiri struggle (also see Chapter 8):

> We believe in a pluralistic society where we not only fight for the Muslims but also for all people living in Kashmir irrespective of their religion. Our struggle is much older than Pakistan. We have a favorable case with strong local support and that is why many Hindus are with us.

Soon after the mass relocation of Pandits by the government was completed, eminent Indian journalist B. G.Verghese wrote in *The Indian Express* (7 February 1993):

> Systematic disinformation about alleged longstanding and continuing vandalizing of Hindu shrines in Kashmir has emerged as a central thrust of the wider BJP-VHP-RSS hate campaign to achieve and sustain a communal polarization in the country.
>
> After persistent effort, I was able to obtain two lists. The first came from a very senior RSS leader who handed me what I understood to be a carefully collated tabulation by his sources. It mentioned 62 [Hindu] temples burnt and damaged in Kashmir by terrorists in 1990 and listed them district wise with remarks such as temple completely burnt, temples razed to the ground, idols desecrated, looted, and so on.
>
> The second list came from the Sanatan Dharam, Jammu and mentioned 6 temples in different parts of the Valley, including one in Srinagar. I made as much inquiries as I could. [I found] only the Sheetalnath Mandir, Habbakadal, was found to have suffered partial damage on November 13, 1990 due to accidental fire.
>
> Two among the most famous and revered temples in Kashmir, Ganapatyar (described in the RSS list as 'demolished') and Dashmani Akhara [...] (described in the RSS list as 'temple burnt, dharmsala burnt') were both unharmed and functional.

At a meeting of the National Integration Council [NIC] in the spring of 1992, BJP President Murli Manohar Joshi repeated the allegation of temples being destroyed in Kashmir. Being a member of the NIC, I was able immediately to challenge his statement and asked him to specify the temples that had been damaged or attacked.

The BJP National Council met in the Gujarat town of Vadodra in the second week of June 1994. Its resolution on J&K showed no sign of understanding the ground realities but an obsessive confidence in violent suppressive measures:

> Immediate apprehension of the guilty and exemplary punishment to the perpetrators of crime anywhere in the state [of J&K]..... Foreign mercenaries must be rooted out. The Doda district should be declared a Disturbed Area. The armed forces must be empowered under the Disturbed Areas Act, and the Armed Forces Special Powers Act.... Immediate constitution of Village Defense Forces, and Special Home Guards through re-employment of ex-servicemen (and) liberal and judicious grant of arms license[s] to the [Hindu] people.

The National Council also advised 'a thorough revamp of the civil services, judicial, administration, police and intelligence network' in J&K. But when BJP later ruled India for over five years, they were unable to achieve any of these illusory goals! Among these goals, fabricating a communal dimension to the Kashmiri struggle was forcefully rejected by Geelani: 'We want to live with our Hindu and Buddhist brothers. We have never pressurized anyone. Hindu brothers who left Kashmir were never told by us to leave the state. It was the Indian government that asked them to leave Kashmir.' He has been the most vocal pro-freedom leader on the issue of Kashmiri Pandits' rights. He told *The Indian Express* (6 November 1999): 'We welcome Pandits as our own, and grieve over their suffering in refugee camps. The spirit of intolerance is foreign to the Kashmiri culture.'

Former MP Kuldip Nayar pointed out that 'The Kashmiri Pandits who migrated from Kashmir, are still living in harrowing conditions outside the town. They are less critical of militants. They say most of them left their homes not because of the militants but because of the Government which promised to provide them rations, accommodation and salary in Jammu itself' (*Deccan Herald*, 14 June 1994).

Cutting across party lines, there is a complete political consensus on India's brutal Kashmir policy. After the dismissal of the Farooq government by Indira Gandhi, Ladli Mohan, an opposition Member of Parliament, said 'the only political party that has supported her is Hindu Mahasabha [RSS].' Even supposed doves like former Indian Prime Minister Inder Kumar Gujral felt that the only way to bring Kashmir back from the brink was to send Jagmohan – for his second stint as Governor. Jagmohan's anti-Muslim posture was not subtle.

Salahuddin expressed heartfelt gratitude 'to those Pandits who didn't fall into the trap of Jagmohan and instead practiced communal harmony and pro-movement attitudes. But those who were duped by Jagmohan shattered the trust of Muslims and sentiments of mutual brotherhood and were scattered in different parts of India,' (*Greater Kashmir*, 5 June 2007).

Salahuddin warned on a number of occasions that some extremist Hindu groups could themselves resort to terrorist acts to create a wedge of hatred between the Muslims and the Kashmir-based Pandits: 'Therefore the Kashmir people and the freedom fighters should always be watchful of this conspiracy and maintain the communal harmony and brotherly atmosphere of Kashmir' (*Greater Kashmir*, 3 June 2007).

Some BJP-inspired Kashmiri Pandits have played a leading role in projecting a completely distorted picture of the situation on the ground in Kashmir. Panun Kashmir is one such organization, closely aligned with BJP/RSS. Its leader Ashok Pandit spoke to the media on 1 June 1994, and the newspapers on the following morning conveyed to millions of Indian readers the following stories:

With the influx of foreign militants into the Valley, especially Afghan mercenaries, the level of cruelty and perversity has only been on the rise. Rape of women has become an attractive reason for the militants to stay on in the Valley. The type of torture inflicted on victims and frequency of beheading, hanging and rape of innocents far surpasses that in either Punjab or the North East [of India].

The Times of India (New Delhi, 2 June 1994)

An Afghan mercenary stormed into a Muslim household and demanded that the young boy of the house be handed over to them for militant training. Upon the refusal from the boy's parents, the boy was tied to the main door of his house and before a huge gathering the boy was cut into 14 pieces.

Free Press Journal (Bombay, 2 June 1994)

No evidence was presented for the incidents mentioned, nor were any details provided that could be checked. Kashmiri militants in fact continued to enjoy widespread support on the street even a decade after the armed uprising began. According to an Honorary Professor at the Delhi School of Economics (cited in *The Hindu*, 29 March 2000): 'As for the militants, they seem to enjoy varying degrees of popular support, partly due to their decent behaviour towards the people (often contrasted with the brutality of the security forces), partly because they are seen to be upholding the common cause – *azadi* [freedom].'

While in power for full five years, the 'BJP did nothing to improve the lot of the Kashmiri [Pandit] refugees, to provide them a sense of security or to create the conditions for them to return to their homes. However, it is always ready to exploit their tragedy in order to justify the victimization of others and sharpen communal divisions in Kashmir and elsewhere in India'.[4]

By contrast, on 2 June 2007, Salahuddin called upon all pro-freedom people to address the problems of Kashmir-based Pandits. He expressed solidarity with them and urged Muslims to befriend and assist them personally. 'We are duty bound to watch and protect the lives, properties, honour and every legitimate interest of 952 families (of Pandits), comprising around 4,000 people, who have not left their motherland.'

Salahuddin gave a striking example to substantiate his argument that the Kashmiri freedom struggle is not communal. During the Partition (1947) there had been more than 37,000 communal riots in India but none in the state of J&K: 'Ours was the only area where the Muslim majority took great care of the Hindu minority, protected their honour and expressed sympathies and solidarity with them on their festivals'(*Greater Kashmir*, 3. June 2007). A Kashmiri Pandit scholar, Balraj Puri testified 'the people of the Valley have turned to Islam in a mark as much of protest as reaffirmation of their identity as a nation. If the rest of the country views their protest as a rise of fundamentalist, pro-Pakistan sentiment alone, then we as Indians have misunderstood the very essence of a secular people. The fact that there have never been any communal riots in the Valley not even during Partition is proof enough.'[5]

In a 19 August 2010 article on *Rediff.com*, Yoginder Sikand corroborates Geelani's claims that, historically, Kashmiri Muslims and Hindus have lived together peacefully. Only BJP/RSS are responsible for creating a well-orchestrated rift between them. 'In the course of a study of Hindu-Muslim relations in Doda, the only district in Jammu and Kashmir where Hindus and Muslims live in almost equal numbers, I have met with numerous self-styled Hindu *sadhus* (priests). Curiously enough, none of them were locals, almost all being from impoverished parts of eastern India who, with some notable exceptions, uniformly thought of Muslims as impure, cowslaying demons, and believed that Hindus ought to have nothing whatsoever to do with them. Most of them were bitterly critical of local [Kashmiri] Hindus who had enjoyed cordial relations with their Muslim neighbours for centuries.'[6]

Indian political parties try to project the three major regions of J&K as culturally or ethnically distinct – the 'Muslim majority' Valley, 'Hindu majority' Jammu and 'Buddhist majority' Ladakh. In reality, Ladakh is 50 per cent Muslim, Jammu around 35 per cent.

More complicated still, three of Jammu's six districts have a Muslim majority (A. G. Noorani, *The Statesman*, 13 July 2000). Geelani has repeatedly said: 'We cannot take anybody along with us forcibly [...] We want [freedom] for the whole of Jammu and Kashmir.... After the plebiscite if [the] majority wants to remain in India we will agree. But first we should be given the right to choose our destiny' (*The Milli Gazette*, 16–31 May 2000).

The propaganda about these ethnically and culturally separate regions is the foreground to murky plans to divide the state on communal lines. Geelani has lashed out at the trifurcation advocates. He urged Kashmiris to be alert to such conspiracies and remain strong in their resolve to achieve freedom for the whole state and all of its people. 'How can we leave our Jammu based Muslim brethren or Dogra [Pandit] brothers in the hands of communal forces like Shiv Sena?' His vision is a liberated Kashmir where all of its people, irrespective of religion, are at peace 'because Islam teaches humanity and not communalism. We want freedom from India [...] so that we build a system where everyone, be it Muslim, Hindu, Sikh, Buddhist or Christian, lives with peace and brotherhood...'(*Greater Kashmir*, 3 June 2007).

The Kashmir government announced a special package for Pandits under which 6,000 youth would be provided employment in the Valley. As of early 2011, about 2,000 Kashmiri Pandit youth shifted back to the Valley: 628 in Islamabad (Anantnag), 164 in Srinagar, 175 in Baramulla, 201 in Kupwara, 135 in Pulwama, 111 in Budgam, 93 in Shopian, 38 in Ganderbal, 9 in Bandipora and 141 in Kulgam district. The Government constructed special residential quarters (called 'Safe Zones') for these Pandits at Sheikhpora (Budgam) Mattan (Islamabad), Vessu (Qazigund) and Hawal (Pulwama). But, one by one, the returning Pandits are leaving the government-provided accommodation and staying instead with Muslim families in the vicinity of their work. 'I have left the government flat allotted to me at Sheikhpora (Budgam) and am staying as a paying guest with a Muslim family near the school where I have been posted,' a Pandit girl posted as teacher in a Budgam village told *Greater Kashmir* (9 March 2011). The girl said she felt safer and more comfortable living with the Muslim family than in a security zone with gun-toting cops around. Evidently, the ruthlessly zealous Jagmohan failed to sow permanent discord between Kashmiri Muslims and Pandits.

On 17 April 2011, Geelani addressed a gathering of Pandits at Migrant Pandit's colony in the south Kashmir district of Kulgam, where he was warmly welcomed by patron of the Kashmir Pandit Amity Council, Sanjay Saraf, who said: 'The Pandits who are here have not returned on the assurances of state government but only because of the assurance of Geelani Sahib and the majority [Muslim] community.' In reply, Geelani said: 'I assure you that you will be fully protected. We will make sure that no harm is done to your lives and property.' He rejected the idea of 'safety zones' as a symbol of mistrust between Muslims and Hindus. He urged Pandits to 'appeal to the government to allow you to return to your original places in villages, towns and cities. We have centuries-old traditions of sharing each others' joys and sorrows. Those traditions are dear to us and have to be re-established. We have to strengthen our bonds.'

Geelani assured them – 'You are not the migrants but the real citizens of this land. None of you will face any harm from your Muslim brothers' – and he did so on the basis of his religious convictions. God does not discriminate between human beings on the basis of religion, caste, colour, wealth or poverty, rural or urban origin. 'Every individual is a human being first and the caste is only for his identification. To be a good human being one must have a good character. [...] Our fight with India is not because it is a Hindu majority country. It is the battle of principles. We are fighting for our rights and the promises that were made to us must be kept.' He said peace cannot be achieved at gunpoint, but had to be established through justice.[7]

Geelani also urged the Pandit community to understand the situation of the Muslim Kashmiris. 'Our peaceful protests are showered with bullets. The security forces do not even spare ten-year-olds. We are not carrying weapons in our hands but are peacefully demanding our rights like India did when it was under the British occupation.' He reminded Pandits that '[Indian] troops have occupied more than 2.8 million kanals of land including that of forests in Kashmir which is not only the property of Kashmiri Muslims but Pandits too. Our natural resources are being exploited. The government and the forces are looting the green gold. The power that we generate is being sold outside the J&K state while we are being denied even our own share of electricity.' He added that even Hindu temples are now in the custody of non-state subjects instead of the Kashmiri Pandits.

Some ill-informed Kashmiri clerics issued a religious edict against Christian missionaries in January 2012. Geelani came out in support of the latter and dispelled the notion that Christians were unsafe in the Valley. He said (*Daily Mail*, 28 January 2012): 'They are a part and parcel of our society and it is our duty to protect them. No Kashmiri can ignore the contribution of schools like Burn Hall, Biscoe and Convent in the education system of the Valley. Unfortunately we have not been able to build educational institutions like these despite having all the available resources.' Madhu Kishwar, a member of Delhi based think-tank the Kashmir Committee said at a seminar in February 2012: 'We appreciate Geelani Sahib for remaining firm on his stand. He has never indulged in double-speak. Minorities have always reposed faith in him' (*Greater Kashmir*, 4 February 2012).

Narinder Singh Khalsa, a senior Democratic Freedom Party leader rejected the allegation that the Muslim leadership of Kashmir had betrayed Pandits: 'Pro-freedom leaders have always taken the leaders from Jammu region into confidence. But on the other hand, Jammu based leadership has always been ignored by the successive regimes. Mainstream leaders for their own vested interests have always divided the people of J&K on communal lines. Despite being the member of a minority [Hindu] community my party deputed me to defend the Kashmir cause in [the] European Union. I am happy that [the] EU admitted that J&K is a disputed territory and it has to be solved in accordance with the wishes and aspirations of the people.' Urging the Kashmiri leadership to unite for the sake of the people, Khalsa said that the time has come for all the pro-freedom leaders to share a common platform: 'Not only Hurriyat leaders but militant leaders also should work collectively for the just and ultimate solution of the Kashmir issue' (*Greater Kashmir*, 4 June 2007).

6

HUMAN WRONGS

UNDER THE RUBRIC of 'public safety' and protecting 'national interest', the notorious Public Safety Act (PSA) in Kashmir grants sweeping powers to the Indian security forces – to enter any house at any time; to interrogate anyone anywhere; to detain anyone for any length of time. South African apartheid regime also enacted the PSA in 1953 to brutalise black Africans.

In Kashmir, Sheikh Abdullah introduced the Ordinance in 1977, which became on 8 April 1978 the PSA after it was passed by the state legislature. President of J&K Bar Association Mian Abdul Qayoom said that in the 1977 elections Ghulam Nabi, then president of the Kashmir Motor Drivers Association, supported the [opposition] Janata Party. Sheikh Abdullah didn't like that and had Ghulam Nabi arrested under the PSA in 1978 – he was its first victim (*Greater Kashmir*, 3 June 2007). Large-scale human rights abuses under the PSA occurred only after the rigged elections of 1987.

Nelson Mandela explained that his movement resorted to armed struggle 'when all other forms of resistance were no longer open to us'.[1] Salahuddin, similarly, explained that it was not until 'after 1989, when we saw that India was not listening to our legitimate voice,' that those protesting for freedom 'picked up weapons as the last resort'.[2]

After the miserable failure of his first stint as Governor of J&K, Jagmohan was reappointed on 19 January 1990. He landed in

Srinagar with a clear plan. That night, various localities of Srinagar were combed by Indian security forces, and the city placed firmly in the grip of state-terror. When, the following morning, thousands of unarmed civilians protested, Indian security forces fired on them indiscriminately from both sides of Sringar's Gawakadal Bridge across the Jhelum River. Nearly 100 people were killed, one of the worst massacres in Kashmir. 'Some died from gunshot, others drowned as they jumped, panic-stricken, into the Jhelum to escape bullets.'[3]

After the shooting was over, the bodies were dumped into trucks and taken to Srinagar's police headquarters for disposal. Among them was an engineer called Farooq Butt who was rescued by some policemen when they saw him breathing. His story and those told by other survivors ran in the foreign press, while the Indian press, by and large, ignored the tragedy, 'making it easier for Jagmohan to pretend that it never happened'.[4]

Just as (according to Nelson Mandela) 'fifty years of non-violence had brought the African people nothing but more repressive legislation, and fewer and fewer rights,' so too for over sixty years for the Kashmiri people the situation has not changed for the better. Kashmiri officials concede that repressive tactics were used to stop the massive regular marches to the UN observer's office. Those tactics do not appear to have worked. On 1 March 1990, an estimated one million people (a quarter of the Valley's population) came out in protest. The government reacted with more repression and more than forty were killed on that day.

On the morning of 21 May 1990, three unidentified youths barged into the home of Mirwaiz Maulvi Farooq (father of Mirwaiz Umar Farooq) at Nagin Lake and shot him at point-blank range. His body was taken to Soura Medical Institute where a restive crowd of over 5,000 gathered. The crowd forcibly took the body of Mirwaiz and their procession wound its way through the downtown areas of Srinagar where a curfew had been imposed. On its route lay the Islamia College, 'requisitioned' by the Indian army and turned into the headquarters of the 69th battalion of the Central Reserve Police Force (CRPF). Seeing a mob heading towards them, the security forces panicked and opened fire, killing fifty-seven. The CRPF men claimed that they retaliated only after militants in the crowed fired on them, a claim for which there is no proof. However, the fifty-seven graves in the martyrs' cemetery in Srinagar provide enough evidence of the occupying armed forces' brutality.

Mirwaiz Maulvi Farooq had joined with Farooq Abdullah in the elections of 1987 and fought together against the pro-freedom grouping, the MUF. Due to this, Maulvi Farooq had begun to sense his end. He offered himself for preventive detention to Jagmohan. But Jagmohan refused on the ground that he did not want to be perceived as anti-Muslim! It is believed that Jagmohan arranged for his killing by Shiv Sena militants.

CRPF was established in 1939 as a firefighting unit to assist central authorities in case the local police failed. In 1990, 103 active battalions of CRPF were spread across the country. The main focus of their training was riot management. The Border Security Force (BSF) was created in the wake of the 1965 war, during which Pakistani forces had overwhelmed the Chad Bet post. It was intended to police the international border between India and Pakistan. Both it and CRPF have played havoc in J&K.

In October 1990, a BSF platoon entered Handwara and 'began shooting indiscriminately and setting houses on fire. Some thirty-six houses and 200 shops were gutted and twenty people lost their lives. Fire brigade personnel who attended were ordered to stay back, and a J&K police officer who called on the BSF to stop was shot dead.'[5] The BSF's contempt for the lives of Muslim Kashmiris, even those serving the state, was also in evidence on the occasion when Divisional Commissioner of Kashmir Wajahat Habibullah, on a visit to the District Magistrate's Office in Sopore, was besieged by militants. According to *Economic and Political Weekly* (6 November 1993), he complained that the army had refused his calls for help. The BSF alleged a lack of manpower in the town as the reason for their refusal.

Clearly, if the security forces can refuse to rescue a top official appointed by New Delhi, they are effectively a law unto themselves. Even J&K police were not spared – rather, the CRPF and BSF humiliated and beat and, in some cases, shot at them. There is an order on record by a Suprintendent of Police, Srinagar, which says: 'If somebody comes to you and files a complaint do not accept that complaint. You cannot accept that [First Incident Report] without the approval of the higher authorities. So, where does the citizen go? He cannot go to the Governor: he has no access to the Governor. He cannot come to the Home Minister [in Delhi]' (reported in *Muslim India*, #148, April 1995).

*6.1 CRPF personnel smashing civilian cars parked
in the Maisuma area of Srinagar on 8 August 2011.*

According to Geelani, on 23 February 1991 at Kunan Pushpora more than a hundred young, middle-aged and elderly women were gang-raped by the Indian armed forces. Among them was the heavily pregnant Zafira Bano who, four days later, gave birth to a baby born with a fractured left arm.

Dukhtaran-i Millat (Daughters of the Community) is a Kashmiri women's organization first set up to promote education and improve religious awareness. It is led by Aasiya Indrabi, who was strongly influenced by the teachings of Geelani. During the uprisings in the 1990s, the group and its firebrand leader took to the streets to protest against the atrocities by Indian security forces, as well as to prove that Muslim women can fight for justice too. This extraordinarily courageous woman has, like other resistance leaders, been in and out of prison; her husband, sentenced to life imprisonment under the Terrorism Act, has never been released. She continues the struggle undaunted.

The worst brutalities by the security forces are committed outside urban areas in remote rural locations where, in some instances, entire villages have been burnt down. It is rare indeed that the media can reach these out of the way places and report about them. However, the human rights organization, Asia Watch, has detailed the case of Muzaffar Ahmad Mirza, an Arabic teacher arrested on 4 October 1991 in Tral village, forty kilometres from Srinagar. 'He was beaten and electric shock applied to his genitals. Then a rod was inserted into his rectum and pushed through to his chest. He was found by the roadside the next day and taken to the Medical College where surgeons attempted to repair his rectum and then carried out surgery to repair the damage to his liver and chest. But he died within two weeks because of complications arising from his injuries. Before Mirza died, he detailed his torture to the international press, and Eyewitness TV filmed his testimony but the programme was later censored.'[6]

Due to their blatant lies, the official Indian media are highly discredited. Senior security officers have publicly admitted this. 'All India Radio and Doordarshan [government owned TV channel] continue to be disbelieved in the Valley and their impact blunted. At times, they lack credibility even in official circles,' wrote Major-General Ray.[7]

While all Kahsmiris suffered at the hands of the Indian security forces, their principal target has been the Jama'at and its leadership. Abdul Jabbar, a fifty-year-old principal of a Jama'at-run school in Baramulla was picked up on 1 July 1992 while doing his morning (fajr) prayer. His nephew Manzur Ahmed Mir narrated the following story:

> They took me along also and they kept beating us up in the car and saying, 'where is the stuff [weapons], where have you hidden it?' They took us to the interrogation centre in the stadium and the beating continued all day. We were given no food or water. Then at about 3.30 p.m. they released me.

When they returned Jabbar's body the next day they did not even bother to hide the signs of torture. His testicles had been crushed, there were signs that he had been given electric shocks on his penis and chunks of flesh appeared to have been scooped out of his buttocks and thighs. His only crime was that he was a member of Jamaat.

In August 1992, Indian security forces launched 'Operation Tiger', a campaign of surprise raids designed to capture and kill suspected militants and terrorize their civilian sympathizers. Summary executions of detainees and indiscriminate attacks on civilians escalated during Operation Tiger and its successor, 'Operation Shiva'. As winter approached, the security forces also engaged in frequent arson attacks, burning down houses, shops and entire neighbourhoods.

According to an Asia Watch report of 1993, security forces repeatedly raided hospitals and other medical facilities, even paediatric and obstetric units. During these raids, they forced doctors at gunpoint to identify recent trauma patients whom they suspected of militant activity. They arrested patients in hospitals, and in some cases disconnected them from life-sustaining treatments. They also discharged weapons within hospital grounds and buildings including operating theatres, thus destroying or damaging medical supplies, transports and equipment. Doctors and other medical staff were frequently threatened, beaten and detained; several of them had been shot dead while on duty; others were tortured.

Many of those receiving medical care may well have been released detainees who had earlier been tortured by the Indian security forces. Torture is widely and routinely practised to coerce information about suspected militants or confessions to militant activity. It is also used to punish detainees believed to support or sympathize with the militants.

Centred in the apple-growing region of the valley is Geelani's hometown Sopur. It has a population of about 100,000 and is a Jama'at stronghold. Geelani won his state assembly seat from here in 1972 and again in 1977. As the Jama'at flag waved from most houses, Sopur had been nicknamed 'Little Pakistan'. 'On a cold 6 January 1993 morning, in a pre-planned operation, cadres of HM approached a BSF bunker [...] and suddenly wrenched away one LMG from the hands of two BSF personnel.... Losing a weapon is a major misdemeanour in the armed forces. Instead of the rational response of sending teams to retrieve the weapon, the BSF personnel began indiscriminate firing.... When the local police officer tried to intervene, the BSF troops threatened to shoot him.... Nearly fifty people died in this incident, most of them non-combatants.'[8]

There are two major flaws in Joshi's report just cited. Firstly, *all* the dead, not 'most', were non-combatants. Secondly, he calls the retaliatory murder of 50 civilians by the BSF an '*incident*', not a '*massacre*'. He criticizes the BSF for failing to initiate a 'rational response', meaning that they did not follow the 'official procedure' laid down in the 'rules of engagement'. But such procedures cannot be defended as 'rational' if they are part and parcel of a policy that is in its entirety irrational. The Indian government's war against the people of Kashmir begins and ends as an atrocity, and proceeds as an atrocity. It does not, by its nature, distinguish combatants and non-combatants – all the people are the enemy. And Joshi knows this:

> The blackest of black operations have been the ruthless counter-terrorist activities undertaken by state agencies.... Some tactics were not specific to Kashmir as they have been used by the police across the country as a means of obtaining information: if a suspect is difficult to trace, hold his family hostage till he surrenders. Shock the suspect with a thrashing, or rough up his wife or parents before him.

> Dead men tell no tales and cannot avenge themselves.... So after interrogation, it became routine to execute the terrorists and declare that they had died in encounters, or at the hands of their compatriots in ambushes when they were being taken to recover hidden weapons or simply that they 'escaped custody'.... Many arrested militants in Kashmir reportedly died in the same way.[9]

Jagmohan's terror tactics failed miserably to dampen the freedom struggle. Girish Chandra Saxena replaced him as Governor of
J&K on 26 May 1990 and turned to the people for help: 'The people
have been complaining about the administration and the security
forces. I explain to them that this harassment is caused to you
mainly because of the combing operations that have to be carried
out because the security forces don't have pinpoint intelligence of
where exactly the militants are in the villages. That is where you can
help' (*The Sunday*, 13 June 1993). In other words, Saxena was telling
Kashmiri civilians, spy for us or face the consequences! A public
relations effort strove to present the security forces' activities as
humane policing under strictly 'rational', disciplined procedures:
'Troops operating in the state are now thoroughly briefed on dos
and don'ts in civilian areas. Soldiers carry a small pocket book
where it is clearly spelt out what they have to do' (*The Asian Age*, 4
June 1994).

The Indian authorities do not have the long experience of the
Israelis in smiling benignly before international public opinion to
explain away their atrocities, nor the resort to 'anti-Semitism' as a
means of silencing critics. Instead, they simply ended any pretence
of transparency. Foreign journals were impounded by customs or
crudely censored for carrying items on Kashmir hitherto considered
innocuous. For example, according to *The Economic Times* (5 June
1994), 'the Bombay customs impounded the *Far Eastern Economic
Review* of June 2. It [...] was penalized for a photograph showing
Kashmiri demonstrators burning the Indian flag.'

Kuldip Nayar reported in *The Radiance Weekly* (June 1993) that
'numerous people, professors, doctors, lawyers, and students have
been picked up by the security forces on mere suspicion and given
the third degree at various interrogation centres before release.
Many have died in the process [i.e. in custody].' While *The Indian
Express* (25 May 1997) admitted that 'none of the nearly 32,000 persons picked up by the security forces and other government agencies for their alleged involvement in militant activities during the
last seven years in Jammu and Kashmir has so far been convicted.'

After five years of mass uprising, a team of human rights activists visited Kashmir in 1994. The team comprised Dr. Ritu Dewan, Professor of Economics at the University of Bombay; Ms. Manimala, a correspondent; Ms. Gouri Choudhry, a social activist; and Sheba Chhachhi, an artist. They reported: 'Every home that we visited in the Valley, rich and poor, told a story of humiliation, loss, pain and death. We are horrified at the violence and terror under which the people, especially women, have lived in for the past five years' (*The Hindu,* 12 June 1994). Kuldip Nayar comments on the psychological effects (*The National Mail,* 8 June 1994):

> As the security forces are busy in their combing operations to catch the militants, the attitude of an ordinary man towards India is hardening because of the havoc, anger and estrangement the forces leave in their wake.
>
> Apart from the detainees, there is a long list of people who are not traceable. Instructions are that within 36 hours the household should be informed if someone connected with it is picked up. But these instructions are only on paper. Parents and wives, in hundreds, go from pillar to post to enquire about their missing son or husband. But there is no news. Even where the authorities have given in writing that their dear ones are in custody, there is no trace of them. Hundreds of *habeas corpus* petitions are pending before law courts. And even when the courts have [issued an] order, there is no compliance.

The New York Times (6 November 1994) observed: 'India's obdurate insistence on resolving a political problem by force has increasingly enmeshed it in a campaign of lawless State terrorism. India was now in the unflattering company of countries that use deadly force to keep their unhappy citizens in line. Summary executions, torture and disappearances.... Regrettably, Washington, instead of raising its voice to defend human rights, has lowered it in an effort to improve commercial and diplomatic ties.'

The Indian occupation forces act outside and above the law, as former Chief Justice of J&K High Court Bahauddin Farooqi remarked (*The Guardian,* 3 August 1991): 'The abuse of human rights here is unprecedented.... In theory we are governed by the constitution, but in practice we are governed by methods unknown to law, unknown to any civilized society.' A prominent Kashmiri lawyer Mir Shafqat Hussain claims that 'I pleaded several thousand cases and managed nearly 6,000 orders from High Court quashing the detentions.' The court's order is first obeyed and then contravened: 'inside the jail there is [a] separate wing of police whose duty is to rearrest the detainee outside the prison. And from here the trauma of the detainee begins again' (*Greater Kashmir*, 3 June 2007).

According to a leaked cable of the US embassy in New Delhi, staff of the International Committee for the Red Cross (ICRC) told some US diplomats they had made 177 visits to detention centres in J&K and elsewhere in India between 2002 and 2004, and had met 1,491 detainees. They had been able to interview 1,296 privately. In 852 cases, the detainees reported ill-treatment. A total of 171 described being beaten and 681 said they had been subjected to one or more of six forms of torture. 498 of them were given electric shocks, 381 were suspended from the ceiling, 294 had muscles in their legs crushed by prison personnel sitting on a bar placed across their thighs, 181 had their legs stretched by 'splitting 180 degrees', 234 were tortured with water, and there were 302 'sexual' cases.

'Numbers add up to more than 681, as many detainees were subjected to more than one form of ill-treatment,' the cable said. The ICRC said all branches of the Indian security forces used these forms of torture. The briefing indicated persistent problems like widespread use of 'IT' (ill-treatment) and 'torture' during interrogation that takes place in the presence of officers. The ICRC had raised these issues with the government of India for more than ten years. The cable said the ICRC has never obtained access to the 'Cargo Building', 'the most notorious detention centre in Srinagar'.

Nelson Mandela recalls finding out, in the middle of 1987, that No. 8115 Orlando West, the house in which he married Winnie had been burned down.[10] Similarly, Geelani's ancestral home at Dooru village in Sopur district was blasted on 19 December 1994 by a charge placed on the outside. Later, a missile was fired at his Srinagar house while the homes of two of his brothers were also gutted. On 1 January 1995, backed by 200 army personnel, four men clad in traditional Kashmiri attire entered Geelani's house in an attempt to kill him. His family took him to a hiding-place inside the house and bolted the door from inside. After searching and firing into the air for some time, the men and the Indian security forces hastily left Geelani's house.[11]

The International Commission of Jurists, Geneva, visited the Valley in March 1995 and issued a report which stated: 'The frequent military crackdowns, the inhuman torture of innocent persons, the indiscriminate shooting at people, the frequent thefts, and the occasional rapes committed by the security forces have increased the disgust and resentment of the people in the Valley.'[12] It is important to keep in mind the sheer scale of the security foces and the extent of their operations. Anuj Chopra reports (*Foreign Policy*, 28 October 2010): 'There are nearly 700,000 Indian security personnel stationed in the region – one for every 20 Kashmiris, one of the highest soldier-to-civilian ratios in the world. Armed with automatic rifles, they occupy schools, hospitals, shopping centers, temples, mosques, cafes, and playgrounds.' The effect on the general population, at least in part intended, is traumatizing: 'about 80 per cent of the Kashmiri population is suffering from mild to severe psychiatric disorders', a study reported (cited in *Muslim India*, #174, June 1997).

Perhaps the worst suffering ensues from the sense that the wrong cannot be righted, because there is no recourse against injustice: 'The High Court Bar complained of [procedures] making a mockery of *habeas corpus* petitions against detention. Out of 19,000 such petitions which were filed, only 2,000 were heard. The rest became infructuous because of the expiry of detention period.' This is a matter of grave concern for all of us: 'Nothing rankles more in the human heart than a brooding sense of injustice. Illness we can put up with but injustice makes us want to pull things down.' (US Supreme Court Justice Brenan, cited in Rajendar Sachar, *The Hindustan Times*, 23 December 1999.)

Hope persists while wrongs and injustices continue to be reported because there is a possibility that, eventually, the wrongs will be addressed. That is why Geelani and his supporters have invested so much energy in short-term and long-term strategies to highlight the plight of Kashmiri detainees in various jails of the country. They have organized protests, seminars and public awareness campaigns on this issue. They have received little if any support from the mainstream media in India:

'Indian press, out of misguided patriotism has always chosen to tell the Indian public less than the whole truth about Kashmir.... Every article seemed written to confirm the general impression of Kashmiris as traitors and secessionists,' admits Tavleen Singh.[13] V. Sudarshan goes further (*The Patriot*, 3 April 1995): 'The only way of getting reports through from the Valley that border on the objective is by getting the reporter to go to Kashmir in order to obtain a first hand understanding. Most newspapers find it more convenient to send their reporters on trips that are organized by the security forces.... The reporters get to see exactly what the Army or the CRPF or the BSF wants them to see, no more or less. The reporters get to meet only those people that the Army wants them to meet. The trips are so managed that it would be very difficult for reporters to be able to present a point of view which is even slightly at variance with the official line.'

As Major-General Ray points out: 'An army reflects the values of its society, the two are inseparable. When military values are degraded upon the battlefields, it is a signal that the values of its society have started to decay.' This has been well demonstrated not only in Kashmir but also in Iraq, Afghanistan, Chechnya and Palestine. Major-General Ray has described the principles and processes behind the training of Indian soldiers:

> Right from early days, the soldier is trained to the doctrine of the application of maximum and unrestricted force. Force is the application of firepower to destroy the enemy. Greater the destruction, better the results and higher the soldiers' own chances of survival [...] A soldier's basic training is designed to breed aggression and violence [...] Soldiers by the very nature of their mental training focus on an 'enemy' who is identifiable. [In the case of Kashmir,

all Kashmiris including its journalists, lawyers, doctors and
police force seem to be identified as enemies.]

The soldier is trained to hate the enemy, to give him no
quarter, to destroy him completely. Greater the hatred,
greater the feeling of superiority of civilization, of race, of
color, or creed, or ego, of power. The enemy soldier alone is
not the target. The state that sustains him, that directs him
to discharge its political directions is also evil – and therefore also an 'enemy' [...]. Such is the intensity and ferocity of
hate that it is often blinding.'[14]

Alija Izetbegovic has reflected that: 'Some people live and die
under such systems without ever knowing what was false and what
was true. Naively believing the press, the authorities, official pro-
nouncements, they live in perpetual delusion, unintentionally and
unconsciously supporting falsehood and injustice.'[15] In Kashmir, it
is often made out that the Indian army has no 'cause', merely a duty
to preserve law and order. On the contrary, it does have a cause,
which the mainsteam media support by obscuring it. General Ray
again: 'The army belongs to the people, never to a government;
accordingly, the army is answerable to the people. Following on
from this logic, the commitment of an army lasts as long as the
commitment of the people lasts. The commitment of the nation
is therefore the cause. This is what is sustaining the morale and
determination of the soldier in Kashmir.'[16]

Vrinda Grover, a senior lawyer and human rights activist, says
(*Greater Kashmir,* 5. November 2007): 'Civil society in India buys
what government gives them. You can't build a nation by fraud
or force. Intellectuals in India should play their part to stop the
rights violations in Kashmir.' Geelani holds the mainstream political parties of J&K equally responsible: 'The National Conference,
the People's Democratic Party [led by former Home Minister
Mufti Sayeed] and the Congress have never uttered a word in this
regard.'[17] He has referred to the state's Human Rights Commission
as a showcase body, without any power to do its job.

Major-General Ray has worked out that '[Kashmiri] militants are not criminals or psychopaths or men with twisted minds. They are unquestionably genuine, normal and straight people, as normal as the neighbour next door, the vegetable seller, the policeman, the banker, the soldier, the bureaucrat and the salesman. The only difference is that militants have a psyche and a logic of their own. This is also borne out of the fact that Kashmiri militants even in captivity are not found distressed. Only 3.22 per cent show symptoms of mental anxiety.'[18] Perhaps this behavioural certificate from Major-General Ray is an indicator that the Kashmiris are engaged in a just cause. It is their conviction of that which enables them to withstand the (so far) two decades of wrongs inflicted upon them by the Indian security forces. They cannot hope for redress of their wrongs from the legal system in the state or in India or in the international order. For all that, the Kashmiris' morale holds and they go on fighting for the justice they have been denied.

India's rulers have proved time and again that they will go to any lengths to malign the Kashmiri freedom movement. They did so with spectacular ferocity on the eve of the high-profile visit to India by Bill Clinton towards the end of his presidency in early 2000 – the beginning of the 'strategic partnership' now settled between the US and India. On 20 March 2000, they killed thirty-nine innocent Sikhs at Chattisinghpora in Kashmir and blamed the bloodbath on Pakistan-backed militants.

This slaughter of innocent Sikhs took place in Islamabad (Anantnag), about fifty kilometres from Srinagar. Then, J&K police picked up five innocent Muslims from nearby villages, killed them and burnt and buried their bodies. It was claimed that these militants were responsible for the Sikh massacre at Chattisinghpora. The local villagers, however, insisted that this was a fake encounter and the victims were innocent villagers. Kashmiri government knew the truth but, initially, refused to listen. When the public pressure increased, the villagers' bodies were exhumed. Their relatives directly confirmed the identity of three. Two others were identified on the basis of the clothes found in their graves. All five had gone missing on the night of the 23 March 2000 from different villages in Islamabad.

6.2 A delegation of Sikh leaders called on Syed Geelani at his Hyderpora residence.

When the indignant villagers marched to protest these extra-judicial killings, the police opened fire and killed a further seven people! Chief Minister Farooq Abdullah ordered judicial inquiries into the incidents, but in the rest of India: 'Except from the media, there was no reaction. There was no sense of shame, no anger, and no grief at the loss of innocent lives. Our political parties did not consider the Anantnag incidents important enough to address. It shows that India's [collective] conscience is not touched by the plight of the people of Kashmir' regretted Bharat Bhushan (*The Hindustan Times*, 20 April 2000)!

The Times of India (editorial, 7 April 2000) was convinced that 'prima facie, the security forces' case [...] seems weak'. Three days later, the *Hindustan Times* editorial was more critical: 'This crime was apparently enacted to boost the official claim that the foreign mercenaries who mowed down the Sikhs at Chattisinghpora in cold blood were in turn killed in an open encounter by our alert security forces.'

In a series of protests, villagers demanded an independent investigation. The security forces killed another eighteen Kashmiris at Barak Pura but protests continued. Eventually, the government appointed the Pandian Commission to (a) investigate the murder of the five unarmed persons branded as the killers of the Sikhs and (b) the shooting and killings at Barak Pura. The Commission found the Indian forces responsible for these murders. Vijay Pushkarna explains why (*The Week*, 16 April 2000): 'Whenever a major incident happens, they [security forces] pick up somebody from somewhere, kill them in such a way that the bodies cannot be recognized, and then claim that the terrorists behind that incident have been killed.' According to a retired government official: '[the] Special Operation Group is desperate to show results [...] Various security agencies claimed to have killed the same prominent militants at different times, at different places [examples follow].'

Further evidence of the lawlessness of the security forces is the unprovoked attack on journalists by the BSF at Magam in Budgan district of central Kashmir. On 10 May 2001, the media had gathered to cover an encounter with militants. Suddenly BSF personnel charged them, trashing their cameras and beating them ruthlessly. Former MP Syed Shahabuddin wrote to the Home Minister on 12 May 2001: 'The assault by the BSF on media reporters and photo journalists at Magam is an indicator of the repression let loose in the state under the existing dispensation.'[19] The targeting of journalists is recognized as a war crime under the Geneva Conventions.

6.3 Daily frisking and humiliation is a part of Kashmiri life.

Geelani himself has narrated the chilling incident on 6 October 2001.[20] The forces of RR-30, Langate surrounded Jagarpura Handware, where Muhammad Ibrahim Dar's family had just moved into a newly built house. The family were woken by the security forces and ordered to make tea for them, which they did. After drinking his tea, the army officer ordered one of Ibrahim Dar's sons, Abdul Majeed, to go out and announce in the locality that there was a crackdown, while Ibrahim himself and his other son Abdul Rashid were asked to sit outside the house. The soldiers went inside and began molesting Abdul Rashid's wife. She cried out, whereupon Abdul Rashid went back in, in an effort to stop the soldiers. They shot him in the head and he died on the spot. Ibrahim then entered the house, began scolding the soldiers and also tried to prevent them from dishonouring his daughter-in-law. He too was shot, in the chest, and died on the spot. Abdul Majeed was later called inside by the soldiers and ordered to drag out the dead bodies of his father and brother. Thereafter, they gang raped another Kashmiri housewife in her own house in front of her own family.

Actions of this kind have no security function whatever. They express a lawless bestiality meant to break the spirit of its victims – 'tactics not dissimilar to those used by the [Nazi] Germans in Europe during World War II'.[21]

At the outset of insurgency, the security forces uprooted Geelani from his native village of Dooru. Thirteen years later Dooru residents still suffer the government's vindictiveness. They complain of collective punishments carried out as a 'political vendetta'. No developmental works have taken place in the village since 1989. Just seven kilometres from Apple Town, Sopur, in north Kashmir, this once-beautiful hamlet and its lush environs are in a terrible state. Link roads connecting the village's 5,000 inhabitants to Sopur are barely passable. It has only one middle school, run under Sarva Shiksa Abhiyan (general education campaign) sponsored by the army, which has never been improved or upgraded. It is impossible for locals to get a government job or positive police verification: 'You will see the name of our village written with "red ink" in every government and police office,' seventy-year-old Ghulam Muhammad told *Greater Kashmir* (10 August 2007). For all that, say the villagers: 'Geelani Sahib has kept our head high. People respect us when they come to know that we are inhabitants of Geelani Sahib's native village.'

In 2006, Shiv Sena and Bajrang Dal activists (allies of BJP) attacked Geelani and disrupted his press conference held in a Jammu hotel with the police force present. The same groups repeated the act in November 2010 at a seminar in New Delhi attended by Arundhati Roy as well as Geelani. As General Ray has observed, 'Unless citizens have the security of their lives, they cannot be expected to repose faith in the administration and police force.'[22]

At another press conference, Geelani condemned the molestation of a girl at Kunan in Bandipore and the killing of four persons, including a pregnant woman in Kupwara in the last week of July 2007. Local residents caught the soldiers responsible and handed them over to the local police. Geelani said: 'these incidents are heart rendering and speak of illegal use of power by occupation forces. I salute the people of Bandipora who despite [the] threat to their lives showed courage and nabbed the culprits red-handed.'

To support the occupation of Kashmir, Indian security forces have established large arms and ammunition depots across the state. In blatant violation of safety norms, many of these depots are located perilously close to populated areas. In one of the largest, Khundru village of Islamabad district, during an 'inspection' of the depot by senior army officers in June 2007, a fire broke out resulting in the death of many civilians and army personnel, with thousands of villagers displaced. One of three government schools in Khundru was destroyed after shells rained on it. Calling this incident an eye-opener for the international community, Geelani said (*Greater Kashmir*, 25 August 2007): 'Kashmir has been turned into an ammunition dump with explosives spread all over the Valley. Anything can happen any time. New Delhi has refused to give any aid to state government for rehabilitating the victims of [the] Khundru blaze. Refusal of New Delhi [to provide financial compensation] is making [Chief Minister] Ghulam Nabi Azad ask the legislators and government employees to donate their salaries for the victims.'

The UN's Convention against Torture and Other Cruel, Inhuman or Degrading Treatment or Punishment was adopted by the

UN General Assembly in 1984 and came into force in 1987 after twenty countries ratified it. India initialled this Convention (14 October 1997) but has still not ratified it. 'This lack of ratification is a bit of an embarrassment as already 145 countries are party to the treaty, while India keeps company with eight other nations in the non-ratified column – Sudan, Comoros, Congo, Dominican Republic, Sao Tome and Principe, Gambia, Nauru and Guinea-Bissau' (Devirupa Mitra, *Hindustan Times*, 11 February 2008).

Amazing stories of our brave armed forces are unending. In the frontier district of Kupwara on 26 September 2007, soldiers of 33 Rashtriya Rifles barged into Magam police station at Handwara and went berserk, because the police had seized nearly 4,800 litres of petrol stolen by security forces from army vehicles in order to sell in the open market! According to police station sources, 'soldiers broke the window panes of the police station and beat to pulp the policemen present there.' Later on, they 'caught hold of the police station Sub Inspector (SI) Abdul Rehman and gave him a severe thrashing. [Others] who tried to rescue the officer were also beaten.'

As they fled the police station, the soldiers took away Rs 35,000, six mobile phones, one digital camera, a wrist watch, one AK-47 rifle, six magazines and 108 rounds. The injured policemen SI Abdul Rehman and constables Muhammad Akbar and Raj Muhammad were rushed to hospital in critical condition. Despite the high cost of resisting the lawlessness of the security forces, Geelani continues to urge the local police to prevent troops from committing criminal acts because it is their duty to combat and prevent crime. Addressing a crowded press conference on 26 September 2007, Geelani said: '[The] army has occupied more than seven hundred thousand kanals [350 square kilometres] of land in the state and there are more than 671 army camps in J&K. I urge the people to stage peaceful demonstrations against this forcible and illegal occupation.'[23]

Geelani appeals to the local police and the local people to resist this huge occupation because the J&K state authorities only defend and excuse it and the atrocities that flow from it. In December 2010 Chief Minister Omar Abdullah claimed that not a single case of custodial torture had been reported during his tenure. Geelani termed this 'a blatant lie'. In a statement, he said: 'Sixty per cent of Kashmiris who were arrested during [the] past two years have been subjected to torture in custody; many persons have even breathed their last in the torture chambers.' Giving specific details, Geelani said out of 150 persons who were killed in 2010, Sameer Ahmad of Batamaloo, Rafiq Ahmad Bangroo, Umar Qayoom of Soura, Tariq Ahmad Dar of Panzla Rafiabad and Inayat Ahmad Khan of Dalgate were arrested and beaten to death. 'By ignoring these killings and sorrowful incidents like Shopian and Machil, Omar Abdullah has demonstrated shamelessness. I want to remind him that [the] majority of the people including students who were arrested since June this year have been subjected to torture in police stations. Even the Hurriyat leaders lodged at Cargo Building had to undergo mental torture. Custodial torture has been common during [the] past 63 years and it reached its extreme in the past two decades.'24

Alluding to an incident on 5 February 2011, Geelani said: 'Innocents killed in Kupwara were buried in the dead of night to hide the crime [...] Instead of punishing the culprits, the authorities are sheltering them on the pretext that they were performing their duty. Have state authorities now given right to the forces to enter any house and molest our daughters? Don't remain under the impression that culprits will be punished. They will be transferred to another post and the issue will die down. How many culprits have been punished since 1989?' The moral indignation in Geelani's question is a proof that his conviction, that truth and justice will triumph, is undimmed. The same conviction has animated the struggle of freedom fighters everywhere. Alija Izetbegovic, for example, said: 'Other people are fighting for their freedom, and more than that, for their survival. Such struggles are usually hard-fought, but seldom lost. Not a single war of liberation in the past 50 years has been lost.'25

Tavleen Singh has criticized the Indian press: 'A policy of self-censorship appears to be operating whereby anything that sounds slightly critical of the security forces seems simply not to make it into the paper.'26 General Ray agrees: 'Banning or restricting the media deepens alienation. In our democracy, every Indian has a right to know what is happening within the country and this freedom cannot be denied.'[27] But the governmet remains unmoved. On 25 May 2011, *The Hindustan Times* reported that 'Indian Customs officers ordered that 28,000 copies of the news weekly [*Economist*, May 2011] should have stickers manually placed over a diagram showing how control of Kashmir' is split between India, Pakistan and China.

India imposes tight restrictions on all printed maps, insisting that they show the whole of Kashmir as part of India. John Micklethwaite, editor-in-chief of *The Economist* told AFP: 'India is meant to be a democracy that approves of freedom of speech. But they take a much more hostile attitude on this matter than either Pakistan or China. [...] This is an act of censorship, and many wise and sensible voices in India see it has no point.'[28]

On 7 August 2011, the Indian army carried out an 'operation' in Hari forest in Surankote *tehsil* of Poonch district, some 220 kilometres north of Jammu, and killed a man whom the army identified as Abu Usman, a divisional commander of the LeT. However, post-mortem identification revealed that the victim was a mentally-challenged Hindu beggar! 'A soldier of the Territorial Army and Special Operation Group of the police had supplied us wrong information, on the basis of which it was claimed that a terrorist has been killed in the encounter,' a spokesman of 16 Corps of the Indian Army told Indo-Asian News Service.

The Poonch incident is similar to what happened in Pathribal in 2005 and Maachil in 2010 when unsuspecting youths were lured from their houses on the pretext of giving them jobs. Then, at a remote spot, an encounter based on 'pinpoint information' took place, the youths were killed, weapons were found and displayed, and the dead described as 'foreign terrorists'. These crimes were exposed and triggered widespread protests. In boilerplate language, the army promised a fair probe and zero tolerance for such wrongdoing, if any. But 'not a single Armyman has been punished in the cases despite a CBI report in Pathribal and a police inquiry report into Maachil' (*Hindustan Times*, 9 August 2011).

The Indian security forces are beginning to realize the futility of fighting Kashmiris. Since 2005, nearly 41,000 BSF personnel – one in five of the total – have resigned their posts, preferring time with their families and looking for better jobs. Over 7,000 left in the first half of 2007; in 2006, nearly 16,200; in 2005 over 17,000. An annual attrition rate of eight per cent 'was alarming but understandable in a force that has a suicide rate that is three times higher than the army,' (*Hindustan Times*, 24 August 2007). 'We are a country that has to be dragged kicking and screaming into safeguarding basic human rights. Nothing could be more unfortunate for a society that sees itself as a modern, liberal democracy' (*Times of India*, 4 June 2012).

TERRORISTS OR FREEDOM FIGHTERS?

Reuters' global news editor Stephen Jukes wrote: 'We all know that one man's terrorist is another man's freedom fighter, and that Reuters upholds the principle that we do not use the word terrorist.'[1] Subhash Chandra Bose was one of the greatest Indian freedom fighters against British occupation. Addressing a rally in Burma in July 1944, he said that 'men, money and materials cannot by themselves bring victory or freedom'. He continued, 'all patriots should have but one desire today – the desire to die so that India should live – the desire to face a martyr's death, so that the path to freedom may be paved with the martyrs' blood. [...] Give me blood and I promise you freedom.'[2]

The British government designated Bose a terrorist. It was also a British government that 'executed, tortured and maimed thousands of people during the 1950s crackdown on Mau Mau rebels [in Kenya]. Among the tens of thousands of people detained, often in appalling conditions, was US President Obama's grandfather, Hussein Onyango Obama' (Associated Press, 18 April 2012).

Human beings need a unified standard that values and respects all human lives equally, not differentiating between acts of injustice against innocent people, whether carried out by individuals or by states, and whatever the religious or political identity of either individuals or states. God made all people equal and made the preservation of basic human rights, even for captives of war, an obligation and a core principle of the Islamic Law.

In an interview to Indian business daily *Economic Times* in October 2003, Geelani affirmed: 'We will continue to fight against the Indian occupation whether I survive or not. [...] The congregation at Martyrs Graveyard, Srinagar after my return from surgery in Mumbai where more than one hundred thousand people gathered was enough to prove our popular support, which gives me [the] strength to fight for freedom.'

'Freedom fighter' is a relative term for those engaged in rebellion against an established government or regime that they consider to be oppressive. As often as not, both sides in an armed conflict will lay claim to represent the popular cause of 'freedom'; even invading foreign armies have usually claimed to be 'liberators', rescuing the local/natives from 'oppression', 'tyranny' and, in modern idiom, 'human rights abuses'. In ordinary usage, the terms 'fight' and 'fighter' mean that the struggle is carried out through violence. However, it is possible to 'fight' with non-violent means. As Nelson Mandela implies, there is a difference between non-violence and pacifism. Pacifists do not use violence ever, even in self-defence: but 'sometimes men and nations, even if non-violent had to defend themselves when they are attacked.'[3] As for the terms 'terrorists' and 'freedom fighters', there is no universally agreed-upon definition. Many organizations accused of committing acts of terrorism themselves claim to be freedom fighters. Further, as Noam Chomsky points out:[4] 'From the U.S. point of view, there is good terrorism and bad terrorism'. Chomsky means that the same actions and policies will be branded 'good' or 'bad' in the US, depending on whether the actors (individuals or states) are, at the time of branding, supportive of or antagonistic to US actions and policies.

The label 'terrorist' is generally negative and therefore used for enemies of the state deploying the label. For example, Winston Churchill in his role as Secretary of State for the Colonies referred to Gandhi as 'seditious' and his party the Congress a 'militant movement'.[5] In the same way the Indian government (which replaced the British Raj) regularly uses the same term to describe people like Geelani and organisaltions like HM.

Especially during the Cold War, the term 'freedom fighters' was widely used by the United States and other Western powers to designate rebels in countries under the control or influence of the Soviet Union or otherwise resistant to the influence of the West. The label was used of, for example, rebels in Hungary, the Contras in Nicaragua, UNITA in Angola and the multi-factional *mujahidin* in Afghanistan during the 1980s.

General Ray wonders: 'A bomber pilot drops atomic bombs on Hiroshima and Nagasaki. A soldier kills and maims the enemy. A terrorist blows himself up in a crowded bus.... Is there a difference? One has the legal sanction to kill, the other does not.' He should also wonder: 'legal sanction' from whom? Just as bomber pilot may have permission from the Pentagon, the 'terrorist' may have permission from his Supreme Commander, sitting as far away from him as the Pentagon is from the Hiroshima bombers! Nevertheless, Ray puts the terrorists' motivation in perspective:

> Society would like to believe that all behaviour that violates societal norms is abnormal. But to think that killing by militants does not meet the approval of a certain section of the society is being gullible. The segment of the population which is aggrieved or deprived whole-heartedly approves and supports the militants' violent means.
>
> Suicide for a cause, for a political goal is a rational act. Such rationality is called martyrdom. A captain who goes down with his ship to the ocean floor is not mentally ill. Neither is the Buddhist monk who immolates himself in the streets of Saigon, or the Gandhi who goes on a fast unto death to extract British concessions. The same can be said of the early Christian martyrs. By the same token, the Hamas human bombs that kill innocent Israeli passengers on Bus 18 are not mad men either. They too are martyrs, they too are normal people.[6]

Geelani's take on this subject is:[7]

1. Attacks on civilians are a matter of concern for all societies and must be prevented or prosecuted and punished

by all means that are themselves lawful.

2. There must be clear, solid proof before anyone is declared a terrorist. Mere suspicion does not excuse the huge numbers of unarmed people being killed by states under the rubric of 'terror suspects'. By designating them 'suspects' the state is in effect admitting that its killing them is outside the law.

3. Any struggle whether political or military, aimed at just and lawful objectives, should not be branded as 'terrorism'.

Zbigniew Brezinski the National Security Advisor to President Carter, says about terrorism: 'The phrase itself is meaningless. It defines neither a geographic context nor our presumed enemies. Terrorism is not an enemy but a technique of warfare – political intimidation through the killing of unarmed non-combatants.'[8] In the context of Kashmir, Indian academic and writer Praful Bidawi has argued (*The Times of India*, 21 September 1999): The Indian government 'suppresses, and often legitimizes, state terrorism, which is far more pervasive and infinitely more destructive than sub-state terrorism. State terrorism is far more organized, intense and institutionalized than anything that guerillas and militants can put together. Many more murders have been committed in this century for reasons of state than of our religious prejudice.'

According to Geelani, 'Nobody supports terrorism. But this does not mean that a justified right should be curbed in the name of countering terrorism. Indian political leaders themselves used force against the British Empire. Bhagat Singh sacrificed his life on the gallows. On 14 April 2000, after my release from an Indian jail, some media personnel asked me what justification there was for infiltration from PaK [Pakistan-administered Kashmir]. I responded: 'Why did India send its troops to East Pakistan to support the [separatist] movement there?" The questioners were left speechless.'[9]

In recent years, India has exploited (rather more blatantly than others) the West's illegal and immoral 'war on terror' to expedite military solutions to its internal and external problems. Praful Bidwai explained this with particular reference to Kashmir (*The Frontline*, 22 October 1999):

> Terrorism has become a bandwagon slogan. In place of the K-word [Kashmir], which long spelt embarrassment, we are told, South Block [India's Foreign Office] has moved on to the T-word [Terrorism]. This gives India respectability, a feel-good proximity to, and a joint project with, the Great Powers, above all the US, no less. This Brave New Campaign against Terrorism has an implicit, unstated, anti-Islamic angle, building as it does on prejudices prevalent in the West, and the need for its right wing to find new enemies to perpetuate high levels of military-nuclear preparations. It confuses popular Islam, first with political Islam, and then the latter with fundamentalism.

The pursuit of this fundamentally flawed approach has earned India many enemies among Muslims at home and abroad. At the same time, it has failed to suppress the spirit of common Kashmiris. There is no doubt that as a result of India's role in the 'war on terror', many Indian politicians and security officials will be tried for 'war crimes' at an appropriate time in the future. India's aligning itself with the West's 'war on terror' respresents not a new decision, a historical shift, but the same policy presented in more explicit rhetoric. The failure to learn from experience (history, one's own or others') was noted in a fine article in *The Hindustan Times* as long ago as 16 June 1994:

> The fact that the Indian anti-insurgency policy has shown little change over the last 45 years is its remarkable feature. The ruling axiom of this strategy is 'wear them out.' The Indian state has developed a fine art [of] combining a military hard line with political inertia till either the local population tires with the insurgents, as has happened in [the] Punjab or the insurgents themselves come to believe that the uprising is proving fruitless and negotiations may be

the preferable solution – as in Nagaland. This strategy has served India fine. However, Kashmir is increasingly showing distinct evidence of becoming a dangerous exception. A pure military strategy, without some bold political initiatives, means that the state has to run twice as hard just to stay at the same place – even the Israelis have discovered that [i.e. that this strategy is hard to sustain].

Ankleswar Aiyar is one of several honest thinkers and writers in India. He wrote an interesting piece on this subject (*The Times of India*, 14 January 2011), putting the terrorism in and by Israel into historical perspective:

> In Palestine, after World War II, Jewish groups (the Haganah, Irgun and Stern Gang) fought for the creation of a Jewish state, bombing hotels and installations and killing civilians. The British, who then governed Palestine, rightly called these Jewish groups terrorists. Many of these terrorists later became leaders of independent Israel – Moshe Dayan, Yitzhak Rabin, Menachem Begin, Ariel Sharon. Ironically, these former terrorists then lambasted terrorism, applying this label only to Arabs fighting for the very same nationhood that the Jews had fought for earlier.

While the Baader-Meinhoff group in Germany, the Red Brigades in Italy, ETA (Basque separtists) in Spain and France, the IRA in Ireland/Britain are often 'near' enough for the Western media to differentiate, and, sometimes, to write sensibly about, the same is not true of Asia and Africa. Africa especially has for so long been ravaged by civil wars that few journalists bother to check carefully before deploying the label 'terrorist'. Possibly the most notorious group is the Lord's Salvation Army in Uganda. In Sri Lanka, the Tamil Tigers long constituted one of the most violent and formidable terrorist groups in the world. They were the first to train children as terrorists. Suicide bombing (widely associated with Muslim Palestinians and Iraqis) was pioneered by the Tamils in fact and used on a large scale: a suicide attack killed Rajiv Gandhi in 1991, another attack killed former Sri Lankan President Bandaranayke. Aiyar clarifies that in India, the militants in Kashmir are Muslim. But they are only one of several militant groups. The Punjab militants, led by Bhindranwale, were Sikhs. The United Liberation Front of Assam is a Hindu terrorist group that targets Muslims. Tripura has witnessed the rise and fall of several terrorist groups, and so have Bodo strongholds in Assam. Christian Mizos mounted an insurrection for decades, and Christian Nagas are still heading militant groups. But most important of all are the Maoist terrorist groups that now exist in no less than 150 out of India's 600 districts. They have attacked police stations, and killed and razed entire villages that oppose them. These are secular terrorists (like the Baader Meinhof Gang or Red Brigades). In terms of membership and area controlled, secular terrorists are far ahead of Muslim terrorists.

(*The Times of India*, 14 January 2011)

Aloke Tikku confirmed this in an article in *The Hindustan Times* (24 January 2011): 'Armed Maoists killed nearly 1,000 people last year, making 2010 the bloodiest year in the history of the movement that began 44 years ago.... Maoists killed 998 people across nine states last year, almost five times the total number of lives lost in terrorist acts in Jammu & Kashmir and the Northeast.' Arundhati Roy observes: 'there are [now] fissures in the consensus amongst Indians. Those fissures have come because people have seen this sort of undeniably mass democratic unarmed protest day after day, year after year in Kashmir. And people are affected by it. They're not easily able to say, "Oh, these are militants, these are Islamists, these are Taliban".'[10]

Muslims are a truly global community with sizeable presence on almost all continents. Thanks to the Western media, they have been projected as the community with an inherent propensity for terrorist violence. But this propaganda is not supported by statistical evidence around the world. For instance, official records of the US agency FBI show that only 6% of terrorist attacks on U.S. soil from

1980 to 2005 were carried out by Muslim extremists. The remaining 94% were from other groups (42% from Latinos, 24% from extreme left wing groups, 7% from extremist Jews, 5% from Communists, and 16% from others).[11]

Like the FBI, Europol annually publishes an EU Terrorism Situation and Trend Report. On their official website, the reports from 2007, 2008, and 2009 can be accessed. The results prove decisively that not all terrorists are Muslims. In fact, 99.6% of terrorist attacks in Europe were by non-Muslim groups; 84.8% of attacks were from separatist groups completely unrelated to Islam. Leftist groups accounted for over sixteen times as much terrorism as radical Islamic groups. Only a measly 0.4% of terrorist attacks from 2007 to 2009 could be attributed to extremist Muslims. On p. 7, the 2009 Europol report states:

> Islamist terrorism is still perceived as being the biggest threat worldwide, despite the fact that the EU only faced one Islamist terrorist attack in 2008. This bomb attack took place in the UK.... Separatist terrorism remains the terrorism area which affects the EU most. This includes Basque separatist terrorism in Spain and France, and Corsican terrorism in France.... Past contacts between ETA and the FARC illustrate the fact that also separatist terrorist organizations seek cooperation partners outside the EU on the basis of common interests.

Trevor Phillips, the head of UK's Equality and Human Rights Commission, confirmed that Muslims are better at integrating into society, while Christians often complain about bias for cynical political gains. He blamed the increasing influence of churches of African and Caribbean immigrants with 'intolerant' views. 'Muslim communities in this country are doing their damnedest to come to terms with their neighbours to try to integrate and they're doing their best to try to develop an idea of Islam that is compatible with living in a modern liberal democracy' (cited in *The Daily Mail*, 20 June 2011).

India is no different where a fierce war on terror i.e. Islam is underway. But according to the crime data for 2012 – released by the National Crime Records Bureau – "personal enmity was behind 3,877 of the 13,448 murders.... Property disputes were the reason for 3,169 murders and love affairs and sexual relations led to 2,549 killings across the country.[12] All fatalities put together in the so called "Islamic terror attacks" will pale against these single year's casualties. Intriguingly, no one seems concerned in India about launching a war on these crimes to save precious human lives!

Aiyar also argues that 'terrorism is certainly not a Muslim monopoly. There are or have been terrorist groups among Christians, Jews, Hindus, Sikhs, and even Buddhists. Secular terrorists (anarchists, Maoists) have been the biggest killers'. He asks 'why then is there such a widespread impression that most or all terrorist groups are Muslim?' In his view there are two reasons: (a) the Indian elite keenly follows the Western media; and (b) the West feels under attack from Islamic groups. Catholic Irish terrorists have killed far more people in Britain than Muslims, yet the subway bombings in London and Madrid are what Europeans remember today. So they focus attention on Islamic militancy. They pay little attention to other forms of terrorism in Africa, Sri Lanka or India because these militants pose no threat to the West.

From an Islamic perspective, to the best of my knowledge, I can sum up this debate:

1. Terrorism is not rooted in any religion. It is not fair for Islam, Christianity, Judaism, Hinduism, or Buddhism to be associated with terrorism. The best way to judge a religion is to read its scripture. These religions, according to their scriptures, propagate a certain way of viewing the Divine and the world, and train their followers to specific principles of morality and spirituality, albeit in different ways and in different idioms. Nevertheless, none of these religions endorses terrorism or any form of violence as a core value.

2. Terrorism is not equal to violence either. According to all rational human beings, some sorts of violence (coercive

force) are valid. For example, violence is necessary to defend ourselves when we are attacked in the street. Force is needed sometimes to arrest and punish criminals (in this case, it is the government's job to do that). Therefore, force in itself is not a vice. The way it is used in a particular situation is what may make it vicious or virtuous.

3. Imagine that some armed invaders enter our locality, kick us out of our own homes, and occupy it. Are we not entitled to self-defence? This self-defence, however, is not supposed to lead us to injustices against other innocent people and should be only against those who invaded our home or who supported the invaders.

4. Terrorism is not restricted to individuals. There are terrorist groups organized at state or sub-state levels. Terrorist governments use armies and mercenaries from among the target groups. For example, Northern Alliance in Afghanistan, Awakening Councils in Iraq, Fatah in Palestine. They are given lethal weapons for use against innocent people. Indian government backed terrorists in Kashmir called 'Ikhwanis'. Once led by Kukka Paray, they have perpetrated the worst of crimes against their own brothers and sisters (see Chapter 8). Similarly, US-funded and Israeli-trained gangs of criminals led by Muhammad Dahlan in Palestinian territories of Gaza and West Bank played havoc among their own compatriots.

5. Terrorism is not restricted to arms and bombs. People can be terrorized and killed by other means, such as hunger, torture, denial of medical care, crippling economic sanctions on a large scale, and so on. For example, over half-a-million Iraqi children were killed by the economic sanctions imposed by the US and UK through the UN.

6. Terrorism is not restricted to non-combat zones. Acts of terrorism can take place in combat zones; rules of war relating to combatants and non-combatants and captives are not respected and observed. Recent examples include

the Abu Ghraib prison in Iraq, Bagram in Afghanistan Camp Delta at Guantanamo Bay (among others less in the news), where the whole world has witnessed the brutality of US state terrorism in complicit silence.

7. Terrorists include presidents, prime ministers, senior government officials and army personnel who take disproportionate measures against whole populations under the rubric of 'security', 'self-defence' or 'international norms.' For example, the murder of 3,000 innocent civilians in New York and Washington on September 11, a great atrocity, does not justify killing huge numbers of people and setting half-a-dozen Muslim countries on fire. Drone attacks killing civilians is the latest form of terrorism.

Aiyar concluded that 'Guerrilla fighters from Mao Zedong to Ho Chi Minh and Fidel Castro [...] were called terrorists until they triumphed. Nothing Muslim about them.'[13] India will not hold talks with Geelani and Salahuddin, because both are labeled 'terrorists'. As Tavleen Singh points out: 'how quickly yesterday's terrorists become today's political leaders. Remember that Farooq Abdullah, now a nationalist hero, was considered a terrorist by Indira Gandhi in 1984. His alleged support for terrorism was the justification [Indira] gave for dismissing his government' (*India Today*, 22 November 2000)!

8

INSURGENCY AND COUNTER-INSURGENCY

FROM 24 OCTOBER 1947 until now, the vast majority of Kashmir Muslims have never accepted the violent occupation of their homeland by Indian forces. How should this refusal have been expressed? Nelson Mandela said: 'The time comes in the life of any nation when there remain only two choices: submit or fight.'[1] When the time came, Geelani and his followers led by HM chose the latter. HM Supreme Commander Salahuddin explained the resort to armed ressistance in this way: 'When someone has occupied your home, destroying your property and degrading your family members, then you have two options: either you vacate your home [i.e submit] or fight.'[2]

'The Islamic position is that all non-violent means of conflict resolution must first be explored. If even after this oppression does not cease, then Muslims are allowed to take up the sword in the cause of justice,' explained Altaf Hussain Tak at the Department of English, Kashmir Univesity.[3] Geelani, in accordance with and within the boundaries of Islamic principles, supported HM's armed struggle to (a) stop Indian brutalities and (b) to establish justice and peace. He played a vital role in turning Kashmir's freedom struggle into an Islamic movement in the 1990s. That is why he is the only politician acceptable to almost all the different factions of militants struggling against the occupation.

What triggered the resort to armed struggle was the crushing of any hope of an alternative, namely the blatant rigging of the 1987 elections in J&K. It is important to understand some of the key events that preceded those elections.

An international cricket match between India and West Indies to be played in Sringar was announced for 13 October 1983. Geelani vociferously opposed, arguing that, as disputed territory, Kashmir could not legitimately host an international match. For India, Srinagar was chosen precisely so as to present Kashmir as 'an integral part of India'. Geelani was arrested and tried in camera so as to avoid the big crowds that would otherwise attend the proceedings. He was jailed for ten months.

Following his release, Kashmiris were still willing to see the dispute settled in a civilized way. Geelani played a leading role in this effort. In the midst of the post-cricket match crackdown, Geelani and other pro-freedom leaders started preparations for the next elections, due in 1987. Geelani succeeded in bringing diverse groups to share a common platform under the banner of the Muslim United Front (MUF). They campaigned with the Qur'an in one hand and the Kashmiri flag in the other. It was a remarkable display of faith and hope. Once elected, as seemed inevitable, Geelani planned peacefully to declare the liberation of Kashmir on the floor of the state assembly.

Salahuddin also contested the 1987 election as the Jama'at's candidate against the then education minister. When the NC hijacked the election, Kashmiris believed they could not attain their freedom through democratic process. Jama'at's President of Jammu region Ghulam Nabi Faridabadi, speaking at a seminar in Jammu, said: 'Salahuddin was all set to win [the] 1987 election with a margin of 10,000 votes. However, he was sent to jail on the directions of New Delhi, and a candidate who had only secured 4,000 votes was announced as winner. [The] 1987 elections were the turning point in the history of Jammu and Kashmir. We were forced to choose [the] bullet instead of [the] ballot'. Tavleen Singh confirmed that 'things were very different after the 1987 election which everyone believed he [Chief Minister Farooq Abdullah] really did rig.'[4] All Kashmiri elections have been rigged, but the one in 1987 was fraudulent to an unprecedented degree. Also unparalleled was the crackdown over the next few months, during which almost all senior MUF leaders were thrown into prison.

Geelani was determined to fight the Indian occupation politically. But Kashmiris, some of his own followers included, now felt the need also to fight militarily against over half-a-million Indian security forces deployed throughout the state. As would soon become obvious, unless the Jama'at took some part, and therefore had some say, in the armed struggle, they would not be able to influence events or to manage their consequences. Nelson Mandela recalls: 'Violence would begin whether we initiated it or not. Would it not be better to guide this violence ourselves, according to principles where we saved lives by attacking symbols of oppression, and not innocent people? If we did not take the lead now, we would soon be latecomers and followers of a movement we did not control.... Only through hardship, sacrifice and militant action can freedom be won.'[5]

The rule of the Dogras had long gone, but the state government setup is still called a Durbar [royal court]. On 7 May each year the Durbar moves from the winter capital Jammu to the summer capital Srinagar. Chief Minister Farooq Abdullah looked out of the window of his office in Srinagar on 7 May 1989 – the capital's streets were deserted in response to a shutdown call by MUF supporters to coincide with Durbar day. Farooq Abdullah turned to one of his most senior bureaucrats and personal friend, Ashok Jaitley, and said. 'This is my government!' Unable to contain his frustration he added something unprintable about the separatists. The storm of anger was deepening, the only question was when and how it would burst. Many Kashmiri youth had already started arming themselves.

After the fiasco of the 1987 state elections, the Kashmiris decided to boycott the national elections in late 1989. The summer of 1989 had passed peacefully enough; the tourist season had been splendid. The rigmarole of meetings within the secretariats of Srinagar and Delhi intensified as the brewing storm signals were picked up and analysed. But they were by no means prepared for the massive endorsement of the election boycott called by the MUF: only five per cent of the electorate voted.

A new coalition government assumed power in New Delhi. In December 1989 Indian Prime Minister V. P. Singh appointed Mufti Mohammad Sayeed, a Kashmiri Muslim, as Home Minister. Militants of the J&K Liberation Front (JKLF) decided to test the nerve of this most powerful Kashmiri Muslim ever in Delhi's history. At four in the afternoon of 8 December 1989, they kidnapped his daughter, Dr. Rubaiya Sayeed, about 500 metres from her home at Nowgam. An hour and a half later, someone claiming to represent the JKLF, called the Srinagar bureau of *The Kashmir Times* demanding the release of Sheikh Abdul Hameed, a JKLF 'area commander' hospitalized at the Sher-e-Kashmir Institute of Medical Sciences. He was arrested after being wounded in an encounter. Also on the JKLF's list for release were: Ghulam Nabi Butt, younger brother of the late Maqbool Butt, Noor Muhammad Kalwal, Muhammed Altaf, and Javed Ahmed Zangar.

Over the next five days, the entire government machinery was activated to get the daughter of India's Home Minister released. The negotiations opened through Zafar Meraj of *The Kashmir Times*. Shabnam Lone, daughter of Abdul Ghani Lone and Maulvi Abbas Ansari of the MUF were also tapped as possible channels. Later, a judge of the Allahabad High Court, Moti Lal Bhat, entered the picture. A friend of Mufti Sayeed, he began negotiating directly with the militants on the Minister's behalf. At 3:30 a.m. on 13 December 1989, two Union Cabinet Ministers, Inder Kumar Gujral and Arif Mohammad Khan, personally flew into Srinagar. They believed that Farooq Abdullah was blocking a deal. Farooq took the view that surrender to the terrorists' demands would open the floodgates for more of the same. But the government of V. P. Singh thought otherwise. A deal was reached with the underground JKLF leadership on the morning of 13 December. At 7 p.m. on that day Dr. Rubaiya Sayeed was set free, exactly two hours after the government released the five militants. Thousands of JKLF supporters gathered at Rajouri Kadal to take the militants out in a triumphant procession before disappearing to their hideouts and then to PaK.

The kidnapping of a young, unmarried woman aroused great anger among Islamically-oriented Kashmiris. Geelani openly condemned this act; Jama'at supporters generally viewed it as contrary to Islamic and Kashmiri values. On the other hand, JKLF militants were in high spirits after bringing the Indian government to its knees. They were itching to convert their movement into a mass uprising. The government, stung by the nationwide outrage at the surrender to terrorism, was equally determined to regain the initiative. Home Ministry orders were clear: to put the fear of Delhi into the heart of every Kashmiri.

Yoginder Sikand (*Economic and Political Weekly*, 20 January 2001) reflected on the circumstance that had led Geelani to consent to armed struggle: 'The armed struggle launched by the JKLF for the independence of Kashmir found mass support among Kashmiri Muslims, disillusioned as they were with Indian rule and with the subversion of democratic institutions in Kashmir. The MUF initially hesitated in joining the armed struggle, directing its four representatives within the state assembly, including Geelani, chief ideologue of the JIJK (Jama'at), to retain their seats so as to be able to air the grievances of the people. However, the rising tide of the JKLF-led struggle soon proved too much for the MUF high command to ignore. In 1989, it instructed its members in the assembly to resign and join the struggle. The JIJK now decided to fully immerse itself in the militant movement. In 1990, it set up its own militant wing, the Hizb-ul Mujahidin (the Army of the Holy Warriors).' Senior Jama'at sources have confirmed to me that the first part of Sikand's report is correct, but the Jama'at never owned HM publicly. Therefore Jama'at's association with HM is disputed.

One of Salahuddin's election campaigners was Mohammad Yasin Malik, who later became the Chairman of JKLF. Salahuddin also mentioned to me that some external factors (beside the hijacking of the 1987 election) had also helped trigger the armed uprising in Kashmir. These included the victory of the Afghan *mujahidin* over the Soviet Union and the Islamic revolution in Iran. Also, as Joshi recalled, 'the once mighty edifice of the Romanian Communist Party just came apart, with its megalomaniacal leader [Ceausescu] caught and executed on 25 December [1989]. The event was viewed on Doordarshan [official Indian TV channel] by the fascinated audience of the Valley, who drew their own conclusions.'[6]

By April 1990, a great deal of blood had flowed and was continuing to flow throughout the state. Geelani wrote: 'Our brave young men started [the] armed struggle only to give a befitting reply to this intoxication of force. [The w]hole nation supported it since it was based on truth and justice. Since Jamaat-e-Islami is a part of Kashmir obviously it also became part of [the] armed resistance.'[7]

The New York Times (22 November 1992) opined that: 'While virtually no one, Indian or foreign diplomat, believes that the guerillas in the Valley can be eliminated by force, it is improbable that the rebels can win a victory by themselves. It is this stand off, New Delhi believes, that will drive exhausted Kashmiris to the negotiating table.' Explaining why that 'exhaustion' was unlikely to come any time soon, K. R. Sunder Rajan wrote (*The Pioneer*, 16 June 1992): 'The Muslims of Kashmir cannot be accused of betraying India. Perhaps they would not have taken to arms if there were other ways to express their feelings. But the National Conference backed by the Central Government, which was out of tune with the feelings of the Muslims, made peaceful protest impossible. This should help us understand why Kashmiri Muslims, whose peacefulness was the subject of innumerable Hindu jokes, have become death-defying guerillas. No amount of force can make Kashmiri Muslims bow to Indian authority.'

That view is confirmed by Oxford-based scholar Sharmila Bose (*The Telegraph*, 5 April 1996), who lists some consequences for India's reputation: 'Deprived of the freedom to choose who would govern them and how, the Kashmiris finally rose in revolt in 1990. New Delhi has tried ever since to militarily crush the people whose political voice it repeatedly stifled. Inevitably, the exercise of military might has solved none of the political problems, but unleashed a reign of repression, detention, torture and killings that has made a travesty of the political and human values India is supposed to stand for and shamed India across the world.'

Staunchly pro-Geelani, HM is the largest militant group

operating in J&K. It was formed on 26 December 1989. Its headquarters are in Muzaffarabad, the capital of PaK. It stands for the integration of Kashmir with Pakistan but, since its formation, it has also worked for the Islamization of Kashmiri society, and esteems Geelani as its ideological inspiration. Indian officials claim that HM was formed as the armed wing of the pro-Pakistan Jama'at at the behest of Pakistan's intelligence agencies – a claim disputed by the HM leadership.

The HM Constitution was approved in June 1990. Mohammed Yusuf Shah, popularly known as Syed Salahuddin, was appointed Patron and Muhammad Ahsan Dar, Chief Commander. Differences between pro-Jama'at and anti-Jama'at elements developed within the HM which led to its split. The pro-Jama'at faction was then led by Salahuddin. The other was led by Hilal Ahmed Mir, who was killed by Indian security forces in a 1993 encounter. Salahuddin is still the Supreme Commander of HM, with Saifullah Khalid and Umar Javaid as Deputies. Ghazi Nasiruddin is its Chief Commander of Operations in the Valley.

HM has been able to tap into a large pool of willing recruits on both sides of the Line of Control. Salahuddin has told me that HM numbers exceed 15,000, all 'highly motivated'. But the Indian government is clueless about the exact number of militants active in J&K. 'The Ministry of Home Affairs has asked the Army, Police and Intelligence Bureau (IB) to reconcile their figures about the number of militants as the numbers put forth by them vary' (*Greater Kashmir*, 24 December 2012). According to Geelani, these highly committed freedom fighters are giving over half-a-million Indian troops more than a run for their money. 'A small body of determined spirits fired by an unquenchable faith in their mission can alter the course of history,' Mohandas Karamchand Gandhi is cited as saying (*Muslim India*, #189, September 1998, 410). It is a common saying that the *mujahidin* are like the grass – the more you cut it, the more it grows.

Because of HM's ideological proximity to Jama'at, both in Kashmir and in Pakistan, some of the youth belonging to Jami'at-i-Tulaba, a student organization, inspired by the idealogy of the Jamaat, were also attracted to the cadre of the Hizb [HM]. Overseas, HM is allegedly backed by Dr. Ghulam Nabi Fai, the Chairman of the US-based Kashmir American Council. However, when I spoke with him in Washington DC, Dr. Fai denied this. He said he does not support one organization against another. He just supports the liberation of Kashmir from 'illegal and immoral Indian occupation'.

At the beginning, in the early 1990s, the HM established contacts with Afghan *mujahidin* groups such as Hizb-i-Islami, which provided some of its recruits with training. Joshi further says: 'Its efforts were boosted by the quality of its commanders – Master Ahsan Dar, Mohammad Ashraf Dar and Maqbool Ilahi – as well as the network of the Jamaat.'[8] Currently, the HM is organized into six divisions: Central Division for Srinagar and Badgram; Northern Division for Kupwara, Bandipora, Baramulla; Southern Division for Islamabad and Pulwama districts; Chenab Division for Udhampur; Gool Gulab Garah and Pir Panjal Division for the Rajouri and Poonch districts; and Doda Division for Doda, Kishtiwar and Banihal. It has a substantial support base in the Kashmir Valley and in the Doda, Rajouri, Poonch districts and parts of Udhampur district in the Jammu region.

Justice Rajender Sachar observed (*Indian Express*, July 1993): 'One may or may not agree with the political views of militants, but it would be unrealistic not to acknowledge that a vast mass of people in Kashmir, including members of various professions, have a warm appreciation for the armed struggle by the militants.' Geelani's just stand is being recognized even by honest non-Muslims. They are joining the fight to establish justice for *all*, not just for Muslims. In a startling revelation, Salahuddin stated in an interview that 'in Jammu many Hindus have been martyred fighting for the HM. These people have realized that Indians are ruthlessly killing children and women to take revenge against the militants. For example, a resident of Prem Nagar, Kuldip Kumar alias Kamran, was martyred in [the] Jammu region. He was our area commander. Kashmiri Sikhs and Christians are also joining our ranks.'[9]

Indian politicians are aware of this, but the media cover it up. In December 2005 Home Minister Sri Prakash Jaiswal admitted in the upper house of the Indian parliament that Hindu youth have joined the militancy 'for monetary considerations or due to criminal bent of mind'.[10] Former Congress Chief Minister of J&K Ghulam Nabi Azad, admitted on TV: 'For the last so many years some politicians and political workers are actively supporting the sympathizers and workers of various militant groups [...] I have identified some politicians who are supporting the overground workers of various militant organizations' (*The Times of India*, 10 August 2007).

According to *The Statesmen* (12 June 1994), 'as the bodies of the killed militants were handed over to the next of kin, people in the area took to [the] streets and protested against the security forces. They raised anti-security forces and pro-freedom slogans.' Rajesh Pilot, the minister in the Indian cabinet holding the Kashmiri portfolio, expected the people of Kashmir to follow the example of the people of Punjab (*The Telegraph*, Calcutta, 27 June 1994): 'Militancy could not be tackled in the real sense till people in Punjab came out openly against it, and I want you [Kashmiris] to do the same thing.' But the uprising against Indian occupation has already lasted over two decades; it has done so on the basis of the widespread public support for it. The following photographs illustrate the widespread and continued public support for the resistance movement.

*8.1 Frequent scenes like this proved the huge public
support that militants enjoy in Kashmir*

HM has conducted a number of operations against Indian military targets in J&K. The group is also blamed for occasional strikes at civilian targets in J&K but has not engaged in armed activities elsewhere in India. However, this may change in the future. According to Salahuddin: 'The irony is, when there is a bomb blast in India then the international community raises an uproar against it. But when Indian forces kill innocent people in Kashmir and rape our sisters and mothers then there is no such reaction from the international community. We have made it clear to the Indian forces that their revenge should be limited to us and not our families. But when they damage our property and kill our family members then we have to retaliate in a manner that we don't want to.'[11] He meant targeting Indian civilians. Vidya Subrahmaniam echoed the implied warning in the *Times of India* (13 July 2000): 'for its part, the BJP must understand that India cannot feel secure when Kashmiris are so insecure.'

Despite claims to the contrary by Indian politicians and security officers, 'the insurgency is running at full tilt, with bomb attacks on the security forces and other official targets.... Hardly a day seems to go by in Srinagar without an explosion. India's efforts to contain the menace are winning it no friends. Kashmiri leaders say the number of custodial killings – essentially, murders of suspected militants held in custody – has risen, a claim backed by human rights groups in Delhi' (*The Economist*, 3 June 2000). The insurgency is largely sustained by the support that 'excesses by the security forces – such as fake encounters and coercive measures against innocents in the name of search and seizure operations – generate in the local population' (*The Hindu*, 12 May 2001, editorial).

In Geelani's view, post-9/11, 'all armed struggles, whether they were just or otherwise, were linked to terrorism. Our struggle too was bracketed with terrorism. Pakistan, which supported us, [it] too, possibly at the instructions of the United States, clubbed our struggle with terrorism. That led to a rethinking in our ranks' (*Arab News*, 17 August 2010). But Salahuddin stressed in his September 2001 interview with the Indian magazine *The Meantime*: 'Any [Pakistani] ruler who compromises on Kashmir will not survive. The

Kashmir mujahideen [...] know [how to] manufacture sensitive and high-intensity devices. We just get diplomatic, moral and political support from Pakistan. We get the bulk of our arms from India itself. There are many Indian NGOs engaged in arms deals.' Earlier, *The Sunday Mail* (12 June 1994) reported a specific incident where militants ambushed the army and walked away with their weapons after killing security personnel:

> On April 1, 1993 the Indian Army's Eighth Division had launched a cordon and search operation in Arampura area. Brigadier H. S. Kanwar was going to inspect the operation in a convoy of four–five vehicles when he was ambushed. The army convoy took a severe beating and four members were killed including a captain. Their weapons were snatched away and one of the vehicles was burnt.

> This shocked Brig. Kanwar and his Commanding Officer, Major-General Mavi. They refused to instruct any army personnel to venture beyond the army outpost at the Degree College which was situated right at the entrance of the Sopore town.

On 2 June 2002, *Washington Post* reported: 'Deputy Secretary of State Richard L. Armitage declared that tensions are down measurably after Pakistan's president, Gen. Pervez Musharraf, promised him that he would permanently end incursions by Islamic militants across the LoC.' Some Kashmiri separatist leaders said Pakistan's crackdown could deprive them of the resources needed to sustain a high-intensity revolt. But *The Washington Post* (3 January 2003) quoted Syed Salahuddin as saying that his fighters were able to 'get what they needed in India and 'sophisticated arms and ammunition are easily available in many markets'. Joshi confirmed that '[the] price of AK-47s in Srinagar ranged from INR 12,000 to 15000, INR 25,000 for LMGs, INR 3,500 to 5,000 for pistols and revolvers.'[12]

Instead of addressing the real issue in a meaningful way, our leadership has continued to deceive the masses. Former Indian naval chief Admiral L. Ramdas boasted (*Frontline*, 3 February 2001): 'It is only a matter of time before both Pakistan and these two groups [LeT and HM] conform because the pressure is building on them. Also, it is only a matter of time before these militants are hounded out by the people of Kashmir.' To the contrary, after two decades of relentless persecution, Kashmiri civilians and militants are not intimidated.

An honest and fair leader, Geelani admits that 'there were lapses and some gross mistakes by the youth [militants].'[13] Nevertheless, massive public support for militants continues unabated. On 25 December 2012 thousands gathered for the funeral of the two HM militants (see below photo) killed at Yamrach village in south Kashmir's Kulgam district. It was the last wish of one of the two slain militants, Mudasir Ahmad, that his funeral prayers be led by Geelani. He addressed this gathering through telephone from New Delhi (*Greater Kashmir*, 26 December 2012).

8.2 The Kashmiri masses carrying the dead body of a militant at his funeral

COUNTER-INSURGENCY

In the hope of recouping its losses in the early stages of its battle with the militants, the Indian government set up counter-insurgency

units, the euphemism for officially-sponsored local terrorist outfits, such as had been successfully deployed in the Punjab at the
height of the Sikh militancy in the 1980s. To execute this desperate
measure, Ajit Kumar Doval was sent to Kashmir in 1990 during
the governorship of General K. V. Krishna Rao. An Indian Police
Service (IPS) officer from the 1968 batch of the Kerala cadre, Ajit
Doval is widely known to be among the very best intelligence
officers India has ever produced – he would serve as the director
of India's Intelligence Bureau in 2004–5. By then he had spent a
decade as the head of its operations wing, and earlier in his career,
spent six years in Pakistan. He was the first police officer in India to
get India's excellence award, Kirti Chakra.

Sumbul in Baramulla district is the village Kashmiris associate
with counter-insurgency because it is the home of Kashmir's top
counter-insurgent Kuka Parray. Originally a folk singer, Parray
jumped on the separatist bandwagon and became a militant and
received some initial training in PaK. Following Ajit's arrival in the
Valley, Parray entered into dialogue with Indian intelligence opera-
tives and formally surrendered to the Indian security forces in 1993.

In late 1992, Geelani warned in a Friday sermon that 'if we have
the courage to fight the Indian security forces, we will also have
to fight those amongst us who are indulging in undesirable activities' (cited in *The Times of India*, 6 November 1992). Responding to
Geelani's warning, militants put in place measures to neutralize the
new threat. *The Pioneer* (24 June 1994) reported: 'Militants are said
to keep a watch on all camps for informants. As a result, nearly 50
informers have been killed by militants. Not surprisingly, less and
less number of people are willing to approach the authorities.'

Around that time, twenty-eight other militants surrendered
and, under the leadership of Parray, formed the pro-government
militia Ikhwan-ul-Muslimin or Muslim Brotherhood (sic). The
Indian government gave full military and financial support, and re-
inforced the group with another former militant Fayaz Nawabadi,
who was released from prison for that purpose. These 'friendlies',
as the Indian soldiers called the 'pro-India militants', gave the intelligence network and counter-insurgency operations in the Valley a

significant boost. The Indian army provided the logistic support they needed to 'liberate' numerous 'occupied zones' under HM control across the Valley:

> Parray, chief of the *Ikhwan-ul-Muslimoon*, a militant group with a difference [...is] fighting for Kashmir's 'liberation' not from India, but from the pro-Pakistan Hizbul Mujahideen and the Jamaat-e-Islami. And in Parray, New Delhi and the army have found a useful ally. [But] sponsoring Parray could prove to be a wrong gamble. Just eight months into his new role, he has transgressed his brief but is not being checked. He is not only alleged to be involved in extortion and looting, his men also run an illegal trade in timber and precious walnut wood right under the nose of the district administration and security forces. (*India Today*, 15 December 1995)

Indeed, by the end of 1995 Parray had not only brought large parts of Baramulla and Islamabad under his jurisdiction, he had also started moving into Srinagar. He effectively controlled the functioning of all major hospitals in Srinagar; local newspapers printed any statement issued by his outfit. The Indian media, though theoretically anxious, fully supported this unconstitutional act of the Indian government. The article cited just above, for example, warns that 'in the end, the Government will have to ensure that he remains what he started out to be, a surrendered militant willing to play the Government's game.' It does not question the game itself or if it should be played by a supposedly democratic government.

By 1996, the Ikhwan militia were openly flaunting their arms around the Kashmir Valley. Kuka Parray became the second most important person in Kashmir after Farooq Abdullah. 'In short, the State sees Parray and his men ruling Kashmir, officially,' wrote Rahul Bedi in *The Pioneer* (1 June 1996). Ikhwanis were feared and abhorred for their ruthless and extortionist ways. It was a high price to pay for the decline in militancy that enabled India to hold elections for the J&K state assembly in 1996. In the run-up to these elections, Parray formed the J&K Awami League party. He successfully challenged the sitting NC candidate M. Akbar Lone in the Sonawari constituency, which includes Parray's hometown Sumbul.

The 'politician' Parray was in all essentials still the 'terrorist' Parray. His gang continued to terrorize common Kashmiris in general and Jama'at associates in particular. On the evening of 14 May 1996, members of Ikhwan knocked on the door of Ghulam Muhammad Wani and abducted his son, Imtiyaz Ahmed. Imtiyaz disappeared without trace. After going from pillar to post, visiting police stations and army officers, Ghulam Muhammad went to the State Human Rights Commission to file a complaint, but that too in vain. He then sold a property, took out a loan and paid a seemingly sympathetic counter-insurgent who promised information about his missing son. But the money, like his son, disappeared.

'My son was a gardener at the forest department, earning Rs 2,000 (US$45) a month; he did no wrong,' said the distraught father. 'It has been 15 years.' A policeman from the Special Task Force (a counter-insurgency wing of the J&K police) came to his house and offered 1,200 rupees ($22) as compensation for the loss of his son! He was also approached by politicians offering him 'aid' in exchange for silence, Ghulam Muhammad told Al Jazeera's Azad Essa.[14]

Government agencies ensured that these Ikhwan criminals were deployed mainly in areas dominated by the Jama'at. Though also very active in Srinagar, their focus remained Pampore, Pulwana, Sopore and Islamabad. An Indian human rights activist sent this report on the ground situation:

> The only inhabitants of the locality [...] are the *sarkari* [government] militants [...] 'renegades', 'counter-insurgents' or 'friendlies', as they are termed. The presence of these extralegal authorities ensures that every resident refuses to go inside the locality.
>
> The residents say they have no one to complain to since the arson and firing were done with the full connivance of

the security forces.... Tales of abuses by 'sarkari militants' are found throughout Pulwana and Anantnag districts where the new terror has intensified in the past two to three months.... The terror is heightened by the fact that there is no perceivable redress.

(Aunohita Mojumdar's Situation Report, *The Statesman*, 15–18 March 1996)

The Indian forces did not use the Ikhwanis only for counter-insurgency operations. They also used them to terrorize the non-combatant local population. A mid-level army officer admitted to the *Asia Times* in September 2003 that 'he had used the *Ikhwanis* to "persuade" locals who had filed baseless complaints against his men to withdraw their charges.' Ordinary Kashmiris have more tales to tell. 'They have made our lives miserable. They extort money from us and if you raise your voice, consider yourself dead,' said Irshad Ahmad, a Sumbul youth. Fayaz Nawabadi was particularly ruthless and, along with notoriety, earned the post of Commander-in-Chief of the Ikhwan. Kuka Parray remained as Supreme Commander. Fayaz walked the streets like a lord – 'Even policemen had to look down while walking past him,' says a resident of Ganderbal.

Fayaz is said to have killed hundreds of innocents. The Ganderbal resident relates that 'if his eyes fell on something he liked, it had to be his.' One day he happened to see and like a new scooter, parked in the Safapora market, belonging to 21-year-old Waseem. 'Waseem would not just let go of his new scooter when Fayaz asked him to give [it]'. Fayaz then walked up to him, held him by his throat, and pumped bullets into him. Waseem fell to the ground. When a shop-keeper raised his voice, he too met the same fate; another likewise. 'Three innocent people died that day.' With three dead bodies on the street to make his point, Fayaz said: 'O [people of] Safapora, whoever goes against us will meet a similar fate.'[15]

Fayaz would be accompanied by his trusted lieutenants, Abdul Hamid Mir alias Nikka Bhai, Mohammad Afzal Mir alias Commander Adil, Ghulam Nabi Mir alias Kaka, among others. The reign of terror engulfed the Sonawari, Safapora, Ganderbal region.

It started a wave of migration from there to the urban areas, with many leaving Kashmir altogether. Saif-u-Din Bhat, a sixty-year-old teacher from Safapora was killed because his brother was associated with HM. Another teacher Abdul Karim Bhat was killed because of links with Jama'at-i-Islami.

Ikhwanis once went to the house of a Jama'at sympathizer in Banyari village. The man they were looking for was not at home. 'The routine would have been to harass the family and leave,' says Yasir, a resident of the area. 'But on that day death was in the air. One of the commanders caught hold of a six-month-old baby of the man. He tossed the infant into the air, and the *Ikhwanis* started firing.' The infant came down in tiny pieces. 'I cannot forget that day,' says Yasir, 'there are no words to express this cruelty.'[16]

Tales of their atrocities abound. 'One more case still resonates in the hearts and minds of people. It always gives me pain,' says Yasir as he recalls. 'There was a girl in Asham, a beautiful girl, Nazima, the daughter of one Ghulam Mohammad Lone. And then Ikhwanis' eyes fell on her.' Nazima was kidnapped. 'For days together no one knew of her,' Yasir says. Details of her state later emerged. It was actually Fayaz who had sought her, and when she resisted him, she was raped by many *Ikhwanis* and she got pregnant.

In the meantime, Ashraf Nawabadi, Fayaz's brother, started pursuing Nazima's sister. She too was kidnapped. 'The family protested. They would not have protested if they knew what was to come next,' says Yasir. The Ikhwanis converged on the Asham market. Pregnant Nazima was dragged out on the street. Fayaz oversaw everything. 'What transpired next is engraved in the psyche of the people there forever,' says Yasir. The eight-month pregnant woman was held forcibly. Then her clothes were torn. After this she was paraded naked. 'Fayaz pulled the trigger, and shot her in the abdomen first. He kept on shooting and shouting...' recalls Yasir. Nazima died on the spot.

Even after such a disgusting incident, no one dared to speak up. That was the peak of Ikhwan terror. 'But nothing is permanent. Whatever goes up, has to come down,' says Yasir. HM cadres were desperately looking to hunt down these criminals. They started eliminating Indian army-sponsored hard-core criminals one by one. Kaka was shot dead in 1994, Nikka Bhai was killed in 1995, and Afzal in 1996. The kingpin, Fayaz, after surviving eighteen attempts on his life, finally met his fate on 17 February 2000. He was blown up in an IED blast in Sumbal, not far from where he had brutally murdered Nazima. According to local residents, the intensity of the blast was such that his body parts could be seen hanging from the power-supply cables running across the street.

But the boss remained alive and well. After having been 'elected' for the J&K assembly, Parray claimed on 7 December 1998: 'I succeeded in achieving this aim as was evident from the successful conduct of the Lok Sabha [Parliamentary] polls. But that was only a beginning; the ultimate goal was restoration of the state legislative assembly. I had to personally go to Delhi and persuade Dr. Farooq Abdullah to come over and fight the assembly polls. I convinced him that my boys had done a commendable job and his or his party's security could not be a major problem.'[17] But international scholars recognized the perils of this flawed government strategy. Michael Krepon, the President of Henry L. Simpson Center and Kashmir Study Group was quoted in *The Hindu* (10 November 1999):

> In the absence of purposeful dialogue between aggrieved parties counter-insurgency operations can have only limited effect. In India this conclusion is not broadly accepted and has not yet translated into changes in government policy. As a result, the Government of India relies heavily on a one-track policy based on counter-insurgency operation. New Delhi's Kashmir policy therefore places a heavy burden on Kashmiris.

The criminal gang the Indian army had fostered was big, but many of its members were on the run. Due to their criminal behaviour, they were fast losing the support of even the Indian security forces themselves. At the same time, their true character was fully exposed to the general public as well. *The Indian Express* (9 December 1999) reported: 'In fact, today, there are many who resent them. Local residents view them with deep suspicion – some even with contempt – for switching sides. Mainstream parties sneer at their recent attempts to jump into electoral politics. Even the Army admits their limited use.... At the peak, there were close to 3,000 of them operating in the Valley [with] different security agencies.... It was later decided that *Ikhwanis* get a uniform salary of approx INR 1500 [US$ 30] per month. Several cases of extortion, looting and harassment by surrendered militants had been reported.'

Within years, these traitors had reached their 'use by' date. The *Indian Express* report continued: 'Six years ago, the *Ikhwans* were the Army's valuable assets, working largely in their shadows. The surrendered militants were of great help in tracking down militants in the Valley. They knew the hideouts and the terrain. Soon, they began getting regular salaries but over the years as their numbers grew, they were increasingly viewed as a liability.' Members of Indian civil society also started writing openly against this menace. 'The role of surrendered militants however is a cause for alarm. Allegations are made of their misdeeds under the protective shield of the Special Task Force [of J&K Police] and Rashtriya Rifles' [of Indian army] (Rajendar Sachar, *Hindustan Times*, 23 December 1999).

Almost all the men of a village in Ganderbal near Srinagar were pro-government militants. HM cadre swooped down on that village one night and wiped out its men. Its residents recall the contribution of their men to fighting militancy. They point out with bitterness that India had left them unarmed to fend for themselves. Several Ikhwanis, discontented with their lot, told *Asia Times* in December 2000 that they had ended up falling between two stools. Parray had accused the authorities of following the policy of 'use and throw away'. His close associate and former MLC, Javed Shah, was killed in Srinagar in August 2003.

Saturday, 13 September 2003 was a day of victory for HM in its battle with the Ikhwanis. Parray was going to inaugurate a cricket match in Baramulla district. A group of HM fighters were hiding near Hajin village; when Parray's vehicle passed, it came under a burst of fire from AK-47s. He was driven to the SKIMS Hospital but succumbed to his injuries on the way. 'Hundreds of our cadre laid down their lives for India, but we have received only harassment and insults in return,' Khurshid, Parray's 26-year-old son told Praveen Swami of *The Hindu* (18 September 2003). Khurshid Parray said 'the message that is going out is that it just doesn't pay to support India.' It is a lesson all Kashmiri traitors have to learn.

Several top Ikhwanis later joined the NC. Khurshid's younger brother Imtiyaz Parray joined the Indian National Congress in April 2010 in the presence of state Chief, Professor Saifuddin Soz. In the meantime, Indian security forces formed Village Defence Committees (VDCs) in various parts of J&K. This was done by providing cash, arms and training to civilians, mainly Hindus of the Jammu region. The VDCs were also targeted and destroyed by HM. Marwan Bishara, Political Editor of Al Jazeera wrote in a 2011 article: 'as highly paid mercenaries and well armed militias confront highly motivated rebels ready to sacrifice all including their lives, history tells us the latter [are] bound to win, if not sooner, then later.' [18]

When asked how he could fault the violence by Ikhwanis as he himself supported the HM, Geelani replied: 'We had been trying for 47 years to solve the [Kashmir] dispute peacefully. But nobody was prepared to listen to us. How can you blame young men who were forced to achieve the objective by taking guns in their hands?' (The *Indian Express*, 18 September 1995). There is no official record but it is estimated that the total number of Kashmiris killed by the *Ikhwani* criminals ran into thousands. All pro-Pakistan militants fought back against the *Ikhwanis*; since Geelani's party were the main target, HM led the fight, which took over seven years to win. 'There is something in the faith of Islam which brings out in its followers a high standard of courage and the will to sacrifice,' Salahi explained.[19]

After finishing off the *Ikhwanis*, Salahuddin was confident that HM could hit any soft target in India at any time. 'But,' he says, 'we have not yet started that because we are fighting the Indian State, not the people of India. We have full sympathy with the people of India. There are 400 million people living below the poverty line in India, and we don't have any animosity against them.'[20] Despite the 'excessive use of military power, [the] Indian army has not been able to bring the insurgency to an end nor have they managed to change the disputed nature of J&K. They could not bring its people closer to India. On the contrary, its disputed position has come to the notice of the whole world. An overwhelming majority of Kashmiris have mentally and emotionally become more hateful [of] India. Excessive use of military force has exposed its real face and intentions,' wrote Geelani.[21]

Speaking to *The Times of India* in early April 1993, the J&K police chief B. S. Bedi had boasted that 91% of the top militants had been arrested or eliminated. He said, at this rate 'it would be reasonable to expect normalcy within six months.' Fifteen years later, on 14 January 2008, Indian army chief General Deepak Kapoor admitted: 'There has been a spate of infiltration bids and violent incidents in J&K over the last two months.' And nineteen years after Bedi's confident assurance, his brilliant successor, the outgoing DGP Kuldeep Khoda again told Indians through the media on 31 May 2012: 'militancy in J&K is in its last phase'![22] Such a remark from the most senior officer of J&K police can mean either of two things: India's top police are incompetent to analyse the ground realities or they are misleading the nation by giving utterly false estimates. In either case they do not deserve the positions they hold.

Geelani recalls 'When on August 19, 1989, the voice of militancy was raised, the then Chief Minister Farooq Abdullah called a meeting and asked us what was happening. An independent member said it was anger at his [Abdullah's] rule; the BJP member said it was rising militancy that should be crushed with a heavy hand. When I was asked, I warned that it was a political problem, which India had not yet addressed. I also warned that if it was not redressed in time, the problem would increase and that is exactly what has happened. India did not heed my words, then. It thought that it was strong and could militarily solve the problem. Now, twenty years have passed and India has utterly failed in curbing the violence. The reason is that it is a mass movement. It is not a movement of a few persons alone.'[23] This has been repeatedly confirmed by Indian analysts – both civilian and security – who have covered Kashmir. For example, Col. Nanda writes: 'the reliability of the police forces of the state and its civil administration was questionable. Their control over the local population was marginal, if at all.'[24]

After 20 years of armed campaign, HM believes their success exceeded their expectations. Indian troops were not able to hamper their movement across the LoC. Salahuddin told me that approximately '37,000 Indian security personnel have been killed by militants over the last twenty years and twice that number wounded. Over 15,000 militants were martyred over the same period.' India's security forces have long been under pressure in J&K. 'They were not sure what they were supposed to be doing in Kashmir.... Most of them ended up reacting like frightened rabbits.'[25]

In addition to the casualties, the security forces have suffered attrition of other kinds. The Indian Home Office admitted that, between 2007 and September 2011, as many as 46,000 officers and personnel took voluntary retirement, while another 5,220 resigned; 461 suicides and 64 instances of fratricides were also recorded. India's 'strategic partner' is sailing in the same boat. The 154 suicides for active-duty US troops in the first 155 days of 2012 outnumber the US forces killed in action in Afghanistan by about 50 per cent, according to statistics obtained by the Associated Press. The 2012 active-duty suicide total of 154 through to June 3 compares to 130 in the same period last year, an 18% increase.

There has to be a good reason for risking one's life. Geelani knows what he believes in: 'One needs to understand the purpose of armed militancy. The militant movement has as its goal: the resolution of the Kashmir issue. Every militant holds his life dearest, yet they are dying for the cause of Kashmir. But if that goal could be achieved through peaceful means why the militants should lay down their lives?'[26] Senior army commanders have clearly and publicly told the Indian political leadership that it is difficult to stop the freedom movement militarily. In line with Geelani's approach, they recommend a political solution to the problem. 'There is no such thing as a military victory in low intensity conflict because such conflicts cannot be resolved by military force. Where the overall objective is to win over the hearts and minds of one's own people, victory cannot ever be measured in militants neutralized and weapons captured. An army can kill all the militants and yet lose the war.'[27]

9

ELECTIONS AND THE PEACE PROCESS

TYRANNIES IN DIFFERENT PARTS of the world have learned over time that the will and spirit of people to resist oppression cannot be tamed by coercion alone. In order to buy time to continue their oppression, they have conjoined coercion with a two-track strategy of arranging 'elections' and 'peace process'. Geelani has taken the view that there should indeed be a process, but it must be a process of justice. For if justice is established, its natural outcome will be peace.

ELECTIONS

Successive Indian governments have projected pro-freedom Kashmiris, led by Geelani, as a troublesome minority. However the overwhelming majority support he enjoys has been demonstrated time and again when he has called for strikes and election boycotts. After the 1987 state elections, the national elections on 22 November 1989 were boycotted: 'Just five votes were cast in all of Sopur, the hometown of Ghulam Rasool Kar, the Congress Party Chief and a member of the state cabinet. Not a single vote was cast in Baramulla. The situation in other centers was no different.'[1] The alienation between people and government appeared comprehensive – and irreversible.

On 18 May 1994, Indian Home Minister S. B. Chavan said in

Jammu: 'No Chief Minister would be imposed from Delhi and only those whom the people would vote to power will govern the State.' He also said (something of a confession): 'Those times are gone when Chief Ministers used to be imposed by Delhi.' A. G. Noorani (*The Statesman*, 10 June 1994) commented that Chavan's assurance is 'meaningless in light of the conduct of his own government'. After a brutal crackdown by Indian security forces, 'the situation from a pure security viewpoint is more comfortable today than it was in previous years, but the stance of the people has hardened – they don't believe that "Indian democracy" offers them space to exist' (Amit Baruah, *The Hindu*, 23 January 1994).

Even those few Kashmiris who voluntarily took part in elections never felt happy with their decision. In remote Warsum village, forty-year-old Choudhary Jalaludin had been a spy for Indian security forces, and no less than seventeen relatives of his had been killed by militants. Yet, though he is against militancy and against Pakistan and for a settlement within the Indian Union, he feels no loyalty to the civil administration. 'Look at the lives we are leading', he complained, pointing to the absence of drinking water, electricity, health care and public transport available in his village. 'Is this the award we get for being loyal citizens,' he queried. 'We have been exploited by our politicians. I challenge any ex MLA, MP or Minister of Kashmir to address even a small group of people without security.' (Reported in *The Times of India*, 5 June 1994.)

In the run-up to 1994 'elections', Indian army chief, General B. C. Joshi had clarified in a statement that 'the Army could manage the security adequately to ensure a reasonable turnout in the rural areas, though the urban areas would be a problem'.[2] There are no international media organizations and observers to record the methods used by the Indian army and Ikhwanis to get rural Kashmiris to vote for the selected candidates on New Delhi's payroll.

In later years, by encouraging the Ikhwanis to play a political role, the security forces intensified the problems in Kashmir. 'The surrendered militants are now behaving like mini warlords. And it is with the help of these surrendered militants that the security forces came up with impressive [voter] turnout figures of 50 to 60%

in some segments... a figure that represents neither the aspirations nor the will of the people' (*India Today*, 15 June 1996).

On 23 May 1996, for the elections held in Baramulla and Islamabad, voters were herded to polling stations by security forces and forced to cast their votes. Reporting from the ground-zero, Harinder Baweja had filed this report (*India Today*, 15 June 1996):

> In the run-up to the election, militant groups had issued threats to stymie the process. They succeeded in some measure: candidates did not come calling on voters. But those who did were the men in olive green [the color of Indian army uniform]. Descending on village after village in the early hours of May 23, their message was the same: Cast your vote, we will come back and inspect the marks on your fingers.
>
> Many residents who were forced to go to the polling booths said that security men had threatened that those who did not vote would never be allowed to open their shops again. And as more and more groups of frightened, fear-stricken people made their way towards the polling stations, it was clear that the elections, after a violence-punctuated gap of seven years, were being held under the shadow of the gun.
>
> It became clear that the administration had carefully plotted its strategy. Herding the voters to booths was only the first step in the drama that unfolded under the overcast skies. Rules were flouted and changed to accommodate the numbers lining up in serpentine queues – people whose names did not figure on the voters' list were allowed to vote....
>
> Given the fact that it was the rigging of the 1987 election that saw the advent of the Kalashnikov [armed uprising] in Kashmir, forcing voters into booths is hardly likely to contain the insurgency that was born of a farcical election. When election agents campaigning for the MUF decided to pick up the gun and launched the movement for independence....

India's self-congratulation for giving Kashmiris the opportunity to elect their own government has sometimes been shameless. Nikhil Chokravarty boasted in *The Hindu* (5 October 1996): 'The situation has changed [...] and one could perceive through several signs that the people [...] had grown tired of tension and violence.... The changed mood ensured to a large measure the possibility of the elections.... Few can deny that, by and large, normal elections took place now and those elected can claim to command the confidence of the electorate.' B. G. Verghese predicted, just before the 1996 elections, that 'the successful conclusion of the polls, with all their limitations, will further set back militancy' (*The Indian Express*, 26 September 1996). This assessment from a seasoned journalist like Verghese is puzzling. The expectation that flawed elections 'with all their limitations' can, as if they were a magic ritual, alter the mood of an oppressed people is an expression of blind faith.

Baweja's conclusion (cited above) recently received support from a highly unexpected source – former Minister of State for Defence and BJP party leader in Kashmir, Chaman Lal Gupta. He told reporters on 22 April 2011: 'Rigged assembly elections of 1987 forced the UJC3 chief Syed Salahuddin to pick up the gun. If we go into the history of Jammu and Kashmir, former minister Ghulam Mohi-ud-Din Shah, who was losing 1987 assembly elections with a huge margin, was declared winner on the directions of the then government. Everybody knows that Syed Salahuddin who was at that time in mainstream [politics] and had contested the election was forced to pick up the gun along with his colleagues following mass rigging of that election by the government' (*Greater Kashmir*, 23 April 2011).

As expected before the state-managed elections, India's favoured candidate Farooq Abdullah was re-instated as its viceroy in Kashmir. Realities on the ground remained unchanged: 'There was a shutdown in Srinagar [...] in spite of the fact that most of the APHC leaders were still behind the bars. The impact of the general strike [...] demonstrated that the secessionist feelings were not completely dead,' (Arun Joshi, *The Times of India*, 14 October 1996). Joshi underplayed the local sentiments. The demand for freedom only got stronger.

Geelani recalled: 'After the 1996 election, which was [another] latent military operation, a so-called civilian government was installed. Government is claiming that conditions have become normal now and the people, having got fed up of the struggle for independence, are joining the mainstream. But the fact is that the so-called civilian government is fully controlled by the army. Military officers have been given full control of the state. [The] Farooq Abdullah government cannot do anything without their approval. The military, paramilitary forces and the gun-wielding renegades are indulging in extreme oppression and tyranny. They have no fear of accountability.' Rita Manchanda confirmed this in 'Hollow Victory for Indian Democracy' in *The Communalism Combat* (October 1996): 'The Hurriyat leaders are arrested, beaten up and hospitalized. The contrast between empty polling booths in the Jamaat-e-Islami strongholds of Sopore and Baramullah and the crowded rush to vote in other polling centers is an ominous portent of a people being forced to choose.'

A team of Indian human rights activists, including representatives of the Committee for the Protection of Democratic Rights, *Lokshahi Hakk Sanghatana*, and A. P. Civil Liberties Committee, reported that 'the Indian army went from house to house on 23rd May, forcibly evicting people from their houses at gunpoint, scuttling them like cattle towards the polling booths. The army had threatened them that if they returned without a mark on their finger, they would be considered sympathizers of [the] militants' (*Muslim India*, #170 (February 1997, 72). According to Geelani, Farooq Abdullah was brought to power in 1996. Thereafter, he played a prominent role in promoting state terrorism by creating the Special Task Force (STF). The STF used methods of such extreme brutality to suppress pro-freedom voices that its very name would cause people to shudder.[4]

After the 1996 elections for the state assembly, elections for the national assembly were held in 1999. *The Indian Express* (6 September 1999) reported: 'Concerted efforts by personnel of BSF, CRPF, Rashtriya Rifles and the Special Operations Group to "enforce" a good voter turnout across the Kangan, Ganderbal and downtown

Srinagar belt paid only marginal returns. *The Indian Express* was witness to numerous instances of Kashmiri voters prodded to the ballot box by AK rifle-wielding *jawans* [security forces]. In the evening, these "voters" would be made to show their fingers to the security forces as testimony of having renewed their membership of democracy. They call it the nail parade.'

Even former NC leader and present Congress chief in Kashmir Saifuddin Soz was compelled to write (*The Frontline*, 13 August 1999): 'It is not possible to ignore the fact that the elections in Kashmir held in 1999 have been a total farce. It was decidedly a situation of mass rigging. The people of Kashmir are convinced that the Election Commission of India indulged in double-standards and ignored all complaints filed with it regarding mass rigging, booth capturing and other malpractices.' Arun Joshi (*Hindustan Times*, 8 September 1999) agreed: 'The low voting percentage in Srinagar Parliamentary constituency has set alarm bells ringing. The APHC was quick to claim that "it was a rejection of the elections and ratification of our point that the Kashmir issue needs to be resolved through implementation of the UN resolutions and not elections".' Retired Delhi High Court Chief Justice Rajendar Sachar made the same point (*Hindustan Times*, 23 December 1999): 'The near fraud of parliamentary elections in 1999 in J&K has shaken the confidence of the people in the state about its commitment to democracy. This was clear to me during my recent visit to Srinagar.'

Indian security agencies have assassinated many Kashmiri leaders to (a) weaken the freedom movement and (b) to engineer splits among their ranks by blaming separatists for those killings. Seventy-year-old Lone was a veteran Kashmiri politician and a senior leader of the APHC. Unlike Geelani, he favoured dialogue with India, supported a ceasefire and showed 'pragmatism' by taking part in elections against the constitution of APHC that he himself helped write. This stand earned him the ire of hard-liners. But the existence of divergent views within a broad political movement is normal and a sign of strength, not weakness. He was killed in early 2002. Indian agencies sought to exploit the divergence among pro-freedom groups by trying to pin the blame for Lone's murder on Geelani.

Another round of 'elections' were held in 2002. *The Washington Post* (28 June 2002) reported: 'India jailed several prominent critics [...] including Geelani [...]. Indian officials had hoped to persuade some moderate Hurriyat figures, including Lone, to field proxy candidates [in the 2002 state legislative elections], but that possibility faded in the aftermath of Lone's killing'

But 2002 elections were no better. 'In which other democracy in the entire world can one find so continuous a record of poll rigging in just one region? How long will New Delhi rely on the renegades [*Ikhwanis*] as instruments of its policy?' asked A. G. Noorani in *Muslim India* (November 2003). In Praful Bidwai's opinion (*The Frontline*, 2 July 1999): 'The Kashmir problem is amenable to a peaceful solution. This can only come about through two processes: first, a change in Indian and Pakistani mindset and a beginning of talks on Kashmir, and second, the involvement of the people of Kashmir in the determination of their fate.'

Kashmiris have endured more 'elections' since then. The prevailing reality behind the façade of elections is summed up in *The Economist* of 29 December 2010: officials in Delhi insist Kashmiris 'have their own land and state, enjoy religious freedom, are by no means the poorest in India and take part in elections, most notably in 2008. But there are severe limits to their democracy. Peaceful protests are prevented, jails are crammed with political detainees, detention without charge is common, phones are partially blocked, the press censored and reporters beaten, broadcasters muffled and curfews imposed. Those who complain too fiercely online are locked away.'

THE PEACE PROCESS

Robert L. Grenier retired in 2006, following a twenty-seven-year career in the CIA. Working backwards through that career: he served as Director of the CIA Counter-Terrorism Center from 2004 to 2006; coordinated CIA activities in Iraq from 2002 to 2004 as the Iraq Mission Manager; was the CIA Chief of Station in Islamabad,

Pakistan before and after the 9/11 attacks; earlier, he was the deputy National Intelligence Officer for the Near East and South Asia, and also served as the CIA's chief of operational training. Grenier is credited with founding the CIA's Counter-Proliferation Division and is now a life member of the Council on Foreign Relations. This introduction is a necessary prelude to appreciating the weight of his views on the cruel game that is called 'the peace process' in the Middle East. After reviewing the secret documents on decades-long Palestine–Israeli 'peace process', Grenier wrote (*The Guardian*, 24 January 2011):

> The picture which clearly emerges from these pages of the Palestinian leadership and of the peace process negotiators themselves is that these are no quislings. For month after month, year after year, through endless, mind-numbing subcommittee meetings and plenary sessions, through interminable exchanges of letters and legal briefs, slogging from hotel meetings in Jerusalem to conferences in Egypt to 'summit meetings' in Washington, the Palestinian negotiators tirelessly advocate on behalf of their people's interests. In the face of Israeli condescension, obfuscation, and endless legalistic pettifogging they continually push back, insisting on application of relevant international law, despite the Israelis' obvious contempt for their international obligations. [...]
>
> The overwhelming conclusion one draws from this record is that the process for a two-state solution is essentially over, that *the history of the peace process is one of abject failure for all concerned.* The Palestinian participants [in the peace process], having lost the most, will likely suffer most.

The entire world knows Geelani's views on this deception. He is a true leader, who speaks the truth he knows. If other pro-freedom Kashmiri leaders will not listen to the truth when he speaks it, will they listen to Grenier?

Geelani strongly believes that any bilateral 'peace process' (between India and Pakistan) will fail to resolve the conflict, in just the way that the Middle East peace process has failed. He has blamed India for not accepting Kashmir as a disputed territory. 'In 1990 when Mr. V. P. Singh spoke about negotiations, Jamaat-e-Islami, while welcoming such a move, put forward some proposals to make negotiations meaningful. I wrote an open letter to Prime Minister Mr. V. P. Singh, wherein I told him that the problem would not be solved by excessive use of force. We should create an atmosphere for talks. Then, during my detention in Allahabad Central Jail, I wrote a detailed letter to Mr Chandrashekhar who succeeded V. P. Singh as the Prime Minister,' recalled Geelani.[5] Nothing came of his pleas.

Geelani believes that there cannot be a peaceful solution until human rights violations such as custodial killings, rapes and arrests are stopped. During the Bosnian war, 'the [Serb] attackers were using negotiations merely as a way *to buy time* and as a cover for continuing the aggression,' Izetbegovic told the UN General Assembly on 27 September 1994.[6] 'India wants to tame Kashmiris [at] gun point. Talks have no importance for it. These have been started for diplomacy and *to buy time*. The so-called peace process has no impact on [the] ground situation. This process is confined to files and newspapers only,' said Geelani at a press conference (*Greater Kashmir*, 8 August 2007).

Nelson Mandela's struggle in South Africa passed through the same phase that Geelani's in Kashmir is passing through. 'We had been fighting the white minority for three quarters of a century. We had been engaged in the armed struggle for more than two decades. Many people on both sides had died. The enemy was strong and resolute. Yet even with all their bombers and tanks, they must have realized that they were on the wrong side of history. We had right on our side, but not yet might. It was clear to me that military victory was a distant if not impossible dream. It simply did not make sense for both sides to lose thousands of men, if not millions of lives in a conflict that was unnecessary.'[7]

When the apartheid regime first realized that it could not forever suppress the freedom spirit, it insisted: renounce violence and the armed struggle, then we will agree to negotiations. Mandela responded: 'The state is responsible for the violence and it is the oppressor, not the oppressed.... If the oppressor uses violence, the oppressed has no alternative but to respond violently.... It is simply a legitimate form of self-defense'.[8] In the same situation, India made similarly conditioned offers and received the same response from the Kashmiris' resistance leader, Geelani.

His conditions for dialogue are (a) illegal killings and detentions to stop forthwith, (b) complete withdrawal of Indian troops, and (c) release of all Kashmiri political prisoners from Indian and Kashmiri jails. These conditions are realistic and reasonable. When South African police, claiming self-defence, shot twelve unarmed demonstrators dead and injured hundreds, on 26 March 1991, in a Johannesburg suburb, a furious Mandela told President F. W. de Klerk that he 'could not talk about negotiations on the one hand and watch our people murdered on the other.' He added that 'the government cannot be both a player and a referee'.[9]

India and Pakistan have been staging the spectacle of 'bilateral talks' for almost half a century. Between December 1962 and May 1963, Foreign Ministers Zulfikar Ali Bhutto and Swaran Singh held five rounds of talks. They acknowledged the disputed nature of J&K and committed to solving it through bilateral dialogue. After the 1965 Indo-Pak war, the UN Security Council enforced a ceasefire on 23 September 1965. For the record, India had about 740 square miles under occupation, against 210 square miles by Pakistan, but the strategic balance was even. The warring parties met at Tashkent to sign the ceasefire and reiterated the need for positive, result-oriented steps. During 1970–1, India openly supported the separatist movement of East Pakistan and helped split up Pakistan. The two governments signed the Shimla Agreement in 1972, again agreeing to solve the dispute over J&K through talks.

After the assassination of Rajiv Gandhi in May 1991, Narasimha Rao became Prime Minister of India. He met his Pakistani counterpart, Nawaz Sharif six times in a period of two years or so. Ministerial level talks and improved economic relations of sorts also went ahead. For Kashmiris themselves, this 'dialogue' process produced nothing. On the ground, nothing changed. Geelani complains that 'over 150 rounds of talks [between India and Pakistan] from 1952 on Kashmir have failed to yield any result so far' (*Greater Kashmir*, 13 December 2010).

Those of a hegemonistic disposition are easily persuaded that disputes are best resolved through force. No surprise then that the BJP-led government triggered an entirely unprovoked nuclear test on 11 May 1998. The decision to do so was taken in high secrecy, even 'then defence minister George Fernandes [a Christian] wasn't told about the tests till the morning they took place' (Praful Bidwai, 2 June 2012, *Rediff.com*). BJP may have imagined this would intimidate Pakistan. But Pakistan responded by exploding its own nuclear device on 28 May 1998. Within a few months of this absurdity BJP Prime Minister Vajpayee travelled by bus to Lahore in February 1999 to sign the 'Lahore Declaration'. The two governments again repeated that all disputed issues including J&K will be solved through bilateral talks. 'Based on the experience of the last sixty years, I had said at that very moment that the fate of this agreement [Lahore Declaration] will not be different from those of Tashkent and Shimla,' recalls Geelani.[10]

For the first time in the history of the Kashmir dispute, the BJP-led government invited Kashmiri pro-freedom leadership for 'talks' in New Delhi. The 'moderate' faction of the Hurriyat grouping got trapped into taking part in the circus. The *Financial Times* (22 November 2003) correctly predicted the outcome: 'The Hurriyat Conference, representing anti-India separatist groups in Kashmir, agreed on November 21, 2003 to hold direct talks with New Delhi in what was labeled a political breakthrough for India. Geelani is almost certain to attack the move. But the moderates in the mainstream Hurriyat are likely to be wary of climbing down from any of their long-standing demands.'

When moderate Kashmiri separatist leaders held talks on 23 January 2004 with Indian Deputy Prime Minister Advani, there was a sense of optimism in their meeting. Abdul Ghani Bhat, one of the five Hurriyat leaders who attended the talks, said they had agreed that the 'sound of the gun should be replaced by the sound of politics.' Geelani had also received an invitation, but refused to be drawn into this never-ending and meaningless deception by New Delhi.

As predicted, India fooled Hurriyat 'leaders' into supporting a joint statement: 'It was agreed that the only way forward is to ensure that all forms of violence at all levels should come to an end. The [Hurriyat] delegation stressed that an honourable and durable solution should be found through dialogue.'[11] Almost ten years later, apart from photo-ops nothing was achieved. About the similar situation in South Africa, Mandela recalled:[12] 'The government seemed prepared to wait indefinitely; their thinking was that the longer we [the freedom movement] waited the more support we would lose.' Geelani described this exercise as 'futile' and promised to continue supporting the freedom struggle against India, while expressing a willingness to attend 'full tripartite talks' between India, Pakistan and Kashmiri groups, a demand long rejected by New Delhi. 'More than 75 per cent of Kashmiris want to join Pakistan,' he claimed. 'So many times Indian Prime Ministers have visited us. But nothing changed.' (Cited in *Financial Times*, 17 November 2004.)

Musharraf started another 'peace process' in Kashmir and significantly weakened the freedom movement. In an interview with a Turkish newspaper on 22 January 2004, he said: 'Pakistan and India ought to be bold enough to move beyond their stated positions [on Kashmir] and show flexibility if we want to reach any conclusion' (*Daily Times*, 22 January 2004). This one-sided 'boldness' brought more misery, more humiliation, more insecurity and more frustration to Kashmiris, according to the *Financial Times* of 23 January 2004.

Geelani complained: 'In the past Pakistan had raised the issue of human rights violations [in Indian held Kashmir], but not any more. The Pakistani media and government have changed their policies because they think that pointing out violations will undermine the "peace process". Pakistan should not be reluctant to say that India was divided on the basis of the two-nation theory. Although India does not admit this fact, it is crystal clear that Pakistan came into being based on this theory. Pakistan seems to be under pressure and its policies are becoming fragile. We do not expect [Pakistan] to indulge in war [with India]; but we want Pakistan to take a principled view and stay firm on that.'[13] The Indian media concur with Geelani's pessimism. 'Beware of supposed breakthroughs. The Tashkent Agreement, the Shimla Agreement and the Lahore Agreement were all hailed as breakthroughs when signed, yet failed to bring peace. No agreements signed by leaders of the two countries are worth the paper they are written on if they do not reflect ground realities' (*The Times of India*, 22 August 2001).

Geelani challenged Musharraf's assertion that Pakistan has not compromised any principles in relation to Kashmir, only changed its strategy. Addressing Musharraf, he said: 'principles are mirrored in strategy and strategies have to match principles. [You say] you have sympathy with the people of J&K, you support their right of self-determination, you support them morally, politically and diplomatically – this is your principle. But your strategy is to shake hands with the people who play with our lives, rape our daughters, arrest our people, kill them and discard their bodies in police stations. You show cordiality with those who have detained 10,000 Kashmiris and we do not know whether they are dead or alive... In 1995 they passed a resolution in both houses of [Indian] parliament reaffirming that J&K is an integral part of India. Whether it's the ruling party or the opposition, unless and until they roll back this resolution, how can they accept J&K as disputed territory?'[14]

Geelani's towering presence bothers India not only within its own borders but even across the border. 'A Hurriyat team was supposed to visit Pakistan in mid-January of 2001 to get the blessing of its government and of militant groups for starting a peace process. But India has so far failed to issue passports to all five delegates the Hurriyat wants to send. India's main worry seems to be that Syed Ali Shah Geelani, a pro-Pakistan hardliner on the proposed delegation, will steal the show in Pakistan, pushing the moderates into the wings' (*The Economist*, 25 January 2001).

As an excuse to delay the settlement of Kashmir dispute, Indian authorities have questioned every now and then who the 'real representatives' of Kashmir are. This is clearly another deceptive posture. 'We're prepared for polls to select the representatives of the Kashmiris, provided these are held under international supervision. But who established that Yasser Arafat was the representative of the Palestinians? Did elections determine that? Who established that Mandela was the representative of the South African blacks?' asked Geelani (*Hindustan Times*, 9 April 2000). He argued that 'if on the call of the APHC or any of its leaders, there is a total general strike throughout the valley, is this not a [measure] that the people of J&K are with us?' Are elections in Kashmir the only measure by which to establish representation? The very same elections about which India's former Law Minister Ram Jethmalani said: 'We have to kill democracy to save democracy'.[15]

The Mirwaiz-led Hurriyat (AHPC) accepted the offer of peace talks from the BJP government in 2005. A Kashmiri delegation consisting, among others, of Umar Farooq, Abdul Ghani Bhatt and Abbas Ansari met with Deputy Prime Minister Advani. 'The result of the meeting was encouraging. The Hurriyat delegation, led by Umar Farooq, agreed that "all forms of violence at all levels should come to an end".... Much the same was agreed at two meetings the Hurriyat held early last year with the previous Indian administration. The violence did not stop, though it has somewhat abated. And the government failed to deliver the promised improvements in human rights. Many Kashmiris, long cynical about India's motives, suspected it simply wanted to divide the Hurriyat and discredit its leaders' (*The Economist*, 8 September 2005).

9.1 'Moderate leaders' meeting with Advani on 23 January 2004 (left to right: Abbas Ansari, Ghulam Bhatt, Advani, Mirwaiz Umar and Lone).

As expected, 'Some separatist leaders have been showing signs of insurgency-fatigue. Mirwaiz Umar Farooq called for a ceasefire and settlement with the Indian authorities. His initiative, however, has enraged Islamists in Pakistan and Kashmiri hardliners such as Geelani, who remains committed to the 18-year-old insurrection' (*Financial Times*, 19 February 2007). This has continued to cement his position as the most respectable leader.

India's former Law Minister Ram Jethmalani met Geelani in New Delhi in April 2007 and shared some details about the US-sponsored 'solution' being cooked up by Indian and Musharraf governments. Geelani told Ram that 'nothing will change on the ground. Indian sovereignty and armed occupation will continue. Troops will be removed from urban areas and redeployed in [the] backyards of cities and towns including [the] LoC. The LoC would be made softer and trade would be allowed between [the] two parts of Kashmir.' But he expressed confidence that neither the people of Pakistan nor its Parliament will approve this 'solution'.

Suggesting a way forward, in a statement on 2 May 2007, Geelani said: 'India is accusing *mujahideen* of spreading disorder but the fact remains that India itself is responsible for disruption of peace and eruption of violence in the state. It is the stubbornness and obduracy of India that disrupted peace in the state,' (*Greater Kashmir*, 3 June 2007). Geelani said the restoration of peace lay in the hands of India only. 'If Indian rulers acknowledge the ground realities and give Kashmiris their right of self-determination, they won't find any freedom loving Kashmiri inimical to peace,' he said.

Geelani's consistency and sincerity have been tested time and again. For example, an officer heading one of the Indian intelligence agencies in Kashmir approached Geelani on 24 March 2002. 'He knew me, as he had interrogated me when I was in jail in Jammu,' recalled Geelani.[16] He said: 'Help me in the peace process.' Geelani 'told him Kashmiris have all the reasons to want peace. But it is not in our hands but in India's hands to bring peace by agreeing to the disputed nature of Kashmir and agreeing to tripartite talks to solve the issue.' The intelligence officer wanted Hurriyat to contest elections. Geelani told him: 'It would not solve the problem. We have tried that method earlier in 1987, but it has failed.' The officer left, saying: 'I have failed to convince you.'

To solve the conflict Geelani has said that India must withdraw its military, end human rights violations, and allow the people of Kashmir to choose India or Pakistan through a plebiscite. Any other solution such as self-rule, joint control, demilitarization, or more autonomy is opposed by Geelani. He admits that wars create problems, but it does not mean that Pakistan should move away from its principled stand. 'I have said many times that we will accept the result of a plebiscite, but India has to accept the results as well,' Geelani emphasizes.[17] In reality, the alienation of the Kashmiri masses has reached such levels that in the opinion of well known Indian journalist Khushwant Singh: 'If there was a plebiscite, the vote would go *heavily* against India and in favour of Pakistan' (*The Telegraph*, 5 February 1990). This is the reason India has backtracked on its promises.

There are elements within the pro-freedom movement inclined to seek independent statehood for Kashmir. But the viability of this option is questioned by even foreign experts. For instance, Stephen P. Cohen, a US expert on South Asia, argued in *The Sunday Observer* (May/June 1990): 'I have always held that an independent Kashmir is an unviable proposition.' While conceding that 'some of the population would prefer independence from both India and Pakistan,' Geelani 'does not believe an independent Kashmir would be feasible, as Kashmir's neighbors including China would not accept it.'[18] Tavleen Singh confirmed that many young people in Kashmir 'admitted to differences between the militant groups on the question of Pakistan but the common goal that every group had was that India should withdraw from Kashmir'.[19]

On the issue of how a plebiscite should be conducted, Vicotria Schofield, the author of *Kashmir in Conflict* (2000) has observed:

> Because of the lack of unanimity among the inhabitants, it has been suggested that if ever the issue were to be resolved by a plebiscite or referendum, a fairer solution might be to hold the plebiscite on a regional basis. Those supporting the independence of the entire state reject this suggestion

because it would inevitably formalize the division of the state which they want to see re-united as one independent political entity. To date, the Government of India has refused to reconsider the possibility of holding a plebiscite. Without, however, holding a plebiscite or referendum it is impossible to determine exactly what proportion of the people support which option.[20]

On Pakistani withdrawal from PaK under the terms of the UN resolutions, Geelani states: 'The UN resolution says that the plebiscite administrator is to be appointed, and that when he takes charge, then Pakistan will be asked to withdraw their forces from PaK. India will also be told that the bulk of its forces in Kashmir should be withdrawn. So let a plebiscite administrator be appointed by the UN, but India is not willing to let that happen.'[21] Geelani has lately stated on record that he is willing to give up his plebiscite demand, should an alternative approach produce tangible results which are acceptable to India, Pakistan and the true representatives of J&K. His flexibility on this point rarely finds a mention in the Indian media.

The Hurriyat party's constitution provides for either a plebiscite or a tri-partite negotiation process. In both cases the parties need to accept the fundamental reality that Kashmir is disputed. As Geelani has noted, the biggest single hurdle remains India's continued description of Kashmir as its integral part. ('It is difficult to negotiate with those who do not share the same frame of reference', Nelson Mandela observed.[22]) Salahuddin also complains that in Indo-Pak talks, Kashmir as a 'core issue has never been discussed on the table. Side issues like the Baglihar Dam, Chenab, the Wullar Barrage, the Indus Waters Treaty and the demilitarization in Siachen are frequently discussed. India is not ready to accept Kashmir as a core issue. Addressing side issues is an Indian way to hinder Kashmiri independence movement.'[23]

In these circumstances, *The Economist* (19 August 2004) conceded the wisdom of Geelani's decision to stay away from the 'peace process': 'The winner in local politics has been the pro-Pakistan,

Islamist tendency represented by Mr Geelani. The losers have been the moderates and those nationalist groups that want independence from both India and Pakistan.' Whether we in India like it or not, that sums up the ground realities in Kashmir.

The Economist (26 August 2010) also presented a crisp comparison of the two shades of pro-freedom leadership in Kashmir: 'Mr Geelani has never wavered in his refusal to compromise with Indian rule. Sheer consistency has earned him a pivotal role.... More moderate separatists, who have engaged in "dialogue" with India, have had nothing to show for it, and ended discredited and compromised.' Against this background, Kashmiri writer Riyaz Ahmed asked in his article 'Crisis of Moderates' (*Greater Kashmir*, 23 March 2011) why Geelani 'continues to be a leader with mass following and enjoys political credibility while the moderates despite all their unilateral claims to moral high ground and possession of the knowledge of the best possible strategy miserably struggle to establish their political bonafides? What is it that makes Geelani important, gets him mass support and also monopolizes separatist politics? And what is it that denies the carping moderates the confidence of the people?'

THE KARGIL FIASCO

THE MOUNTAINOUS REGION of Kargil is a part of the disputed state of J&K. It is situated between Srinagar and Leh, approximately 420 kilometres from Srinagar. Leh is the supply centre for the Siachen glacier. The peaks in the Kargil area range between 13 and 18,000 feet in height. One third of Kargil, including the Muskoh valley, Sando, Kaksar and upper Batalik, is glacial, while over one half is rocky terrain. The territory is inaccessible for eight months in a year; the temperature falling to extremes of -50°C. India quietly occupied Siachen in 1984 as these ice-clad mountains were left out of the purview of the ceasefire agreement between India and Pakistan. The BBC (10 September 1998) reported that as a costly mistake because India is spending over US$1 million every day to sustain its occupation. It costs over INR 500 (US$ 10) to supply a loaf of bread to each Indian soldier posted there, while a large number of their fellow citizens starve to death every year across India.

'On June 2, 1998, the Intelligence Bureau [IB, the internal arm of the Indian Intelligence network] dispatched a note to the [BJP] Prime Minister [Vajpayee] with details about Pakistani logistics-building efforts along the LoC in the area opposite Kargil,' reports a study by the Centre for Land Warfare Studies (CLAWS) (*Greater Kashmir*, 28 November 2011). The CLAWS study added: '[IB] predicted that, having acquired a nuclear umbrella, Pakistan was likely to push militants into Kargil. The note was personally signed by the then-IB chief. In protocol terms, a sign that its contents were extraordinarily sensitive and warranted follow-up action.' The study titled 'Perils of Prediction, Indian Intelligence and the Kargil Crisis', said that Research and Analysis Wing (RAW, the external arm of the Indian Intelligence network) had also warned in its October 1998 assessment that the Pakistan army might launch 'a limited swift offensive with possible support of alliance partners' [i.e. militants]. However in its next six-monthly threat assessment, RAW omitted any reference to a 'limited offensive' and depicted the Pakistani threat as consisting only of 'mercenaries' [i.e. militants alone].[1]

In May 1999, ten years after the armed insurgency started in Kashmir, militants took over the mountainous peaks of Kargil, Drass and Batalik, and offered stiff resistance when Indian forces tried to move forward. Aware that all of them were local Kashmiri militants, the Indian army made ambitious announcements of evicting them within forty-eight or seventy-two hours. The militants dug in. Prior to launching a full-fledged assault, more than 40,000 soldiers were moved into the Kargil sector. Even Kashmiri youth linked to the Ikhwanis were sent to Kargil and Drass. During the fifty-five-day encounter that followed, militants held the better positions on the higher peaks, while Indian forces at the foothills struggled to move upward under fire. Transporting arms and ammunitions also proved tough.

The Indian army, realizing that their initial assessments and target timelines were unachievable, resorted to airpower. To justify that deployment the government began presenting the incident as a Pakistani army incursion. With this spin, Indian forces deployed Russian MIG 21 and MIG 27 and French Mirage 2000 fighter jets, besides Swedish Bofors guns. Brigadier Gurmeet Kanwal observes (in an article on Rediff.com, 2 February 2013): 'The Indian army launched some of the fiercest attacks in the annals of military history to take back high altitude mountain peaks from aggressors.' Aerial bombing continued till the second week of July, 1999. The militants managed to shoot down two MIG fighters and one army helicopter. In early 2013, some Musharraf-era retired Pakistan army officers admitted the involvement of Pakistani army, but the credibility of their claims is questionable.

This conflict brought India and Pakistan to the brink of nuclear war, putting the most populous region in the world at high risk. The BJP government, together with other political parties, tried to spin this war as another terror-project of Pakistan. The US, UK, France, Russia and other countries called for an immediate ceasefire. For the first time ever, the Russian Parliament offered mediation. The wider implications of the conflict were evident. US President Bill Clinton invited both Indian and Pakistani Prime Ministers for talks in Washington. Nawaz Sharif instantly complied; Vajpayee refused to go! After the Clinton–Nawaz talks, a joint statement was issued to the effect that all fighters should be recalled from the Kargil front, and that India and Pakistan should hold talks within the framework of the Shimla Agreement and Lahore Declaration. The US President made a commitment to use his 'personal influence' to solve the Kashmir issue. Militants retreated. Nothing happened. Another pledge broken, another assurance unfulfilled!

Temporary ups and downs are part and parcel of any long drawn out conflict. They must not be viewed – by either side – as permanent gains or losses till the fight reaches the finishing line. Head of the Palestine resistance movement Hamas, Khaled Meshal, agrees: 'It is normal for any resistance that operates in its people's interest... to sometimes escalate, other times retreat a bit.'[2] But the Pakistani masses are very touchy about the Kashmir issue. They reacted strongly against the joint statement in Washington. Many political parties including Jama'at, People's Party and Tahrik-i-Insaf took to the streets. Effigies of Clinton and Nawaz Sharif were burnt in Karachi. Nawaz was labeled a traitor to the Kashmiri struggle. He tried to sell the Washington statement as a big leap forward in the internationalization of the Kashmir issue. But Kashmir has been an internationalized issue for the last sixty years!

'Interestingly, when the Kargil operations were over, the very same nuclear hawks [in BJP] seized the argument that the nuclear weapons have greatly restrained the two countries from escalating into a major war. But they conveniently forget the fact that there was no war between 1972 and 1998, and the nuclear tests [1998] have greatly enhanced Pakistan's self-confidence in undertaking a cross-border operation in Kashmir' (K. M. Sethi, *The Economic & Political Weekly*, 11 September 1999). Media reports indicate that the Kargil attacks cost India about INR 80 billion (approximately US$ 1.8 billion) with more than 500 Indian soldiers dead. Ordinary Indians have a right to know the underlying triggers for the Kargil attacks, which entailed such heavy human and financial costs.

The Kargil attacks necessitated a year-round vigil by Indian forces in this sector. Defence analysts believe guarding the high peaks from Dras to Batalik is costing more than guarding the Siachen glacier. Against INR 50 million operational cost a day for Siachen, the estimated operational cost of manning peaks from Zojila to Turtuk lies between INR 120 and 150 million per day! Siachen has 108 posts. Hundreds of Indian soldiers have died in Siachen and over 10,000 have been permanently disabled over the years. According to the then Indian Environment Minister Jairam Ramesh: 'What Pakistan has been able to do is to convert Kargil into a Siachen for us to defend at considerable extra cost, and revive world interest in Kashmir' (*India Today*, 26 July 1999).

All this massive spending is being committed to keep Kashmir as an 'integral part of India' at gun point! Over the last sixty years, billions of dollars have been spent to maintain a military presence in the state, upgrade combat machinery, not to mention thousands of human lives on both sides of the LoC. However, 'good equipment and numerical strength cannot win a battle if morale is low' asserts Salahi.[3] This is evident from the increased number of suicides and farcitides within the Indian security forces.

During the month of June 1999 alone, a total of 276 houses were burnt down by Indian security forces in J&K. On 30 June 1999, then Prime Minister Vajpayee brazenly stated 'Kashmir problem and Kargil are two different issues.' Geelani put this question to the naïve Vajpayee: 'Is Kargil not a part of Jammu & Kashmir?' Praful Bidwai (*The Frontline* 2 July 1999) agreed: 'There is a link between the Kargil crisis and the Kashmir [dispute]. It just will not do to pretend that there is no outstanding issue or dispute in Kashmir.' Addressing the Indian public during the Kargil conflict, Geelani wrote:

Human life to us is the most valuable [...] commodity in the world. It is a crime in our view to differentiate between humans on the basis of colour, ethnicity, language, religion, caste and regionalism. We feel sad whenever a human life is lost. You too must be feeling sorry when bodies of your relatives [Indian soldiers] reach you. This is a natural feeling. You must be thinking about Kashmiris as terrorists who must be expelled [from Kargil peaks] at any cost. You may not be aware that we [have been] ruthlessly crushed by Indian security forces for the last ten years. You might have been under the delusion that young Indian soldiers are performing a heroic duty by defending the borders in J&K.

In reality, Indian soldiers are punishing us for demanding what your leaders promised us, i.e. [the] right of self determination. The honour of our mothers, sisters and daughters is being outraged by Indian forces. Daughters are being dishonoured in front of their parents. Wives have been molested in front of their shackled husbands. Thousands of women have been gang raped. Our youth are made to sit on burning stoves in interrogation centres. Rollers are moved over their bodies. Iron rods are inserted in their bodies. They are suspended from roofs. The entire villages are being reduced to ashes. One Jalianwala Bagh [massacre of unarmed Indians by British forces] shook the entire Indian nation which triggered demand for freedom from Britain. Many Jalianwala Baghs are being repeated on a regular basis in Kashmir.

Let the Kashmiris exercise their rights. If the majority opts for India, we will have no grievance. We will be happy to live as citizens of India. If the majority votes for secession, Indian people and government will have to gracefully accept this decision. This is a democratic demand which India professes. If Kargil summits are recaptured by your army using airpower and Bofors guns, will this solve the problem? No and never. The entire J&K is Kargil. If you do not solve this problem, you will achieve nothing by recapturing Kargil.[4]

For Muslim militants, the most important lesson to be learnt from the battle of Uhud is that 'Muslims must not be complacent. Only believing in God does not ensure victory in battle unless [the fighters] are well prepared and willing to make the necessary sacrifice,' counsels Salahi.[5] The price of complacency is most evident in the battle of Hunayn when Muslims almost converted victory into defeat, and were rebuked in the Qur'an (9: 25-6):

> On the day of Hunayn when you were pleased with your numbers, you noticed that it was no avail to you. The vast expanse of the earth seemed narrow to you and you began to flee. Then God sent down His reassurance and tranquility on His Messenger and on the believers, and He dispatched soldiers whom you did not see who inflicted suffering on the unbelievers.

Turning to Kashmiris during the Kargil conflict, Geelani appealed:

> Our struggle continues since 1947. We [have been] offering great and unparalleled sacrifices for the last ten years. Our freedom fighters have performed great heroic deeds of bravery and military strategy on Kargil as well as other fronts. The joint statement in Washington will never influence our overall struggle. Ours is an indigenous struggle.[6]

> History bears testimony that for lasting success, a revolution has to be conceived and executed indigenously. We are grateful to the nations that are providing us political, moral and diplomatic support to liberate us from the clutches of slavery. Let those nations realize that our struggle will continue regardless of the hurdles. Their policies should be formulated based on this fact. Every nook and corner of our territory is peppered with the graves of martyrs. We will not betray their souls. Nor shall we let anyone bargain with their sacred blood.

> In our struggle, we must observe human and moral values whatever the state of affairs. We should never allow this

sacred struggle to be tainted with communal colour. We
have to foster unity and cohesion in our ranks. We must
pursue our goals with conviction and determination. We
have to purify our hearts and minds having full faith in our
legitimate stand, without being influenced by the power
and awe of occupation forces. Allah is the only triumphant
and subduing force in the whole universe. We have to make
ourselves eligible [for] His help through complete reliance
on Him and by acting upon his injunctions and guidance.
You will then see that if one door is closed, a thousand
doors will open up and we will succeed in attaining our
legitimate and equitable goals, *insha'Allah*.[7]

In Pritish Nandy's view (*The Times of India*, 27 February 2011):
'We are slowly becoming, like the US, a country where everyone,
from teachers to healers to rock stars believe that God sent them to
this planet with the sole mission of making money. The scramble
for lucre has become so obsessive, so obscene that the dignity of
many professions has simply vanished.' The Indian administration's insatiably corrupt officers never miss an opportunity to
plunder the country – not even during national crises! They are
the real terrorists. But they are never demonized by the media or
harassed by security forces. For instance, Madhya Pradesh cadre
Indian Administrative Service (IAS) Officer Arvind Joshi was a
joint secretary in the defense ministry during the Kargil attacks
in 1999. The income tax department has identified stolen wealth
valued at INR 3.6 billion (close to US$ 70 million) when his house
and other properties were raided in February 2010. The unlawful
wealth accrued by just one state officer, who has been 'serving the
country' for thirty-two years, includes twenty-five flats in Bhopal,
New Delhi and Guwahati, 400 acres of land in Madhya Pradesh,
and a wide range of investments.

The issue is not corruption among law enforcers alone, but also
among law makers. 'One hundred and sixty-two MPs in the Lok
Sabha [lower house of Parliament] and more than 40 in the Rajya
Sabha [upper house] have pending criminal cases against them,

and several others face serious allegations of corruption. How can we expect them to ever pass bills to strengthen the criminal justice system or to punish corruption? There is a direct conflict of interest' (Arvind Kejriwal, May 2012).[8]

Ever since Pakistan was established as an independent state, some of our fellow-citizens in India have been cursing its existence and dreaming and plotting its failure. For example, Vidya Subramaniam was quoted in *The Times of India* (30 July 2000) as saying, 'post-Kargil, Pakistan is so bankrupt that it must sue for peace or fail as a state.' Eleven years later, neither has happened; as *The Economist* (April 2011) noted: 'After all, Pakistan has been in decline for many years, and has not tumbled into the abyss.' Yet it remains true that Pakistan *is* tottering. But then so is India: facing over two-dozen insurgencies covering over 45% of our national territory! It is bad manners to curse one's neighbours – let us not do it, and let Pakistanis refrain likewise.

11

CEASEFIRE

'THE FACT THAT the militants have been successful in thwarting the mighty Indian forces and in bringing about a stalemate reveals the government's weakness,' writes Gautam Navlakha in *Economic and Political Weekly* (17 September 1994). In such situations, repressive regimes seek face-saving escape routes, as they are too insecure to own up to mistakes and say 'let's start afresh'. Instead, they play games to get temporary relief from criticism for their failure, while prolonging the sufferings of the occupied peoples. Alongside the near-farcical failures of staged elections and 'peace process' circuses, ceasefires engineered from time to time are another time-honoured tactic. In 2000, it was tried in Kashmir and failed miserably.

Salahi has reflected on the lessons that can be learnt from the battles fought by Muslims under the command of the Prophet himself. At Uhud, the believers turned a potential victory into a near defeat as a result of the failure of one group to adhere to the Commander's orders. Salahi writes: 'Every military commander maintains that strict obedience by all his troops is absolutely necessary for the success of his plan, whether offensive or defensive. Obedience by all soldiers in war is taken for granted. Without it, no army can achieve victory even against a weaker enemy [...] and God's unfailing rule was that He supported the believers as long as they supported Him and His cause with all their hearts.'[1]

The militants in Kashmir are not bloodthirsty killers; they are simply fighting for the freedom that we in India promised them. Post Kargil, Indian intelligence agencies approached Hizbul Mujahideen [HM] in the summer of 2000 for a ceasefire. The senior HM leadership decided, in a change of tactic, to consider a truce. There was a willingness to test India's readiness to settle the dispute through negotiation. The political leadership of HM agreed to meet in Srinagar and issue a declaration thereafter. However, HM's newly-appointed Operational Commander for Srinagar, Abdul Majeed Dar, violated some 'critical covenants of *Jihad*' and unilaterally announced a ceasefire for three months on 24 July 2000. On reflection, Dar's announcement appeared to be premature and was potentially disastrous for the freedom movement as a whole.

In a meeting with me, Geelani confirmed that Dar had met him a couple of days before his July 2000 announcement. Since an important Jama'at *shura* (Executive Council) was due in a week's time, Geelani asked Dar to wait till after that meeting. Surprisingly, Dar went ahead with the announcement, disregarding the advice of Geelani. This sent conflicting signals to militant cadres on the ground and their supporters within and outside Kashmir. Exercising the highest level of wisdom, maturity and vision, both Salahuddin and Geelani did not immediately oppose the ceasefire in a public way. Rather, militants on the ground and senior Jama'at leadership were quietly informed that this move by Dar did not have the blessing of Geelani or Salahuddin.

'God has assured the believers of victory against any enemy, as long as they serve Him with sincerity of action and purpose. Whenever they give priority to their own narrow interests, He leaves them to their own priorities', Salahi reminds Muslim activists struggling for justice worldwide.[2] Due to HM Supreme Commander Salahuddin's unshakeable resolve during the Kashmir dispute, and also his proximity to Geelani, the Indian government has always sought to sideline him. In order to undermine his hold on the most dedicated and disciplined militant outfit in J&K, India tried to engineer a split by arranging this ceasefire with Dar. India had hoped that a large number of HM cadres would switch their loyalties from Geelani and Salahuddin to the Dar camp. Their hopes proved to be vain.

India was obviously trying to engineer a split between the ranks of the most cohesive and ideologically strong armed group. During the short-lived ceasefire, 'the Home Secretary Pandey met with the five representatives of HM at Srinagar. The Delhi government had arranged Fazal-ul-Haque Qureshi, a former member of the Al-Fateh, to be the go-between for that meeting,' wrote Nanda.[3] Indian security forces repeatedly violated the ceasefire and HM's move towards peace did not yield any positive results for Kashmiris. 'The cease-fire is just a stunt to deceive the world. The reign of government terror continues,' Geelani said in the course of a Friday sermon at Baramulla mosque.

As expected, it was called off by Salahuddin on 8 August 2000. Soon after, HM's leadership decided to expel Dar for his premature ceasefire declaration. Dar suffered a major blow when the Special Operation Group killed his deputy, Masood, who had led the HM delegation at the talks with India. Farooq Mircha, another Dar aide, disappeared mysteriously some months later.

After the ceasefire was called off, Salahuddin continued to show maximum possible flexiblity, which is a core Islamic value. He said (cited in The Times of India, 20 January 2001): 'Of course, my personal viewpoint is that it is better for Kashmir to be part of Pakistan, but we cannot force this by guns. Once India agrees to a settlement, we will make sure Azad Kashmir and the northern areas are also part of [the settlement].... No doubt people in Kashmir want peace but not the peace of slavery. They know that three wars have been fought between India and Pakistan over Kashmir. The fourth could well be nuclear. Who doesn't want peace? Peace will not come from ceasefires but from solving the core problem of Kashmir. Don't forget that there was peace in Kashmir till 1989. The Kashmiris took recourse to the gun because of their disappointment with all political and diplomatic attempts to solve the problem.'

HM's July 2000 ceasefire was not the first one tried in J&K. Javed Ahmed Mir, a senior JKLF leader reminded the Indian government that, after JKLF announced a cease-fire [in 1994] more than 600 JKLF activists were martyred by Indian security agencies and thousands of activists were arrested. He warned that making ceasefire a precondition for dialogue was not practical at all. He added: Salahuddin is very much aware of how JKLF was betrayed after it announced the ceasefire. For instance, JKLF executive member and prominent human rights activist Jaleel Andrabi was killed by the Indian army in 1996 – shot in the head and his eyes gouged out.

The US State Department spokesman, Nicholas Burns issued a statement on 29 March 1996, condemning that killing. He called on the government of India to conduct a full and transparent investigation into the abduction and murder of Andrabi. He expressed the hope that Andrabi's murderers would be quickly apprehended. But Andrabi's murderer, Major Avtar Singh of 35 Rashtriya Rifles, coolly migrated to the US and settled down with his family in the backyard of Mr Burns, in Fresno County, California. Singh owned and operated Jay Truck Lines, a trucking company in Selma. After learning of his whereabouts, the J&K High Court had earlier ordered the extradition of Major Avtar. But Fresno County Sheriff Margaret Mims confirmed that 'Indian officials chose not to try to extradite him'.[4] After peacefully living in the US for more than a decade, early morning on 9 June 2012, Singh killed his wife, and two children aged 3 and 15 before killing himself (NBC News, 9 June 2012).[5]

Anyways, 'the ceasefire during the holy month of Ramadan or its extension for a few days or even months or a bus journey to Lahore are at worst futile pieces of deception and at best image building exercises and clever moves on the international chess board. Unless the frozen postures of the past are abandoned and fresh mechanisms created for the settlement of the problem there is no hope of peace and prosperity,' wrote India's former Law Minister Ram Jethmalani in *The Asian Age* (18 January 2001). Twelve years on, his observation remains apt and to the point.

Islam expects its adherents to exert every possible effort to bring about victory. The generation of the Prophet's Companions clearly understood this principle and acted accordingly. Every time they met with their enemies, they prayed God to grant them either victory or martyrdom. Pursuing their 'use and throw' policy, the Indian security forces killed Dar on Sunday, 22 March 2003 in Sopore.

Police sources in Srinagar said that Dar, along with his mother and sister, had gone to Noorbagh locality to supervise the construction of his house. It is no surprise that the Indian government blames Salahuddin for his murder.

It is believed that JKLF was once supported by India against HM. Due to their secular ideology, the Indian authorities expected them to play the same puppet role that the National Conference has historically played for India. 'In Delhi political circles there was talk of elections in which JKLF would be allowed to win and come to power and then be compelled to crack down on the other militants. This would make JKLF lose popularity and pave the wave for the re-emergence of a National Conference government, with or without the Congress,' opined Gautam Navlakha (*Economic & Political Weekly*, 17 September 1994).

Both Geelani and Salahuddin carry so much authority and influence in Kashmir that senior JKLF leader Javid Ahmed Mir himself urged New Delhi to hold talks with Salahuddin. When its adversaries begin to recognize HM as a force to be reckoned with, it is the greatest testimony to its strength and popularity. 'Salahuddin has got a role to play in [any] final resolution and without his inclusion Kashmir issue cannot be resolved,' Mir said. He added: 'New Delhi setting preconditions for holding a dialogue with Hizbul-Mujahideen shows that it is not sincere [about] resolving the Kashmir issue.' Mir claimed that Salahuddin too has shown an inclination towards holding a dialogue but he has got no response from New Delhi' (*Greater Kashmir*, 5 September 2007).

It seems that the opportunity that JKLF declined was eagerly seized by Mufti Saeed, leader of the People's Democratic Party, and his daughter Mehbooba Saeed. They came to power in J&K through another rigged election in 2004. During their tenure as new viceroys of India, Mufti's government did exactly what JKLF had been expected to do, not just to militants but to all freedom fighters. It even handed over Kashmiri land to Amarnath Yatra Trust, which is responsible for arranging an annual Hindu pilgrimage. Led by Geelani, the Kashmiris protested, and a massive wave of agitation proceeded across Kashmir in 2008 (details in Chapter 16).

12

THE HURRIYAT SPLIT AND
EFFORTS TOWARDS UNITY

AFTER EXHAUSTING ALL peaceful means to resolve the Kashmir dispute over four decades, and the hijacking of state assembly elections in 1987, armed struggle was the only option. Kashmiris paid a hefty price for demanding freedom. Pro-freedom leaders were jailed. Some youth crossed into PaK with a view to getting military training. Among those who stayed behind many were either slaughtered by the Indian security forces or stuffed into prisons across India. There was a need to guide the Kashmiri masses and channel their demands in a coherent manner. Geelani was one of the moving spirits behind the formation of the All Party Hurriyat Conference (APHC) in 1993, a political platform comprising twenty-three Kashmiri political and social organizations. The APHC 'agreed to have Geelani [...] as their leader.'¹ It was meant to press with one voice for implementation of the promised plebiscite.

However, the challenge was immense – for instance, the JKLF stood for independent statehood for J&K, while the Jama'at envisioned a full merger of J&K with Pakistan. Jama'at was one of the key constituents of APHC, which nevertheless clearly had a majority of secular elements. Despite recognizing Geelani's leadership abilities, bias prevailed over rationality. As a result, Mirwaiz Umar Farooq was elevated to this crucial position. It is widely believed that Geelani privately opposed the election as the first Chairman of the APHC of Mirwaiz Umar Farooq. Geelani's opposition was not based on personal rivalry. Being a veteran pro-freedom leader and a seasoned politician, Geelani knew the risk of electing a completely 'green' and immature leader: Umar was just twenty-one.

Geelani did not harbour any delusions about himself or his party either. People associated with Jama'at-i-Islami 'have never claimed, nor are they in a position to claim, that they are free from any weakness, fault, evils and lapses,' he wrote.[2] But Mirwaiz Umar had little understanding of the Kashmir dispute. He had virtually no following beyond a small group of worshippers who prayed in the Jamia Masjid (central mosque) in downtown Srinagar. For a complicated issue like Kashmir, an intelligent, informed, widely acceptable and morally strong leadership was required.

Experience is the foundation of leadership and 'loyalty to the organisation takes precedence over loyalty to an individual,' Nelson Mandela observed.[3] No organization other than Jama'at and no individual other than Geelani satisfied those conditions at that time in Kashmir. However, in the interest of unity, Geelani accepted Umar's election once the Jama'at's Executive Council gave its consent. A great visionary that he is, right at the inception of APHC 'Geelani made it clear that Jama'at's support to Hurriyat was 'conditional' and that the moment we feel that it is going in the wrong direction, we will withdraw.'[4] Within few years, his apprehensions were confirmed when Mirwaiz Umar made a series of mistakes – among others, his embrace of Musharraf's flawed stand on Kashmir.

Unity is a good, but among resistance movements, a fleeting one. In India as in South Africa and resistance movements elsewhere, there were different groups representing different shades of ideology and viewpoint. The occupying forces are of course aware of this reality and make the most of it to distract, obstruct and (when possible) crush freedom movements. India, under the tutelage of Israel (itself constantly refusing to enter into a meaningful negotiation on the pretext that Palestinians are not united), has repeatedly refused to enter into a result-oriented dialogue with Kashmiris.

The Indian government has played every trick to rope separatists into its fold. In one such incident, Yaseen Malik was abducted by some gunmen in June 1994 from a hospital ward where he was receiving treatment. This was the time when pro-government militia (*Ikhwanis*) were at their peak of power. They controlled most of the hospitals in the Valley. The plan was to trigger infighting between various militant outfits. The pro-Jama'at HM was blamed for this abduction. HM spokesman denied any involvement: 'Now these people [Ikhwanis] have conspired to abduct and eliminate Yasin Malik. They abducted him from his hospital room and they themselves rescued him in a similar manner. Sheikh Abdullah and his men used to enact such dramas to project individuals and gain public sympathy.'

The spokesman promised that if the JKLF came forward with evidence of the involvement of HM people, HM would not hesitate to present them for trial. He went to say that Yasin Malik's recent statements made it clear that he wanted to run from the armed struggle and 'wrap' himself in politics. But HM, though it had lost about 10,000 men during the first five years of its armed campaign, would 'at no cost allow the *Jehad* to be turned into "Gandhian politics",' a veiled reference to Yasin Malik's fast unto death to press for his demands.

While this 'hero-making' drama was unfolding in Srinagar, India's Minister of State for Internal Security, Rajesh Pilot, said in an interview in New Delhi that 'he was willing to talk to Yasin Malik, who was recently released from Delhi's Tihar Jail. The emergence of a moderate leader like Malik could be just what the Indian government is looking for. New Delhi hopes to hold elections in Kashmir by the end of the year,' (*The Asian Age*, 4 June 1994). Ashok Jaitley, a prominent civil servant of Kashmir cadre went to the extent of suggesting in the early 1990s that JKLF would one day play the same role of bringing Kashmir back to India as NC had played in the past. This forecast proved true only to the extent that, on 16 July 1992, JKLF members set fire to the central office of Jama'at in the Batmaloo area of Srinagar.

Six years after its formation, Geelani's own election as the second chairman of APHC was not smooth either. The late leader of People's Conference Abdul Ghani Lone raised several objections.

When Geelani became APHC Chairman, the Indian media projected APHC as an assemblage of hardliners and soft-liners, an opportunity that the Indian government sought to exploit: for example, it allowed some APHC leaders to travel freely outside India while routinely denying travel documents to others, notably Geelani. For India the presence of the openly pro-Pakistan Geelani in APHC was not acceptable.

Lone also obstructed Geelani's re-election as APHC chair. Over time, the true colours of other Kashmiri pro-freedom 'leaders' became clearer. When Professor A. G. Bhatt succeeded Geelani as the third Chairman of APHC, differences emerged between Geelani and other members of the APHC's decision-making body, the Executive Council. As mentioned earlier, Prime Minister Vajpayee declared non-initiation of combat operations from November 2000, and start a 'peace process'. But Vajpayee, and his party BJP, knew that Geelani will not dilute his principled stand. Secular elements of APHC petitioned Jama'at chief G. M. Bhat against Geelani's 'indiscipline'. It seems that 'moderates' in AHPC had been instructed to get rid of the 'extremist'.

Geelani has been consistent about the direction in which Kashmiri politics should move. In a speech in February 2001, he said (*The Hindu*, 24 February 2001): 'The time has come when the people in Kashmir have to decide whether to support secular politics or politics based on Islamic principles', and he asked the people to extend their 'full support to the politics supported by religious tenets'. The predictable reaction from the leadership of the People's Conference was to claim that Geelani was becoming isolated, had lost even the support of his own party (a reference to Jama'at chief, G. M. Bhat's perceived differences with Geelani), and was therefore resorting to populist sentiments. This was a bizarre claim. Even in New Delhi there is acceptance of the strength and depth of Geelani's support base: he was (and remains) the 'game changer' in Kashmir.

Some APHC 'leaders' were playing a double-game. After a year's detention in Birsa Munda Jail, Ranchi, Geelani was released in April 2003. When he reached Srinagar, Professor A. G. Bhatt visited him at his home and confided to him that People's Conference would be fielding candidates in the 2002 state assembly elections. Since the APHC's constitution expressly prohibits contesting elections during the Indian occupation, Geelani demanded the immediate expulsion of People's Conference from APHC. However, there was little support for Geelani's stand from other members of the APHC Executive Council. Then, after some days, Abbas Ansari was declared the new Chairman, and Bhatt began speaking out in favour of People's Conference (not the impression he had given Geelani in private). This double-game by Bhatt facilitated the meaningless 'dialogue' which ensued between India and APHC led by Abbas Ansari.

According to Geelani, 'some Hurriyat leaders were not following the Constitution [of APHC] in letter and spirit. Different members were expressing different opinions. Such behaviour encouraged India to approach them individually. Unfortunately, some leaders were getting influenced and making statements that they should not have made. India is not to be blamed for this, we are.'[5] Such underhanded politicking led to the split in the APHC. Geelani launched Tahrik-i-Hurriyat-i-Kashmir (THK) on 7 August 2004. THK is a relatively smaller but powerful alliance of pro-Pakistan parties. For pro-freedom Kashmiris, this split was a clear setback. Almost all sincere Kashmiris have since been demanding unity.

Difficult decisions are part of the burden of leadership. 'As a leader, one must sometimes take actions that are unpopular, or whose results will not be known for years to come. There are victories whose glory lies only in the fact that they are known to those who win them.'[6]

Leaders from across the LoC (PaK) have also been pushing for unity among the pro-freedom leadership. 'I'm not against the unity,' Geelani insisted, 'but they must understand that Kashmiris have sacrificed their lives only for freedom and [the] right to self-determination.' And he affirmed the points on which there should be unity: 'I am not against talks but for dialogue to be meaningful India should accept J&K as a disputed territory, withdraw its forces and unconditionally release the [political] detainees' (*Greater Kashmir*, 30 June 2007). 'This is the foundation for unity,' he declared.

Geelani is a practising Muslim. He yearns for unity among various factions more than anyone else, but insists that 'Self governance, joint control and soft borders cannot be the basis for the unity,' (*Greater Kashmir*, 19 May 2007). He was speaking to the media at his Hyderpora residence in Srinagar where he was put under house arrest to prevent him from addressing a Friday congregation at the Tourist Reception Centre mosque. Seven years on, events proved Geelani right (once again) when Abdul Ghani Lone's son and political successor Sajjad Lone contested parliamentary elections in 2009! His People's Conference is still a constituent of APHC, but blatantly violated its own constitution.

In a more idealistic way, Salahi counsels: 'Muslims may have different points of view, but such differences must not be allowed to alienate any group of them from the other. They must always feel that any Muslim remains a brother with whom they have the strongest of ties.'[7] In Geelani's view, such an ideal unity is possible only by following the Qur'an and the lifestyle of God's Messenger.

Geelani said, unity among the different elements of Hurriyat was improbable 'because the parties that form the Hurriyat Conference have different mottos. For instance, the Jama'at has as its motto the propagation of Islam while JKLF is a secular organisation believing in an independent Kashmir.' Geelani rejects the charge that the lack of unity has become an obstacle to resolution of the dispute: 'Division among pro-freedom leaders can't hinder the resolution of [the] Kashmir dispute. We were united for ten years but no state authority approached us for resolving the Kashmir issue.'

Democratic Freedom Party chief Shabbir Ahmad Shah visited Geelani's residence in the middle of 2007 to ask after his health. Shah wanted a unified APHC. Geelani told him: 'I am ready for unification but go and ask Umar Farooq if he subscribes to my stand [on the] right to self-determination. Although unity is necessary for carrying forward the ongoing freedom struggle, instead of unity for the sake of unity we are desirous of unity that is based on principles. "Islam" and "plebiscite in Kashmir" can provide [the] strong basis for a viable unity.' (*Greater Kashmir*, 16 June 2007) Since then, there has been no word from Shah. Showing continued immaturity,

Umar Farooq and Maulana Abbas Ansari held a rally in Kashmir in late 2007 and repeated their acceptance of Musharraf's four-point programme to reach a settlement of the Kashmir dispute. In January 2008, Shah also joined APHC led by Umar Farooq.

Salahuddin believes that both sides should seriously think through the factors that triggered the division of APHC, and complains that some elements in the Mirwaiz-led Hurriyat still talk about Musharraf's four-point formula. He emphasizes that the Hurriyat constitution of 1993 is clearly against making any bilateral agreement (i.e. with India alone), and he assures Kashmiris that if the right of self-determination is not compromised then Geelani would be the first to embrace unity. He alleged that there were certain elements within APHC who were in fact serving Indian interests. As it turned out, the unity of APHC without the Jama'at was not strongly enough founded to last.

By 2011, the Mirwaiz-led Hurriyat was in complete disarray. Maulvi Abbas Ansari, former 'moderate' Chairman of APHC, is the patron of Ittehad-ul-Muslimeen (IuM), one of the founding members of APHC and represented on its Executive Council. Ansari had led the APHC delegation to meet Advani in 2004. He again agreed to play the same role in the next staging of India's interlocutors drama in 2010 (details in the last chapter). This time, 'The Hurriyat Executive Council had taken a decision to suspend the IuM for meeting the interlocutors. I as a chairman of the Hurriyat today issued notice to head of IuM, Masroor Abbas Ansari, asking him to explain why they violated the Hurriyat decision,' Mirwaiz told *Greater Kashmir* on 21 April 2011.

In reply, Abbas Ansari said he feels 'liberated' after the expulsion of IuM from Hurriyat. Poor Kashmiris! They thought Ansari was fighting for Kashmir's liberation from India; it appears he was fighting for only IuM's liberation from Mirwaiz's Hurriyat!

At another meeting of Mirwaiz's APHC on 31 May 2012, more showcause notices were served. This time to A. G. Bhat, Nayeem Khan and Azam Inquilabi, and disciplinary actions were demanded against Shabbir Shah. Bilal Lone did not even attend that meeting. Perhaps the next step is for Mirwaiz Umar to issue a notice against himself as he is the only 'disciplined' leader left in his Hurriyat. Without consulting their own senior colleagues, a delegation of APHC led by Mirwaiz Umar left for Islamabad in December 2012 for the purpose of 'discussing' the Kashmir issue with Pakistani leadership. Nayeem Khan complained: 'There is no democratic setup in the Hurriyat (M)' (*Greater Kashmir*, 25 December 2012). Geelani was also invited. He refused to visit Pakistan citing a 'weak' government and upcoming elections there.

While the circus is on within Mirwaiz-led APHC, Geelani and his supporters have their hearts and minds fixed on their just goal: a plebiscite as promised by the UN and the international community six decades ago.

13

AILING BUT NOT CAVING IN

IN THE FACE of endless internal and external challenges, Geelani has refused to compromise on his basic principles. Leading one of the hardest fought liberation struggles of this century has taken a toll on his health. He had a pacemaker placed in his heart in 1997. In 2003, an infection forced doctors to remove his left kidney.

Doctors recommended that he go overseas for treatment. His passport was seized by the Indian government in 1981 on the ground of alleged 'anti-India' activities. With the exception of his hajj pilgrimage in 2006, he has never been allowed to leave India. In international law, Article 12 of the International Covenant on Civil and Political Rights guarantees an individual the right to free travel. But India, with its increasing global clout, has grossly violated its international treaty obligations. After Prime Minister Manmohan Singh intervened, the Indian government returned Geelani's passport.

During a regular check-up in April 2007, doctors discovered that Geelani's remaining kidney had developed a malignant cancer in its early stages, but life threatening. He needed urgent surgery. Doctors at New Delhi's Apollo Hospital advised him to travel to either the UK or the USA for specialized treatment. However his request for a visa was turned down by the US embassy in New Delhi on the grounds that he has 'failed to renounce violence'. This decision by the world's most powerful (and loudest) champion of democracy, freedom of speech and human rights is shocking. A prominent Indian columnist Veer Sanghvi wrote in *Hindustan Times* (10 June 2007): 'at no time in its history has America been so hated all over the world'. After Geelani's health deteriorated he went to Mumbai where doctors at the Tata Memorial Hospital successfully performed surgery on his right kidney.

Geelani has always opposed meaningless talks between 'moderate' separatists and New Delhi. His principled approach has led some Indian commentators to speculate that he is becoming increasingly isolated in Kashmiri affairs. As mentioned in the previous chapter, this myth is also promoted by some 'moderates' among the Kashmiri pro-freedom leadership. Geelani returned to Sringar, after successful surgery in Mumbai, on a Sunday summer morning in 2007: tens of thousands of Kashmiris thronged the airport to receive him, and a large crowd chanting pro-Pakistan slogans attended a rally to welcome him back.

13.1 Syed Geelani addressing a public rally in Kashmir

Supporters chanted 'Long live Geelani' and 'Geelani lead us, we will follow you' as he emerged from Srinagar's high-security airport. Geelani was driven straight to the martyrs' graveyard in Srinagar. An estimated 100,000 people had gathered to listen to him. He is beyond doubt Kashmir's most popular leader.

After offering prayers for the thousands of militants, separatists and civilians buried in that graveyard, Geelani told the crowd: 'We will take the ongoing struggle to its logical end. We will not allow any sellout. Our ultimate goal is freedom from India' (*Greater Kashmir*, 23 April 2007). Indian troops were confined to their bunkers to avoid trouble. The massive rally was presented as a victory by Geelani supporters over Umar Farooq. 'Today's rally is a referendum that [the] people are with us. They want a straight solution to the Kashmir dispute, and that is freedom from India,' said Masarrat Alam, a close aide of Geelani (*Gulf Times* of Qatar, 23 April 2007).

After the rally, a senior Kashmir police officer said a case had been registered against Geelani for holding the rally without permission and for the anti-India slogans at the event. 'We will take action in due course of time,' said the officer, who wished to remain unnamed. This is the freedom of expression that 'the largest democracy in the world' accords to the citizens of a territory it insists is an 'integral part'. 'Strong regimes do not condemn people for the spoken word; weak ones are afraid, and resort to violence in an attempt to prolong their existence,' believed Izetbegovic.[1]

Subsequently, many senior associates of Geelani were detained under the PSA immediately after welcoming their leader. Later (18 May), Geelani was placed under house arrest for 'violating the law' by speaking to his supporters in their own homeland! Since 2004, he has been put under house arrest over 150 times. 'No other pro-freedom leader has been [given] such treatment. They are targeting me to stop me from reaching out to my people. This shows how much venom they possess against me.' He also said: 'So far, 17 attempts have been made on my life but I am safe and sound by the grace of Allah' (*Greater Kashmir*, 14 November 2007).

The freedom struggle, Mandela says, is 'not merely a question of making speeches, holding meetings, passing resolutions... but of militant mass action, and above all, the willingness to suffer and sacrifice.'[2] Geelani has certainly lived up to this standard. In 2008 he was diagnosed with renal cancer.

14

A BILATERAL OR INTERNATIONAL ISSUE?

VISIONARIES AMONG INDIA'S POLITICIANS understood the nature of the Kashmir dispute and advised its rulers sincerely and in a timely manner. However, their advice fell mostly on deaf ears. Jayaprakash Narayan is reported to have said (*Hindustan Times*, 20 April, 1964):

> Neither India nor Pakistan can live and grow unless there is friendship and cooperation between them. The lack of such relationship between them has, among other things, upset the power balance in South and South East Asia, depriving the sub-continent of the role that history and geography had destined it to play. The result was the tilting of the balance in favour of China – a most unhealthy state of affairs [for the region]. The Kashmir question has to be viewed in the broad perspective.

Kashmir lies at the middle of the Sino-Indian–Pakistani arc and hence could be seen as a focus of regional ambitions between the three countries over power and hydro resources. Conflicts involving these three major states tend to define and structure the regional distribution of power.

India's first Prime Minister Nehru made a pledge to the people of Kashmir in these words: 'If, after a proper plebiscite, the people of Kashmir said, "We do not want to be with India", we are committed to accept that. We all accept it though it might pain us. We will not send any army against them. We will accept that, however hurt we might feel about it, we will change the Constitution, if necessary' (statement to the Indian Parliament, 26 June 1952).

Those fine promises aside, in September 1961, the US ambassador was informed at a dinner meeting with Nehru that the most India could do is accept the LoC as an international border. After India's humiliation at the hands of China in the 1962 war, the US needed to befriend India. Carl Kaysen, the Deputy Assistant for National Security Affairs told the US President in a 3 November 1962 memo:

> We are really not able to support their [Pakistan's] demand for a settlement via plebiscite, and that their best opportunity for settlement on terms something like ratification of the *status quo* may be passing from their grasp. This will be a difficult and painful process, but it is the one we must push through.[1]

Thanks to the firm stand of Geelani, together with a vast majority of Kashmiris solidly behind him, this 1962 option has been successfully resisted for half a century. The main thrust of the Western powers' policy remained to put pressure on Pakistan, rather than on India: 'In June 1992, [US] Secretary of State James Baker shot off a letter to the Pakistan government, warning that it could be branded a "state sponsor of terrorism" if it did not desist from aiding the Kashmiri militants'.[2] However, *The Wall Street Journal* (20 September 1995) rationalized the need for internationalization of the Kashmir dispute:

> We generally frown on efforts to internationalize bilateral disputes. But if ever a case cried out for a bit of outside interference, it is Kashmir. Specifically, it may be time to resurrect one of the first U.N. resolutions ever passed, and let the people of Kashmir hold a plebiscite on self-determination. Why? Because as it stands now, Kashmir is a proxy fight between the two rogue nuclear states [the US was aware of Indo-Pak nuclear capabilities much before it became official]. The best way to reduce the likelihood of

that scenario is to whisk Kashmir out of its regional setting and make it an international issue. This would not involve such a big leap or precedent. The plebiscite resolution is already on the books. U.N. observers have been in the region since 1949, manning the world's oldest U.N. cease-fire line, between Pakistani Kashmir and the larger disputed section on the Indian side.

Ironically, US Senator Bill Bradly (Democrat), a public policy maker of national stature, said (*The Pioneer*, 24 June 1994): 'India is a very diverse country like the US. You can say what you want about plebiscite in Kashmir. But the reality is if you had a plebiscite in Kashmir, you would have to have it elsewhere.' He was responding to questions at a luncheon hosted by the Centre for National Policy, a Washington-based liberal think-tank. 'A society as diverse as India would fragment,' Bradley said, if the plebiscite idea won, and 'this is a challenge posed not only to the US and India but also to other countries.' This argument is clearly a deliberate attempt to distort the facts and mislead international public opinion.

Lee Hamilton, Chair of the House Foreign Affairs Committee, said in his foreign policy address that the UN resolutions on Kashmir, which Pakistan kept pushing for, had become obsolete and declared that the 1972 Shimla accord between India and Pakistan 'can and should be the basis for ending this conflict' (*Hindustan Times*, 9 June 1994). Geelani disagreed. In his view: 'If someone says that with passage of time, the resolutions have lost their relevance, then the United Nations has itself become irrelevant with passage of time....'[3] After experiencing similar bias, wrote Izetbegovic: 'The international community obviously doesn't have the courage to act according to the truth, rather they do things the easy way for them.... But this is not a long term solution for problems. Only truth and courage move things forward.'[4]

Shimon Peres, the current President of Israel, visited India in May 1993. Besides laying the foundation for a drastically changed US stand on Kashmir, he reportedly told BJP leaders that the only way to solve the Kashmir problem is to change the demographic character of the Valley by carrying out a massive re-settlement of non-Muslims. Peres discussed this concept very thoroughly in a long meeting with L. K. Advani. Advani relished Peres' idea, basically to replicate Israeli practice of 'demographic transformation' in the occupied Palestinian territories. Emboldened by Advani's favourable response, Peres also made these observations in the presence of Agriculture Minister, Balram Jakhar, Minister of State for External Affairs, R. L. Bhatia and many others during the official dinner. But Peres may not be aware that long before this 1993 meeting with Advani, India has been trying to change the demographics of J&K. Here are some statistics:

Year	Total Population	Muslim	Percentage
1951	3,253,852	2,277,694	70.00
1961	3,560,976	2,421,463	68.00
1971	4,616,632	3,000,810	65.00
1981	5,967,389	3,789,291	63.50
1991*	7,718,700	4,785,594	62.00

Source: Census of India. *There was no census in J&K in 1991. These numbers are extrapolations. India did not report the population split in 2001 and 2011 censuses.

New Delhi sometimes tested the patience of even its viceroys in J&K. None other than Chief Minister Farooq Abdullah disputed the figures of the 1981 Census in the State Assembly on 7 December 1988. The ratio of non-Muslims to Muslims, which in 1961 was 1:2.1 in J&K, had increased to 1:1.8 in 1981. 'This wrong information has been given by the Government of India. I deny these figures as Chief Minister' The Statesman (9 June 1994) reported Farooq Abdullah as saying. 'These doubts about the census reports in J&K were not baseless. In fact, the Kashmiri intelligentsia were aware of the plans of many Indian political leaders, bureaucrats, professionals and businessmen to change the existing composition of [the] population in J&K, which at present has a Muslim majority' (The Radiance Views Weekly, 2–8 January 1994).

'Whether we like it or not, Kashmir today has become an international issue. There is no point blaming Pakistan if we cannot put our own house in order [...] There is no harm in taking the issue to international fora and putting forth our point of view. Before we do this, of course, we must have a point of view.... We will have to tell our own people what the truth is, in black and white,' admitted Rajat Sharma (*The Sunday Observer*, 2 October 1994). 'What seems clear is that the present stand of the Indian Government is a trifle contradictory. In international fora, mediation is rejected on the grounds that Pakistan and India have agreed to resolve the Kashmir dispute bilaterally. When Pakistan approaches India for talks, it is told that Kashmir is an internal matter (despite India's own claim to PaK). Within India, however, Kashmir is treated like a colony, unworthy of democratic rights' (*The Hindu*, 29 March 2000).

Western leaders continued to push Pakistan to stop 'cross-border terrorism'. *The New Age* editorial, 26 May 2000, explains the US interest in Kashmir: 'The US [...] desires to not only assume the mediator's role but also to pave the way for a foothold for the Pentagon in [...] Kashmir, the ideal place, being very close to China, Russia, India, Pakistan, Afghanistan and Iran, a gateway to the Central Asia republics as well.' Al Jazeera's senior political analyst Marwan Bishara reminds us that 'interests, not human rights, are the centre of superpower calculation.'[5]

But this self-serving superpower is overstretched, militarily and economically. At the present time, there are officially 737 U.S. military bases in 132 of the 190 member states of the UN. The actual number probably exceeds 1,000. All this under a US$ 14 trillion debt burden! Russia has been India's consistent supporter on Kashmir issue. President Vladimir Putin said, on his arrival in India (3 October 2000): 'In our opinion, this [terrorism] is clearly a manifestation of much larger international problem [read Islam]; our views coincide with those of India. We believe that terrorism has shifted to this region. That is why we [India and Russia] will have to coordinate efforts to combat terrorism both militarily and politically'.[6]

MIT Professor Noam Chomsky presented some alarming ideas including 'some sort of federal arrangement, keeping the line of control, with semi-autonomous regions loosely federated with each other'; even 'a broader South Asian federation could be a direction in which things could move'.[7] This would effectively turn the clock back to pre-1947 and put the people of Pakistan under Indian subordination. This has been the original game plan of successive post-Cold War US administrations and a critical component of its 'new world order'.[8] Gwynne Dyer wrote (*Arab News*, 28 August 2007): 'in fact, India is the keystone of the new US strategy in Asia, and Washington will do almost anything to keep it in place.'

'The US is undoubtedly anxious about the Islamic "fundamentalism" emanating from Pakistan and radiating into Kashmir. It is therefore more sympathetic toward Indian positions than ever before; a sympathy which is greatly enhanced because of its profit-making interest in the Indian economy', explained Aijaz Ahmed in *The Frontline* (March 2001). Geelani believes 'The US should be told in clear and unambiguous terms that its policies at international level are not based on justice and fair play. They are always biased and based on its own national, social and economic interests. Universal human and moral values are completely ignored in pursuit of such policies.'[9]

Given the scale of US interest in the Indian economy, no realistic person could expect the US to play the role of honest broker in the Kashmir dispute. *Washington Post* of October 4, 1994 reported: 'Assistant Secretary of State Robin Raphel angered Indian officials last spring when she made public statements in the United States criticizing India's human rights record in Kashmir. But later, Raphel and other U.S. officials have muted public discussion of the issue at the same time that senior officials have been leading delegations of American business leaders to India.' Former UK Prime Minister Tony Blair makes it abundantly clear (*Financial Times*, 10 January 2008): 'Nowadays, the intersection between politics and the economy in different parts of the world, including the emerging markets, is very strong.'

The UK is the chief maker of the Palestine and Kashmir disputes. Its antagonism towards Muslims was evident also in the aftermath of the war in the Balkans. The Muslims in Bosnia-Herzogovina represented 43.74% of the population but, after the war initiated by Serbian aggression ended, were offered only 26.36% of the disputed territory. Izetbegovic wrote of this outcome: 'The message from the three great powers, particularly Great Britain, was that there was no way out for Bosnia except to negotiate and to accept whatever was offered. This message was equivalent to blackmail.'[10] British writer and popular historian William Dalrymple admits that 'in the last 300 years there have been more instances of Muslim countries being invaded than them being invaders themselves. The British are partly responsible for stereotyping Islam. They have a lot to answer [for].'[11]

Even Samuel Huntington, an ardent Western hawk, recognized that 'the West won the world not by the superiority of its ideas or values or religion [...] but rather by its superiority in applying organized violence.'[12] This organized violence is orchestrated by holding joint military exercises and joint invasions on sovereign nations, mainly Muslim. A joint Indo-British exercise was conducted in the summer of 2007 in Leh region of J&K. Geelani protested: 'No such exercises can be taken up in the entire state of J&K till this issue is settled. By doing so India is violating the United Nations resolutions and is trying to strengthen its occupation.'

Huntington went on to say, 'Westerners often forget this fact [supremacy in organized violence]; non-Westerners [read Muslims] never do.'[13] Being directly in the line of fire during the Bosnian war, Izetbegovic agreed: 'When genocide occurred [...] they shamefully remained in silence.... They would like it to be forgotten. Perhaps they can forget, but we must not and we cannot.' He also explained why – 'because a forgotten genocide repeats itself.'[14]

Since the mid-1990s, US policy has shifted more openly in favour of India. Frank G. Wisner, the US ambassador to India, gave a speech to the Command and Staff College at Quetta, Pakistan in July 1996. He told the assembled top brass of the Pakistani army that it was imperative for Pakistan to move from 'confrontation to reconciliation' with India. He said the solution lay 'not in revisiting the troubled history of the Kashmir dispute but through a fresh look at your assumptions so that you can arrive at new conclusions. After nearly 50 years, there are certain fundamental realities that will not be changed.' He clearly meant that Kashmiris and Pakistan must forget about the right of self-determination; they must simply accept India's illegal occupation and continued oppression.

Wisner and other international leaders should know that with the shift in political power, everything changes, including 'fundamental realities'. A series of reverses in American designs in Iraq, Afghanistan, Egypt and Gaza are just a few examples. Muslims are beginning to wake up, to differentiate between friends and foes, and to take responsibility for shaping their own destiny. Muslim sacrifices have clearly turned the tide against the West's hegemony in global affairs. Philip Stephens admitted in the *Financial Times* (1 June 2012) that 'the wars in Iraq and Afghanistan and the political awakening in the Arab World have greatly weakened [Western] capacity to effect change' in the Islamic world.

As Pakistan's significance faded after the accomplishment of US strategic objectives in Afghanistan, the pro-India tilt of US policy in the region has become more pronounced. Some analysts suspect that there exists a joint American–Indian–Israeli agenda for South Asia, which is going to hurt Pakistan in the long run. The fourth Indo-Pak war had been averted, because of the deterrence parity between the two countries. But it may be just a lull before another storm, given the absence of any progress in a just settlement of the Kashmir dispute.

The 2001 Kargil crisis over Kashmir was the closest that the world has come to an actual nuclear exchange since the Cuban stand-off. Indeed, Richard Kerr, Deputy Director of the CIA at the time, mentioned that 'it was far more frightening than the Cuban Missile Crisis', the tense nuclear stand-off in 1962 between the US and the Soviet Union. Thus, along with the Arab–Israeli struggle over Palestine, Kashmir has been the most protracted and militarized regional dispute in the post-war era. India's contention that Kashmir is an integral part of India has been rejected not merely by the people of Kashmir, but also by some honest international leaders. For instance, Helen Clark, the former Prime Minster of New Zealand said on 15 October 2004: 'It is perfectly obvious to the whole world that Kashmir is a flashpoint for tensions between the two countries. Most countries do not regard it as simply an internal affair [of India].'[15] Similarly, 'India has failed to convince even a friend like Mandela of its case on Kashmir,' noted an editorial of *India Today* (cited in *Muslim India*, #192, October 1998). Contrary to fair and just international opinion, clandestine Israeli guidance and support to successive Indian governments against Geelani and his resistance movement continued. A high-level Israeli military delegation visited India in the second week of June 2007 to discuss counter-militancy and anti-infiltration strategies in J&K. The delegation was led by Israeli Deputy Chief of General Staff Major-General Moshe Kaplinsky, who visited strategically sensitive places, including the Nagrota Headquarters of the 16 Corps responsible for guarding the LoC south of the Pir Panjal range in J&K. The Israelis shared their experiences of tackling infiltration and militancy. They also reviewed the functioning of the large number of Israeli-origin anti-infiltration and night-vision devices deployed along the LoC. 'Besides military alliance, the contacts between secretive agencies and religious extremists of the two countries are increasing day by day,' Geelani said (*Greater Kashmir*, 16 June 2007).

Just a week before candidate Obama became President Obama in 2008, he announced that Kashmir would be among his 'critical tasks'. He visited India in November 2010. As expected, the world's most articulate leader and Nobel "peace" laureaute did not even mention the slaughter of 118 unarmed Kashmiri protestors on the streets of Kashmir in the summer of 2010 (details in the last chapter). His statement on 7 November 2010 in New Delhi was ambiguous, 'Kashmir is a longstanding dispute between India and Pakistan. I believe both Pakistan and India have an interest in reducing tensions between the two countries' (*Indian Express*, 8 November 2010).

Some people believe that an international body of the size of the Organization of Islamic Conference (OIC) should be able to exert enough pressure on India to arrive at a just solution and promptly end the misery of Kashmiris. It has fifty-seven member countries and was established in September 1969 to address the social, political and economic issues of Muslims worldwide. It came into existence in response to an arson attack by Israeli terrorists on the al-Aqsa mosque in Jerusalem. It is headquartered in the Saudi port city of Jeddah and is heavily influenced by Saudi rulers. It is the second largest international organization in the world after the UN. Its first charter was created in 1972.

At the peak of the Bosnian war in 1993, a special Ministerial Meeting of the OIC on Bosnia-Herzegovina was held in Islamabad on 12–13 July. The communiqué issued after the meeting made references to Kashmir also. According to an Indian official: 'We contacted a number of OIC member countries which participated in the meeting. These friendly countries have indicated to us that the communiqué's references to Kashmir were discussed at the Special Meeting and were imposed on us at the last minute as a Pakistani proposal. They [the friendly Muslim countries] did not wish to raise a controversy, but they have clarified to us that they do not question the territorial integrity of India.'

The OIC is a weak and ineffective organization. On 23 January 1993, it requested India's permission to visit J&K and investigate human rights abuses. The impotent OIC General Secretariat was bluntly told by Delhi that 'no purpose would be served by the visit of the OIC to Kashmir, which is an integral part of India.' The Indian government informed the OIC that investigation of any human rights violations was the sole responsibility of the Indian authorities and that the OIC's suggestion was unacceptable. Indian commentator K. K. Katyal again exposed OIC's internal functioning: 'The collective anti-India noise at the OIC, it was found, did not conform to the views expressed by individual members of the grouping in their bilateral talks with India. The relationship between India and most of them was governed by economic and other powerful factors and there was a marked keenness to strengthen those [bilateral] ties' (*The Hindu*, 11 December 1997).

Geelani complained: 'There was a role for [the] OIC in October 2000 to forge unity among Muslims when [the] USA attacked Afghanistan after 9/11. But it remained a mute spectator. Now the situation has gone out of their hands and they cannot do anything at this juncture.'[16] Indeed, OIC members have long been quietly toeing the line indicated for them by the US. For example, in the Hazratbal crisis in Kashmir, Indian security forces besieged the famous Kashmiri shrine. A US chargé d'affaires Ken Brill 'informed the Indian government that American missions had been asked to convey to OIC member countries to refrain from making provocative statements on the issue'.[17] This demonstrates the extent to which Muslim governments representing 1.6 billion people are so cowed by the US that they dare not protest even on matters that are of no direct concern to the US, except that the US as global hegemon has an interest in ensuring that the pattern of compliance is kept intact.

In June 2007, President Bush announced the appointment of a special US envoy to OIC 'to share with them America's views and values'. Given the history of American hostility towards Islam, this sharing can only weaken an already febile organization. Reflecting on thirty-eight years of non-achievement, its Secretary-General Ekmeleddin Ihsanoglu lamented: 'The OIC cannot participate in a Formula 1 Race with a 1972 model broken engine and flat tires. We need a new vehicle to participate in today's international races' (*Arab News*, 4 June 2007). OIC has passed dozens of resolutions voicing 'concern' about Indian atrocities in Kashmir. However, all such resolutions have been ineffectual as India has never allowed an OIC fact-finding mission to visit Kashmir. The OIC has not been able to resolve bilateral disputes between neighboring Muslim states either, let alone burning global issues like Palestine and Kashmir. It may be fair to say that, the 'Organization' achieves only 'Conference', that is, talk among national leaders.

Similarly, the twenty-two-nation 'Arab League represents Arab governments and not Arab people', as Professor Khaled Fahmy of the American University in Cairo observed.[18] It has been the tragedy of Muslims throughout recent centuries that their political leaders have often worked against the interests of the very people they represent in order to preserve their own positions of leadership, which are secured by foreign powers.

India's recent emergence as an economic power is wholly dependent on the oil supplied by Arab-Muslim states. *The Times of*

India (10 February 2008) reports: 'Most of [the oil] comes from the Persian Gulf [Saudi Arabia, Iran, Iraq and UAE] [...] India needs to source as much energy as it possibly can, because power, or lack thereof, could become the greatest hindrance to India's economic story.' Referring to the Arab world, Geelani believes 'Some of these countries are economic heavyweights and oil-producing countries. We expect them to pay special attention to what is happening in Kashmir' (*Arab News*, 17 August 2010).

But the reality is quite the opposite. The Arab League's ambassador to India, Ahmed Salem al-Wahishi, told reporters in Srinagar on 16 May 2011: 'The League of Arab States has no position on the specific question of Jammu and Kashmir. We are looking forward to peaceful coexistence and tolerance in the whole region.'[19] On 19 February 2013, UAE reached an agreement for US$ 2 billion investments and 'establishment of a strategic oil reserve in India' (*Gulf News*, 20 February 2013).

Despite supplying over 70% of India's oil imports, the Arab rulers have never attempted to criticize, let alone check, the atrocities on Muslims in India generally and Kashmiris in particular. No surprise that some Indians believe that 'Pakistan has no powerful friends. Even the Saudis are trying to influence the Pakistani and Kashmiri fundamentalist forces to moderate their position, vis-à-vis Kashmir and India' (Pradip Bose, *The Janta*, 21 January 2001). They are focused on securing their corrupt regimes, if necessary by behaving as Western puppets. Chomsky confirms that 'the wealth of the [GCC] region is supposed to flow to the West with a kind of payoff (commission) to the local managers [rulers].'

Undeterred by the OIC and the Arabs' hopeless state, Geelani is optimistic about the future of the Muslim *ummah*. He said in 2009: 'India's occupation in Kashmir has to end and within a couple of years some radical changes will take place in the world. America will have to leave from Iraq and Afghanistan'. After this statement of Geelani, the US/NATO have indeed been humiliated in both these countries. Following the Arab uprisings, the puppet rulers of some Arab states have gone, others are on their way out; it remains to be seen if the new rulers can act independently of the West.

Jayaprakash Narayan (cited at the beginning of this chapter) had predicted Chinese strategic interest in Kashmir way back in 1964. Lately, China has begun flexing its muscle as a counterweight to the US - at least in its own backyard. In 2010, China declared its intention by issuing stapled visas to Kashmiris visiting China. Despite many protests from India, China has refused to stamp its visas for Kashmiri travelers on Indian passports. This is China's way of telling the world that it does not consider Kashmir 'an integral part of India'.

It is often mentioned that China is a stakeholder in Kashmir because it occupies 3,800 square kilometres of Aksai Chin in addition to 5,180 square kilometres of the Karakoram Range which Pakistan 'gifted' to China in 1963. All this leads to questions that are asked in New Delhi in hushed tones: What if China were to start supporting the struggle in Kashmir more actively? Would India be able to combat China's clout? Stapled Chinese visas don't mean inconvenience for Kashmiris. It signifies hope for some. Says Kashmiri academic G. N. War: 'It tells us that China has not bought the Indian line that Kashmir is part of India. It sent a message to Kashmiris that China recognizes their plight, that it knows Kashmir is a disputed territory' (*Times of India*, 15 January 2011).

Another notable gesture was the Chinese denial of a visa to Indian army officer Lt.-Gen. Jaiswal in October 2010. Jaiswal held the Northern Command in the Indian army. Many atrocities by India's army in Kashmir were committed under his jurisdiction. Additionally, Chinese maps given to tourists in Tibet show the region being bordered by Nepal, Myanmar, India and Kashmir. The presence of the Chinese army in the northern areas, growing investments in PaK, from tunnels, roads to hydroelectric projects, has added to the growing Chinese support.

Nanda notes that China is leaning towards Pakistan and 'its call for a virtual international intervention in Kashmir is seconding Pakistan's demand and rejecting India's approach of bilateralism.'[20] Elaborating China's stand on the Kashmir dispute, its Assistant Foreign Minister Wang Yi said: 'the only way out is the peaceful settlement with the help from the international community....

I believe the peaceful settlement [...] will not only reduce tension there [it] will do good not only to the two countries but also to the development of South Asia' (*The Hindu*, 12 September 2000).

As explained earlier, J&K gets the merest pittance for the hydel power it supplies to the Indian grid. China's activities in PaK are seen by some as an alternative to this exploitation by India. A college teacher who did not want to be identified was quoted in a 15 January 2011 *Times of India* report: 'China is developing a mega hydel project in the Neelum Valley in Muzzafarbad. Tomorrow, if Kashmir were to be independent, China could finance projects here. An independent Kashmir could sustain itself by just selling power to India.' Such arguments offer a sort of answer to the question of how a landlocked Kashmir could survive. Kashmiri columnist Javed Iqbal recently wrote about the Chinese plan to link Gwadar, the Chinese-built mega-port in Balochistan to a highway in Karakoram. Many see this as a highway to prosperity. 'We will again be part of a new silk route,' is an oft-expressed hope in J&K.

Another important development is bothering Geelani. 'Compared with much of South Asia [Kashmir] has many rivers and relatively few people,' (*The Economist*, 19 November 2011). Although India has the Indus Water Treaty with Pakistan for sharing Kashmir's water resources, India is at various stages of building up to 60 dams across J&K. This will provide much needed electricity to India; it could also deprive Pakistan of much needed water.' Geelani is aware of this looming threat to the region and has repeatedly warned Indian authorities against this. A February 2011 report prepared for the American Senate observed that 'the cumulative effect of [many dam] projects could give India the ability to store enough water to limit the supply to Pakistan at crucial moments in the growing season'. The report therefore concludes that dams are a source of 'significant bilateral tension'.[21]

Like Egypt, Pakistan 'exists around a single great river, though the Indus is nearly twice the Nile's size when it reaches the sea. It waters over 80% of Pakistan's 22m hectares (54m acres) of irrigated land, using canals built by the British. In turn that farming provides 21% of the country's GDP, as well as livelihoods for a big proportion of its 180m people. Many of them are already thirsty. On average each Indian gets just 1,730 cubic metres of fresh water a year, less than a quarter of the global average of 8,209 cubic metres. Yet that looks bountiful compared with each Pakistani's share: a mere 1,000 cubic metres.'[22] *The Economist* continues to argue that 'countries downstream have genuine reasons to fret. Pakistan is exposed.' Fairness demands that India only take whatever fairly belongs to us, and give whatever fairly belongs to others – whether they are Muslims, Christians, Jews or others.

According to Maj. Gen. Afsir Karim, 'The latest US game-plan [is] to wrench the entire territory of Jammu and Kashmir, including the northern areas, and create a new independent state that will depend on the US (and its Western allies) to re-conquer its old colonial possessions, albeit in a new economic world order. Also [to] acquire new strategic vantage points vis-à-vis Tibet, Sinkiang and the Central Asian republics.'[23] But India seems unwilling to either solve or internationalize the dispute. C. Raja Mohan is a strategic affairs expert in India. He says a potential deal with Pakistan has five main elements: (1) no change in the territorial lay-out of Kashmir, which is currently divided into Pakistani and Indian areas; (2) creating a 'soft border' across the LoC that separates the two sides; (3) greater autonomy and self-governance within both Indian and Pakistani-controlled parts of the state; (4) a cross LoC consultative mechanism; and (5) demilitarization of Kashmir at a pace determined by the decline in cross-border terrorism. Geelani suggests a broader approach for solving global disputes, including J&K:

1. All hurdles being faced by the UN since 1945 in fulfilling its stated goal of maintaining global peace and settling international disputes should be removed. Veto powers of the five permanent members of its Security Council should be abolished. This unsustainable concentration of power within five non-Muslim states has not allowed the solution to even a single dispute related to 1.6 billion Muslims to their satisfaction.

2. Mutual differences among Muslims have been fully exploited by US and its allies for intervention. Efforts should be made at OIC level to settle such mutual disputes and differences. All brotherly members of OIC should sit together and try to analyse the causes of their disputes in an honest manner to find amicable solutions.

3. I fully understand that the US and its allies or members of OIC will not frame their policies in accordance with my suggestions and demands based on truth and justice. Nor will they refrain from carrying out their plans because facts and reasons rarely move those who are intoxicated with power and authority. But it should be recorded in the pages of history how badly the so-called champions of world peace and justice smashed their own rules.[24]

14.1 Syed Geelani welcoming a Japanese diplomat at his residence in the Kashmiri style.

Oxford scholar Bose also counselled in The Telegraph (5 April 1996): 'Accepted wisdom has it that all territorial disputes anywhere are ultimately resolved through negotiation, and Kashmir ultimately will be no exception. However, the actual resolution of the conflict can only come through international participation, in the form of pressure, supervision and peace keeping. Finally, there is no long term solution without a popular referendum that includes the option of independence for all or part of the territory. The Kashmir conflict is the defining political and moral issue of these times in this region. It is not India's only problem, but without resolving it the country can have no peace, security or prosperity of any lasting value in South Asia, nor any pride in the strength of Indian civilization.' The Kashmiri freedom struggle, advised Arundhati Roy, 'has to get out of its ghetto and make alliances with what's going on, not just in India but in the rest of the world.'[25]

15

THE BOTTOM LINE

THE *HINDUSTAN TIMES* of 30 April and 15 May 1964 asked a simple question and offered a straightforward answer. The question: if we are so sure of the verdict of the Kashmiri people, why are we so opposed to giving them an opportunity to give it? The answer: a plebiscite would start the process of disintegration of the country. Few things have been said in the course of this controversy more silly than the presumption that Kashmiris, given a free choice, would choose to join with India. Instead of such silliness, we in India should find the courage to face facts honestly and deal with them on the basis of the ideals and fundamental principles that guided the freedom movement that gave birth to this country.

After the uprisings gained momentum, Justice Rajender Sachar issued a timely warning in *The Indian Express* (July 1993). That warning remains relevant:

> India will remain the loser unless the face that it presents to the people of Kashmir Valley is humane, compassionate and understanding. At present that face is ugly and insensitive.

> Another cause of bitterness is the conviction in Kashmir that howsoever viciously the security forces act, the administration will condone it. This is denied by the Government which says that action has been taken even against Commanding Officers, who have been given two to ten years prison terms. But neither the victims, nor the public is

aware of any such action. Is it wonder if people are skeptical of such claims by the Government?

The facile excuse that the security forces will be demoralized by the publication of this is perverse. In a democracy, the morale of the people is the first requisite, especially when a large number of people have lost faith in the impartiality and working of the administration.

Unfortunately, 'the Indian attitude to Kashmir is based on emotion rather than information' declares Tavleen Singh.[1] Som Benegal made an equally blunt statement in *Hindustan Times* (21 November 1993):

> Kashmir is lost. This is a truth that many of my countrymen will find hard to swallow.
>
> The bitter truth is that we may at great, continuing and self-defeating cost hold the sullen body of Kashmir captive, but its heart, soul and spirit are lost to us. It is no use fooling ourselves that militant groups are all Muslim, most of them bent on merger with Pakistan but also that there are those who want *azadi*. Anyone can see that the alienation of Kashmir, whether Muslims, Hindu, Buddhist or whatever, from India is complete. Those who speak for India cannot go beyond inaudible whispers. To amplify these whispers with megawatt loudspeakers carry no credible message to the Kashmir people.
>
> Right from the beginning they were reluctant to admit they were Indians, though they carried Indian passports, they referred to us as 'you Indians' and to themselves as 'we Kashmiris'. As a wise and mature nation we should stop parroting about Kashmir being an integral part of India and the only solution being under Shimla Pact; it has produced nothing but hot air. And finally, we must not lose sight of the fact that what matters most is the happiness of the people of the Valley.

Just five years into the mass uprisings, Geelani made it clear that 'We did not launch the present movement just for fun. We have some objectives, we have some dreams and unless that objective and that dream is realized, I mean people of this state getting the absolute right of deciding their own political future, we will go on with our job, and use all possible means to achieve our goal.' He was speaking by telephone to *Kashmir Today* (London) in September 1994. Almost twenty years after this statement, like a true Muslim and a true leader, Geelani has not moved one inch from his principled stand.

The Indian establishment might claim, 'Well, it has been almost twenty years since the above prophecy of Som Benegal. But Kashmir is still with us!' True, the piece of real estate is still with us. But are the inhabitants of that piece of land still with us? The answer is written all over J&K. So the real question is: what should be done? Pradip Bose's answer (*The Janata*, 6 March 1994) is even more relevant today than when first published:

> 'Face, facts, otherwise they will stab you in the back', says a Danish proverb. India's inability to face unpleasant facts about Kashmir for over four decades, has now created the possibility of her being 'stabbed in the back', which might prove to be fatal for the Indian Republic.
>
> What are the facts? The first and the most important is the overwhelming majority of the people in the Kashmir Valley, who are Muslims, have now been completely alienated from India.
>
> Second, for four and half decades the Indian people have been told that Kashmir is an integral part of India. Is this strictly correct? If it is a fact, then why does India permit UN observers to be stationed in Kashmir and not in other parts of the country, such as Punjab and Nagaland, which have also witnessed secessionist movements?
>
> Third, India through Lord Mountbatten and Pandit Nehru, had given a solemn assurance that the Kashmiri people would be allowed to decide whether they would like to

remain with India, or opt for Pakistan. This commitment was never kept.

Fourth, there is no doubt that Pakistan is training and arming Kashmiri militants and sending them across the border to create disturbances. But how does one explain the open defiance of the people there, including women and children, who risk their lives to face India's mighty armed forces empty handed? [Pakistani] intelligence agencies can certainly motivate, train and arm number of guerillas to fight against a government, but it can never organize mass upsurges and sustain them over a long period of time.

Nothing could be better if the Kashmir problem could be solved through the Shimla Agreement. However, without Pakistan's active cooperation no advance can be made. If it does not work, then other alternatives have to be looked into and no option should be ruled out.

Sarmila Bose argued (*The Telegraph*, 5 April 1996): 'The Indian Army in the Kashmir Valley is an army of occupation and like all armies of occupation will some day be forced to vacate the areas it presently occupies. Military occupation of Kashmir, besides being enormously costly in monetary terms, is costing the nation in many other ways. Human rights violations, inevitable in militarily occupied areas, in the Kashmir valley isolate us internationally and brutalize the nation.'

The Director-General of BSF, D. K. Arya, admitted as early on in the uprising as 9 April 1994: 'Political process is the only answer to militancy. We are no answer.' As a patriot, I completely agree with T. V. Rajeswar that 'The Kashmir dispute should not dictate the destiny of the entire nation. The welfare and future of the people of the entire country should be given more importance' (*Hindustan Times*, 17 July 1998).

In a realistic manner, Ram Dhamija argued: 'Both the borders and society in Kashmir have kept changing through the different periods. This was partly a result of invasions, occupation and migrations. In history there is nothing sacred about such changes.

And changes could be brought about today also through the means and methods of discussion and through a process of give and take, allowing for factors on the ground, including the aspirations of the people who are now resident in Kashmir' (*The Pioneer*, 17 July 2000). Ram Jethmalani (*The Asian Age*, 18 January 2001) also asked and answered the right question succinctly: 'Can India put an end to insurgency and terrorism at a bearable cost and should we, even if we can, hold in bondage a large number of people who owe us no loyalty or emotional attachment? To my mind the answer to both these questions is a strong "No".'

Throughout Kashmiri freedom struggle, pragmatic intellectuals have advised successive Indian governments to take a realistic stand on this dispute. In October 2010, Arundhati Roy addressed a convention of political activists and Kashmiri separatists in New Delhi. She told the audience: 'Kashmir has never been an integral part of India'. That, she said, is a 'historical fact'. Geelani was Roy's co-panelist at the event. She supported Geelani's demand for a plebiscite and urged the Indian government to accept the choice of Kashmiris. In the world's largest democracy, all hell broke loose. The 'patriotic' sections of Indian society – who are gradually taking this nation towards moral, social, political and economic bankruptcy – demanded her blood. As expected, BJP demanded that she be arrested for inciting 'disaffection' against the government, a 'perfect case of sedition'. The Indian government led by Congress agreed, and found her statement 'bordering sedition'. The Indian media remained largely on the fence!

'Sedition, a charge that is obsolete in most democratic societies, is often employed to squelch dissenting voices in totalitarian cultures. So it's disquieting when there are boisterous calls to use it to curb politically unpalatable opinions in a liberal democracy like India', wrote Anuj Chopra about this episode in *Foreign Policy* (28 October 2010). Defending free speech, the essence of secular democracy, Pritish Nandy wrote in *Hindustan Times* (12 January 2011): 'Arundhati Roy has also been accused of sedition because of her views on Kashmir. I have never agreed with her but to accuse her of sedition is absolute nonsense. The issues she has raised are certainly worth thinking about, even if we choose to reject them. The very fact that they are not part of the hysterical majority view makes them that much more important. For democracy is not only about accepting the majority view. It's also about respecting minority views, however wrong they may appear to be.' Indian minorities have been desperately waiting to breathe in such a democracy, Mr Nandy!

Roy, undeterred, doubled down. She issued a written statement (*Greater Kashmir*, 27 October 2010): 'I spoke about justice for the people of Kashmir who live under one of the most brutal military occupations in the world. [...] Kashmiris live in the terror of what is becoming a police state. [...] Pity the nation that has to silence its writers for speaking their minds.' In the end, the government blinked and announced that it would not press charges against her. Nandy rightly asked (*Times of India*, 10 January 2011): 'What is it about us that we call such people anti-national? Or is it because they shame us all by doing the right things? Why is it that we get so angry when Arundhati Roy raises issues that we feel are beyond political debate? Is it seditious to do so in a country that's so boastful of its democratic traditions?' Courageous and prudent Indians like Roy and Nandy have shown us that it may be risky to stand up for justice, but it is not that harmful, in the end.

But as I have shown throughout this book India is not a democracy for every Indian. Holding elections every five years must not be equated with democracy. Democracy means equal safety, equal security and equal opportunity for all citizens. It does not mean safety for some, security for some, and opportunities for some. India is a democracy for only the ruling cabals. The Indian establishment is dominated by stubborn and corrupt individuals with a pedestrian outlook. Let alone granting the right of self-determination, we are not even keeping our promise of giving Kashmiris decent social infrastructure. A severe earthquake in October 2005 damaged the already dilapidated infrastructure of the state. After five years, the J&K government had been able to restore just 18% of the schools damaged in north Kashmir districts of Baramulla, Bandipora and Kupwara. These are not statistics from Pakistan's ISI. They come from the J&K state's Directorate of Economics and Statistics (November 2010).

All said and done, 'there is nothing more futile in politics than to talk about wonderful but unattainable ideas.... A realistic compromise is better than a handful of ideal prescriptions that remain only on paper,' wrote Alija Izetbegovic.[2] Pakistani political analyst Tahir Amin identifies 'four principal obstacles in the resolution of Kashmir dispute: (a) lack of unity among the Kashmiri resistance forces; (b) Indian intransigence; (c) absence of a coherent long-term Pakistani policy towards Kashmir; and (d) lack of a hospitable international environment.' In his view, the 'prospect of settlement would increase only when the cost of occupation becomes unbearable for India.'[3]

Till then, 'Indo-Pak relations have dark clouds surrounding them. Pakistan calls Kashmir the core issue. India says J&K is an integral part of India. The world calls J&K a disputed territory,' writes Nanda.[4] In these circumstances, how long Kashmiris continue to suffer depends upon how patient and determined they are. When consoling and counseling his people in Bosnia, Izetbegovic told them: 'We must not be too impatient. In these years, the destiny of our people for the next century is being made, and this requires less emotion and more thinking, determination and patience.... Law and justice are finally stronger than anarchy and force, but we have to endure.... There is no magical solution, there is only patience and hard work.'[5] His advice is no less relevant to oppressed Kashmiris.

On the sixtieth anniversary of Indo-Pak independence, Geelani said: 'Sixty years have gone by since India and Pakistan achieved independence. But we need to see our people in these countries independent. Actually both countries are still slaves to policies and strategies adopted by British rulers during their occupation of India.' India and Pakistan claim to be on the path of progress and development, but 'progress cannot be measured in terms of economic growth but security to its people, their religion, property and lives. People continue to be victims of leadership in both countries' (*Greater Kashmir*, 2 September 2007).

Ankleswar Aiyer confirms Geelani's assessment of the Kashmiri uprisings. In his view British imperialist power used to cite economic activities as 'evidence that most Indians simply wanted jobs and a decent life. The Raj built the biggest railway and canal networks in the world. It said most Indians were satisfied with economic development, and that independence was demanded by a noisy minority. This is uncomfortably similar to the official Indian response to the Kashmiri demand for *azadi* (independence).'[6]

The US is the only country that can *quickly* right this historical wrong. But in an article, Robert Grenier, the former counter-terrorism director of CIA, put the current US somersault on Kashmir into perspective: 'The US, which has never been willing to do more than repeat sterile formulas in favour of a negotiated settlement in Kashmir, has not been willing in recent years even to do that, such is its lust for a "strategic relationship" with India.'[7] Bilateralism yields results only when both parties are committed to achieving results. India and Pakistan have held more than 160 rounds of bilateral discussions. India is clearly buying more and more time to perpetuate its illegal occupation. Pakistan is internally weak due to its own wrongdoings. Both these facts are corroborated by Ajai Shukla (*Business Standard*; 14 January 2013): India's 'Ministry of External Affairs emphasized that the Indo-Pak dialogue should not be disturbed, since it is going India's way. Discussions focus on the issues important to India (commercial ties, terrorism...) while there is lesser emphasis on the issues that New Delhi wanted to avoid (Kashmir, ...).'

Innocent Indians, Pakistanis and Kashmiris have been paying a hefty price for this never-ending bilateralism. Kashmiris are facing massacres, gang rapes and detentions. India and Pakistan are suffering low development on account of high defense budgets. A senior administrator in Srinagar put it this way: 'The truth is that the Kashmiri does have a case. Give me my rightful place in the sun, give me my dignity, my religious sensibilities, my cultural identity. Don't impose yourselves on me.' That is a legitimate demand everyone can understand.

16

NOT THE END

As THE CHAPTER TITLE indicates, I do not draw any conclusions from the discourse presented in this book, nor have I any solutions to offer as such. The reason is simple: too many shifting elements, regionally and internationally, are presently in play that will influence outcomes for this 'paradise on fire'. In this chapter, therefore, I only present the latest events with Geelani and Kashmir in roughly chronological order.

'The world respects those who understand and can defend their interests. It has little respect for others, much as it may praise them,' wrote the Chairman of Bajaj Auto, Rahul Bajaj (*The Economic Times*, 17 December 2007). Freedom struggles do go on for decades if not for centuries. For example, Algeria was liberated from the clutches of France only after seventy-five years of bloody struggle and some fifteen million deaths. India's own freedom struggle with British colonial power lasted almost a century. Eritrea fought a bloody thirty-two-year war with Ethiopia before it achieved independence in 1993. The South African example is also fresh in our memories where black Africans fought the apartheid regime for over fifty years before achieving a resounding victory. Therefore, Kashmiri freedom fighters and the masses behind them have to keep their spirits high for a long haul. If they do, their oppressors will have to, one day, leave the lands they occupy by force.

Former Indian parliamentarian Kuldip Nayar wrote way back

on 8 June 1994 in *The National Mail*: 'Militancy has spread all over, as an Urdu daily editor says, "Every boy and girl, from the age of 12 to 30 is a militant even if he or she does not wield a gun." He explained that militancy was only an expression for defiance. It may take some other shape. 'Even if all guns become silent, India should not believe that it has normalized the situation in Kashmir.' In Geelani's view, 'people who are advising India to adopt a humanistic and moralistic stand are the real well-wishers of India. Kashmiris wish India a bright future and want it to become strong and powerful. This cannot be achieved through the use of Agni missiles and atomic weapons but through protection and respect for human and moral values.'

'Mr Kuldip Nayar is quite well-known to us. He is my personal friend, for whom I have great regard and affection,' wrote Geelani in *The Oppressed Nation* (p. 40). Former Indian Law Minister and currently a BJP Member of Parliament Ram Jethmalani visited Geelani's residence on 5 June 2011. Addressing a press conference after the meeting, Jethmalani admitted: 'such atrocities were not perpetrated [even] in Nazi Germany. We were deeply pained to hear about the continuing human rights abuses and indiscriminate arrests of innocents. Kashmiris are living in an atmosphere of terror and tyranny.' In an earlier article in *The Mainstream* (11 January 1997), Balraj Puri explained the plain truth: 'Participation in elections as such does not reflect [any] decline in the strength of the "*Azadi*" movement.' Thirteen years later, *The Economist* (26 August 2010) made the same point: 'When turnout in an election for the [J&K] state government in 2008 reached an unprecedented 60%, many Indians misread this as belated Kashmiri acquiescence in Indian rule.'

Geelani explains why elections do not reflect the reality: 'Elections are being held in the presence of hundreds of thousands of Indian army men in order to scare us and divert us from the goals which our martyrs cherished. They want us to put our seal of approval [on] slavery [to] India, get ourselves included in the category of sellers of honour by voting and supporting those criminals who looted [the] chastity of our mothers, sisters and daughters. By taking part in elections we will be giving historians the opportunity of writing in future that the overwhelming majority of J&K, finding themselves completely helpless and powerless, surrendered and supported the tyrants, despots and rapists. By demonstrating cowardly character as a community, we shall tarnish our image in the history forever.'

Those who surrender to the charade of elections do not enjoy the support of the people; those who reject that charade do. Accordingly, Geelani challenged the J&K Chief Minister to come out among the people (*Greater Kashmir*, 9 May 2012): 'If at all Omar Abdullah is really keen to see our representative character, he should put an end to my house arrest and give Hurriyat permission to hold a public meeting at Lal Chowk here. If he [Omar] is really [the] peoples' representative let him come out of [his] security ring and address a public meeting. Once his security is removed he will find it difficult to move even from [his residence in] Sonawar to [his office at the] Civil Secretariat.'

One of the many Hindu deities is said to reside in the Amarnath caves of Kashmir. Hindus hold a religious procession to this place every year under the management of a Trust established for this purpose. In May 2008 Kashmir's puppet government led by Mufti Sayeed gave the shrine's overseers the right to build facilities on a ninety-eight-acre state-owned site along the procession route. Kashmiri Muslims viewed this as a present loss of territory to non-Kashmiri Hindus, and a future threat, given the prospect of Hindu settlement in the area that would erode the Muslims' demographic majority in the state. After India's further compliance with the advice of Israeli President Shimon Peres to change the demographic balance, 'Kashmir has erupted in protest over a plan to transfer 40 hectares of forest department land to the managing board of a Hindu cave shrine,' reported the *Financial Times* (25 August 2008).

Geelani protested. Kashmiris followed him. Trigger-happy Indian security forces responded in their usual style: at least thirty-seven unarmed civilians were killed. The protesters eventually forced the government to revoke the land transfer. This in turn infuriated the Hindus of Jammu. 'Hindu militants rioted across the district, blocking the highway that links the Kashmir valley to the rest of India. This "economic blockade" created a sense of siege in the Valley. Hindu nationalists [BJP] had made a grim economic reality of the separatists' political dream' (*The Economist*, 21 August 2008). Geelani saw an opportunity. If the path to Jammu was blocked, he advised Kashmiris to march to Muzaffarabad, the capital of PaK. On 11 August 2008, the Indian security forces fired on the march killing four, including a senior pro-freedom leader, Sheikh Abdul Aziz.

Fifteen more Kashmiris were killed in further protests the next day. Geelani led even bigger protests. Almost a million Kashmiris poured onto the streets of Srinagar. Seeing the unprecedented reaction of Kashmiris, for the first time in over sixty years, mainstream Indian media openly discussed the possibility of a plebiscite. Thanks to the determined leadership of Geelani, Kashmiris got a step closer to their goal. Not there, yet. But the distance is shrinking!

On 11 June 2010, another crisis erupted. A seventeen-year-old Kashmiri boy, Tufail Mattoo, was walking home past a demonstration. He was killed by a tear-gas shell fired by the Indian security forces. The incident triggered a cycle of protests, shootings, baton charges and firing of tear-gas shells, curfews and political strikes that closed down entire cities. Kashmiri leaders, most notably Geelani, were put under house arrest.

'Kashmir,' wrote John Elliott, 'seems doomed to many more years of uncertainty, with periods of violence alternating with relative calm. That means that prospects for the state's youth are bleak, while the prospects of them becoming increasingly militant are considerable. After two decades of troubles, generations of youth have grown up in a stone-throwing culture where baiting and attacking security forces, and being viciously attacked and killed in return, is part of regular life from the age of nine or ten' (*Financial Times*, 16 July 2010). This surely conveys a story at odds with the official Indian version. The Indian government and media would have us believe that the squads of stone-throwing Kashmiri youth are hired or sponsored by our mischievous neighbour.

In the same article, Elliott continues: 'A few years ago, I was told by a senior British diplomat that peace could never come to Kashmir till the Indian government acknowledged, to itself and publicly, that its security forces had been involved in appalling human rights abuses. That, said the diplomat, was the lesson of Northern Ireland where London only made progress on a settlement after it made that acknowledgement. Sadly, the behaviour of the security forces in just the last few days, let alone the last 20 years, shows that neither the current Kashmir government [led by NC's Omar Abdullah] nor India's Home Ministry is prepared for such a *mea culpa* on human rights abuses.'

The abuses continued. 'Four tumultuous months later, India staunched the outpouring of rage in its only Muslim-majority province, but at a price. Troops fired repeatedly into crowds, killing 110 protesters and bystanders, and injuring at least 1,000 more. Strict curfews and separatist strikes have disrupted education, commerce and social life,' wrote Amy Kazmi in *Financial Times* (24 October 2010). After this *Financial Times* report, eight more Kashmiris lost their lives in that cycle of state-terrorism. The Indian government blamed Geelani for inciting violence. Geelani replied: 'It was due to the brutal murders of youth in [the] Machil fake encounter – Wamiq Farooq, Zahid Farooq, Inayat Khan and Tufail Matoo – by the forces that forced people to take to [the] streets... and stage protests' (*Greater Kashmir*, 17 August 2010).

In an interview with Saudi Arabian English daily, Geelani rationalized the changed tactics of Kashmiri youth. He said (*Arab News*, 17 August 2010): 'We took a conscious decision not to take up arms because we were afraid that our pious struggle would again be dubbed as terrorism by India and the outside world – the way it was declared in post 9/11 era. So we opted for the path of peaceful struggle, which is what we are leading now. We want to run India out of excuses. Because the struggle in 1988 was armed, India justified the disproportionate use of military force. Now nobody can dare call us terrorists. This struggle has been on for the last two months. You will appreciate the fact that not one man in uniform [security personnel] has been killed at the hands of our men. [The murdered Kashmiris] include women, children and the elderly.

This is a carnage and the world's so-called largest democracy is committing this.'

Anuj Chopra confirmed in *Foreign Policy* (28 October 2010): 'The most recent wave of anti-India rage was led not by Pakistan-sponsored militants, but by Kashmir's homegrown youth – most of them teenagers – who hurled stones at Indian security personnel while zealously shouting independence slogans. They took to the streets in defiance of stern curfews and even shoot-on-sight orders.' In a statement, Geelani castigated New Delhi for illegally using state power to suppress the peaceful agitation of Kashmiris. He said: 'For this purpose, the NC has been directed [by New Delhi] to help the police and Army. The NC leaders in collusion with the concerned [Police] Station House Officers prepare the list of youth, who have taken part in the agitation since June this year. These youth are asked to report to the Police Stations and then arrested' (*Greater Kashmir*, 14 December 2010).

16.1 A delegation of Indian parliamentarians called on Syed Geelani in 2010 at his residence in Srinagar.

Geelani alleged that the cases being registered against most of the arrested youth on the recommendation of the NC activists were frivolous, and moreover the youth were being 'forced to pay ransom for their release. This is a dangerous campaign to ruin the professional career of our younger generation. The FIRs become a lifelong problem for [the] youth,' he said (ibid.). He complained that 'Kashmiris have been successful in giving a pure peaceful direction to the movement', but 'instead of respecting the transition of our movement, New Delhi and its agents in Kashmir are adamant on their policy [of using excessive force] which has categorically failed in [the] past 63 years.' By using the security apparatus to further its interests 'the NC is displaying its sheer shortsightedness. As a political party, the NC should fight Hurriyat's peaceful programs at the political level only.' Geelani also made the point that the government's silence over the excesses by the security forces is tantamount to a crime against humanity (*Greater Kashmir*, 20 December 2010).

Balraj Puri reminded the Indian government way back – in *The Radiance Views Weekly* of 3–9 March 1996 – that the limitations of force to solve Kashmir problem 'have become fairly evident. Whatever achievement may be claimed by the Indian security forces, it will be an illusion to conclude that force alone can end popular alienation in the Valley.'

The 'international community' also remained at best silent about or even, at worst, supportive of, state terrorism. UN Secretary-General Ban Ki-Moon issued a statement to the effect that the government of India was taking all measures to protect human rights in Kashmir. Geelani, addressing reporters at his Hyderpora residence, said: 'The statement of Ban Ki-Moon is totally unrealistic and devoid of facts. He has given [a] clean chit, rather a certificate, to India that it is protecting human rights in the Valley. Holding such a high and responsible position, he has not done justice to his job by overlooking the ground realities in Kashmir and Wikileaks disclosure on custodial torture of the Kashmiris.' The UN he said had adopted a posture of 'criminal silence' over the killing of innocents in Kashmir (*ibid.*). Looking at a blatantly biased history of UN, discussed earlier in the book, this was not at all surprising!

Geelani pointed out (for the benefit of Ban Ki-Moon) that: 'In the last two decades, over one lakh Kashmiris were killed by Indian security forces. Most of them were civilians. The forces even did not spare the non-Muslims to defame our just and sacred movement. The massacre of 35 Sikhs in Chittisinghpora and subsequent killing of five locals to cover up the crime is still fresh in our minds. How can Ban Ki-Moon forget [the] rape and killings of Aasiya and Neelofar and fake encounter killings of three youth of Nadihal at Machil? The troopers pumped bullets on the unarmed youth and teenagers killing 118 of them. They imposed curfew for 90 days and conducted arbitrary arrests. I want to tell Ban Ki-Moon that these are measures undertaken by New Delhi to crush the resolve of Kashmiris and not to protect the[ir] human rights' (ibid.). Geelani went on to affirm that, even if Ban Ki-Moon or others take no note of human rights abuses in the Valley, their indifference will not dent the resolve of Kashmiris.

Due to his bold and consistently principled stand, Geelani has been the undisputed leader of Kashmiris. But in recent years, his stock has soared even among Indians. MensXP.com is a web portal of the New Delhi-based Xpert Media Technology Private Limited. In association with Samsung Galaxy Tab, it launched 'X51: India's Most Influential Men of 2010.' A December 2010 survey on this web portal rated Syed Ali Geelani as the most influential politician in India, ahead of some prominent stalwarts of mainstream politics including Prime Minister Manmohan Singh. Talking to *Greater Kashmir* (9 December 2010), the managing director, Xpert Media Technology, Angad Bhatia said 'X51' had received unprecedented traffic over the previous two weeks. 'More than 32,000 votes were cast. Geelani is leading in Politics with 9.3 points [followed in second place] by Prime Minister Manmohan Singh with 6.19 points,' he said. Bhatia was savvy enough to add that it is debatable whether Geelani is Indian or not!

The survey also revealed that Rahul Gandhi scored 5.64 points, (the current President of India) Pranab Mukherjee 4.65, J&K Chief Minister Omar Abdullah 3.06 and Maoist leader Kobad Ghandi 3.47. Bhatia said currently Geelani is highest in the politics category and also overall. He said voting is in the hands of the public. 'Anybody may choose to rank him at whatever number between 1 and 10,' he said. The survey (in addition to the votes) has also attracted thousands of comments from people across the country. One voter, Omar Bhat, commented about Geelani: 'I never liked his Pakistan line, but his character, integrity, resilience and principled stand make me salute him.' Another voter termed Geelani 'a brave politician'. Bhatia said 'X51' was flooded by people commenting in favour of Geelani. 'One in every two comments on X51 is for Geelani,' he said.

At a press conference in Srinagar, Geelani warned that the youth were angry and frustrated that they are punished 'just for peacefully expressing their views' on how the dispute should be resolved. Geelani at this time has categorically told the Kashmiri youth to be patient and desist from any recourse to violence. He expalined: 'New Delhi has prepared a sketch and wants the Kashmiris to fill colours in it. By using oppressive measures to crush our peaceful agitation, New Delhi wants to push Kashmiris towards violence with the sole aim of further crushing our movement militarily and [to] mislead the international community. I urge the youth to foil the evil designs and carry the movement forward peacefully' (*Greater Kashmir*, 11 January 2011).

Geelani complained that, at the instruction of New Delhi, the J&K authorities had launched a crackdown on his party workers: '51 [of our] prominent leaders and activists are languishing in jails. Today is my 127th day of house arrest. Youth are arrested and shifted to Jammu jails. [...] the jail authorities of Kot Balwal, Udhampur, Amphalla and Kathua are resorting to political vengeance against the Kashmiri detainees by harassing and maltreating them. This shows the real face of India's so-called democracy' (ibid.). The president of the J&K High Court Bar Association, advocate Mian Abdul Qayoom, had been arrested in July last year and not released, despite the quashing of the case filed against him under the Public Safety Act (PSA). 'He has been lodged at a Police Station in Jammu and twice attacked by the activists of BJP. Mian Qayoom is being punished for giving voice to the suppressed people of Kashmir,' Geelani claimed (ibid.).

A March 2011 Amnesty International (AI) report, *A Lawless Law: Detention Under the Jammu and Kashmir Public Safety Act (PSA)*, says:

'It is widely understood amongst the legal community in Srinagar that confessions and disclosure statements made in police custody are a result of torture and other ill-treatment.' Geelani complained that the youth were being implicated in false cases, with the police turning the arrests into a business – many were arrested and released after paying hefty amounts, and fearful of speaking to the media because of the threat to their lives. The NC Working Committee had passed a resolution in 2011 to release all the detainees, but the 'resolution is yet to be implemented. This clearly shows that the Chief Minister [Omar Abdullah] or his party has no authority to prevent misuse of power by the police and troopers as they directly take dictation from New Delhi to suppress the people,' Geelani said (ibid.).

His assessement is supported by Anuj Chopra (*Foreign Policy*, 28 October 2010): 'Kashmir has its own government, but it is just as directly controlled by New Delhi as the army, paramilitary forces, and intelligence agencies that have descended upon the state.' Geelani warned the District Magistrates: 'They blindly oblige the police by imposing PSA on Kashmiris. They should bear in mind that they might be holding top posts but one day they will be answerable to Almighty [God]' (*Greater Kashmir*, 11 January 2011).

Former cabinet minister and a member of the Indian Parliament, Ram Vilas Paswan visited Geelani at his Hyderpora residence on 27 April 2011. Geelani briefed him about the atrocities being suffered by Kashmiris. Paswan then asked of the government: 'What have they done about the Armed Forces Special Powers Act (AFSPA) and the youth booked under PSA? Why don't they release those who are not involved in any heinous crimes?' (*Greater Kashmir*, 28 April 2011). Geelani has often questioned the vision of Kashmiri masses and their ability to patiently withstand the Indian onslaught.

In *The Oppressed Nation* (pp. 29-30), Geelani reflected on the reasons why Shaikh Abdullah, in spite of committing gigantic blunders in the management of the Kashmir dispute, had remained, *during his life,* the most acclaimed figure on the political horizon of the Kashmiri people: 'In my opinion the vision of our nation is not very broad and mature. Maturity of thought and vision is not achieved through academics [alone]. Education, no doubt, broadens our mind and outlook. It creates awareness, increases our knowledge, enables us to think about [the] problems of our life and helps us adopt proper means to lead a better and comfortable life. But maturity of thought and vision cannot, in any case, be acquired only by education and knowledge [...] I very well remember when [former Soviet Prime Minister Nikolai] Bulganin and [former Soviet President Nikita] Khrushchev visited Kashmir [in December 1955], our people did not express the slightest feeling that they were in fact our enemies who had deprived us of our fundamental rights. People came out in hordes [...] Mosques were empty even at the time of Friday prayers.'

Addressing a seminar in Srinagar, Geelani criticized those Kashmiris who get distracted from the main focus of freedom struggle: 'While chanting *Hum Kya Chahatai Hain? Azadi!* (What do we want: freedom) the discourse instantly makes a transition to *Hum Kya Chahatai Hain? Transformer!* (What do we want: electricity)! We have to fix our priorities. We should not mix up our cause with developmental activities, jobs and elections. When we have [put on] the mantle of supporting the just cause, we should ensure to sustain it at any cost' (*Greater Kashmir*, 11 January 2011). He went on: 'developmental activities including construction of roads, fly-overs and bridges have nothing to do with the ongoing movement. We can survive on grass to protect our identity, culture and religion. We will continue to fight peacefully till we achieve [the] right to self-determination.' There seems to be a wide consensus that Geelani is right about this: 'Development in itself will not fix Kashmir,' said *The Economist* (29 December 2010); so also Anuj Chopra (*Foreign Policy*, 28 October 2010): 'material inducements and a modicum of political representation cannot heal Kashmir's existential scars, much less expunge the spirit of *azadi*.'

The March 2011 AI report (referred to above) also states that the state of 'Jammu and Kashmir was holding hundreds of people without charge or trial in order to keep them out of circulation.' It alleges that a contentious PSA allows security forces to detain individuals although the state has insufficient evidence for a trial.

Under this law, AI says, between 8,000 and 20,000 people have been detained over the past two decades, with 322 people held between January and September of 2010 alone. Govind Acharya, an AI India specialist says detentions under the PSA can last for up to two years. But the numbers of enforced disappearances are ominously similar i.e. upto 20,000.

However, the Indian political leadership remains in denial mode. Reacting to Geelani's complaints about Kashmiri detainees, India's Harvard-educated Home Minster P. C. Chidambaram said (21 June 2011): 'I don't know wherefrom Geelani has got all these figures. The numbers quoted by him are highly exaggerated. [Geelani] should file an application under [the] Right to Information (RTI) Act and seek information about the actual number of political prisoners languishing in different jails. I reiterate that only 123 plus 45 (168) persons are currently serving imprisonment under different provisions of the law' (*Greater Kashmir*, 22 June 2011). This shows how far removed from realities on the ground the country's political elite are. Security forces in Kashmir are openly flaunting the rulings of even the High Court; is it likely that an RTI request would be of any use when those who are illegally detained are never taken into custody on the record?

After the peace process circus with 'moderate' leaders fizzled out in mid-2000s, the Indian government appointed a team of 'interlocutors' in 2010, commissioned to 'find out' what the demands of Kashmiris are! Are we a nation of dumb idiots that we do not know or do not understand what the Kashmiris have been demanding for over sixty years? In reality, India is a nation of compassionate, honest and peaceful inhabitants. But our rulers have taken us all for a ride since independence. The panel of interlocutors included journalist Dileep Padgaonkar, academic Radha Kumar and former Election Commissioner M. M. Ansari. They visited Kashmir every month to meet various 'thought leaders' among Kashmiris. They tried to meet Geelani, but he refused, calling the exercise futile, since the interlocutors have no power and no function, except to draw hefty salaries.

Anuj Chopra agrees that the interlocutors are worthy and

eminent members of civil society, but in his view, this gesture is 'essentially toothless. Their mandate does not include assessing militarization and military governance, without which the suffering and outrage of Kashmiris will not go away,' (*Foreign Policy*, 28 October 2010). Padgaonkar wrote to Geelani in February 2011 inviting him to 'choose date, time and venue for talks,' adding: 'If you don't want to meet us, we are eager to hear from you and you can send your proposal to us in a written format' (*Greater Kashmir*, 21 February 2011). Geelani, after already refusing to meet them earlier, completely ignored this invitation. The Mirwaiz-led Hurriyat, having learned their lesson the hard way after facing humiliation by engaging in the 2004 'peace process', also followed Geelani in staying away from this new circus orchestrated by India.

In the end, Interlocutors presented their report to the Indian government and Dileep Padgaonkar told the media in December 2011 (*Greater Kashmir*, 27 December 2011): 'During our various visits to Jammu and Kashmir we met nearly 700 delegations. Most Kashmiris want change in [the] status quo.' What a revelation! It is not just Geelani; even mainstream politicians have no delusions about India's intentions. A senior mainstream leader, Engineer Abdul Rashid himself admitted: 'Kashmiris had nothing to celebrate about the Interlocutors' report and the[ir] panel was constituted just to divert attention from the unrest of 2010' (*Greater Kashmir*, 15 April 2012).

Geelani maintained that the summer 2010 agitation was a reaction to the killings of innocents in the Valley: 'How could people remain silent when innocent Kashmiris were being killed. We should not take the agitation of five months as [a] yardstick of our movement as [that] was only a reaction to the killings. Our movement [has been] going on for [the] past 63 years [...]' (*Greater Kashmir*, 11 January 2011). Paswan admitted that perceptions about Kashmir were fast changing in India. 'Our purpose is to tell the masses that innocents and students are being killed in Kashmir and the 118 youth killed last year were not terrorists. Kashmir is not about terrorism,' (*Greater Kashmir*, 28 April 2011).

India cannot shut its eyes and ignore Geelani forever. His

recognition as the voice of Kashmiris is becoming increasingly evident. In the first week of March 2011, he was invited to New Delhi to speak on the Kashmir dispute in the two-day high profile *India Today Conclave* themed 'The Changing Balance of Power'. In the invitation to participate, the Editorial Director of *India Today* and *Headlines Today*, M. J. Akbar, explained that 'the Conclave is an international event aimed at charting a bold new future through a free and frank exchange of ideas between the finest minds of the world.' The organizers maintained that against the backdrop of last year's summer unrest, Kashmir remains an emotive issue driving Pakistan and India to obsessive actions and reactions. They underscored the need to explore options for a lasting settlement of the dispute.

Spanning many sessions, the Conclave invitees were (among others) Prime Minister Manmohan Singh, Gujarat Chief Minister Narendar Modi, former Pakistan Ambassador to Afghanistan and High Commissioner to India Aziz Ahmed Khan, and Pakistani writer and activist Fatima Bhutto. Geelani's co-panelists were former J&K Chief Minister and present Renewable Energy Minister Dr Farooq Abdullah and former Cabinet Minister Arif Muhammad Khan. Needless to say, Geelani presented the Kashmiri dispute from his perspective in his usual forceful style.

Every year for India's Independence Day celebrations, Kashmiris hoist the Pakistani flag at Lal Chowk (the main square) in Srinagar. This gesture is meant to express their love for Pakistan and turning away from the occupying power and its forces. In January 2011, to provoke Kashmiris, the BJP tried to hoist the Indian flag at Lal Chowk. Geelani taunted: 'BJP hoisting a flag in the presence of one million Indian soldiers in the Valley is no brave act and there is nothing courageous about it' (*Greater Kashmir*, 24 January 2011).

Geelani repeated his party's policy to peacefully carry forward the ongoing movement: in the face of provocations 'we have been urging the people to keep their protests peaceful and even refrain from raising provocative slogans during demonstrations. This was evident during the last year's summer unrest where 118 un-armed youth and teenagers fell to the bullets while none of [the] security force personnel and police were killed. This has infuriated the Indian leadership and communal parties including BJP who are hell-bent upon instigating Kashmiris by their communal politics' (*Greater Kashmir*, 25 January 2011). Geelani said that, instead of (a) accepting Kashmir as a dispute, (b) releasing all the Kashmiris languishing in jails, and (c) demilitarization to improve the situation, New Delhi has given a 'free hand to its forces and communal parties to suppress the ongoing peaceful movement'.

Reviewing recent events, Geelani said: the Kashmir 'dispute will linger on till [the] last Indian soldier leaves the state. But more than the Indian soldiers the J&K police have been at the forefront of unleashing atrocities on the Kashmiris. The police are behaving as more loyal than the king. History and future generations of Kashmir will never forgive them' (ibid.).

As mentioned earlier, thousands of innocent Kashmiris have disappeared without a trace over the last twenty years. In 2011, over 2,000 unmarked graves across J&K were discovered. *New York Times* (8 July 2012) took a shot at the Indian government and its 'strategic partners': 'Had the graves been found under Col. Muammar el-Qaddafi's compound in Libya or in the rubble of Homs in Syria, there surely would have been an uproar. But when over 2,000 skeletons appear in the conflict-ridden backyard of the world's largest democracy, no one bats an eye.'

Geelani insists that unless there is complete demilitarization of the state, the Kashmir dispute cannot be resolved. During a visit to his hometown Sopore on 27 March 2011, Geelani reminded Kashmiris that 'even the British occupied India for over a century, carried on massacres and jailed its leaders including Mahatma Gandhi and Maulana Abul Kalam Azad. But India finally achieved independence. Right of self-determination is our inalienable right and we can achieve it if we maintain steadfastness and unity' (*Greater Kashmir*, 28 March 2011).

Geelani has been a thorn in the flesh of the Indian authorities for a very long time. They have frequently resorted to cheap and vindictive methods to neutralize or silence him. They cooked up a fanciful income tax case against him (not for the first time) in May

2011. Hurriyat spokesman, Ayaz Akbar said that the government, having failed to coerce Geelani into abandoning his position, was now resorting to psychological pressure through the Income Tax Department: 'Such tactics had neither succeeded in the past to tame Geelani, nor can they succeed in future. Geelani's whole life has always been open and evident. No aspect of his life has ever remained concealed or mysterious. Indian rulers know well that accusations could be leveled against Geelani but these could not be proved in any court of the world' (*Greater Kashmir*, 11 May 2011).

Akbar also repeated that Geelani has not built up any assets or property over the last twenty years. He reminded Indian authorities that 'Geelani's own house, which he had constructed in 1970s at Duroo, Sopore, was razed to the ground in a blast by the army in 1996. The raid on [his] Hyderpora office in 2002 was more of a war type than income tax raid. At that time, a claim was made about recovery of certain things. Geelani was taken to Ranchi Jail of Jharkhand and his son-in-law Altaf Ahmad Shah to Kote Balwal Jail, Jammu. Geelani was then released after nine months because of serious illness. Before conducting [the raid], a high-profile New Delhi envoy had met Geelani at [his] Hyderpora office and tried to persuade him [to hold] talks. But when Geelani refused to deviate from his stand, the income tax drama was staged to teach him a lesson. He was then shifted to jail thousands of miles away from his home' (*Greater Kashmir*, 28 March 2011).

While Kashmir is burning, India's notorious neighbour is also on fire. Tarun Vijay, a top RSS ideologue taunts Pakistan in his 20 February 2008 *Times of India* column. Thanks to the Musharrafs and Zardaris, he writes, 'It is the army and the US which decide the fate of this Islamic republic with Allah often taking a backseat as he [Allah] watches the sordid dramas.' Pakistan is perhaps at its weakest point since its humiliation at the hands of India in 1971. This is not good news for any neighborhood. 'India has deep stakes in the stability of Pakistan. An unstable Pakistan is much more dangerous for the Indian interests,' confirmed Binoo Joshi (*Greater Kashmir*, 9 May 2011).

Armed with strong faith and courage, Afghans have once again humiliated foreign invaders. The US-led NATO war on Afghanistan has now lasted almost twice as long as World War Two. But a politically and militarily weak and misguided leadership has brought nuclear-powered Pakistan to its knees. Virtually the whole country is under the sway of the US, while its people are staggering under a severe debt burden. Under the last PPP regime, Pakistan has reportedly borrowed more in the last four years than it had over the previous sixty years of its existence!

The Economist (2 April 2011) reports that '30,000 people have been killed in the past four years in terrorism, sectarianism and army attacks on the terrorists' in Pakistan. The numbers are growing fast: former Prime Minister Gilani admitted in late 2011, 'We lost 35,000 precious lives, including 5,000 security personnel, and incurred damage of billions of dollars [...] as a result of our participation in the war on terror.'[1] As if this price for being passive followers of American policy was not enough, US forces killed twenty-four Pakistani soldiers in late November 2011. Adding insult to injury, a US Congressional Committee in its budgetary proposals for the year 2013 prohibited economic and security assistance to Pakistan 'unless the government of Pakistan is cooperating with the US on counterterrorism efforts and other issues'.[2]

As citizens of India, we should take comfort in the fact that the people of Pakistan still do not see us as the greatest threat to their country. A July 2009 Gallup survey in Pakistan clearly showed that 60% of Pakistanis see America as 'the greatest threat for Pakistan'. A mere 18% view India as the greatest threat.

BJP top-gun Advani preached 'hot pursuit' of Kashmiri militants across the border into PaK. But he never dared to practice what he preached when he became the Deputy Prime Minister of India. Bruce Riedel, a Senior Fellow at the US think-tank the Brookings Institution explains why: 'So far, India has shown remarkable restraint and it's not out of love for Mahatma Gandhi, although Indians do love Mahatma Gandhi,' he said. 'But because India's generals, politicians and diplomats can't figure out a way to strike back against Pakistan without triggering a full-scale conflict that has the potential to become nuclearised'.[3] Clearly it is not our 'restraint' but our fear of retaliation by Pakistan that has deterred us from Advani's favoured 'hot pursuit' policy.

Compared to Pakistan, Iran is a weaker country, but has strong political and military leadership. 'The only Muslim country that refuses to cave under American pressure is Iran,' said Geelani in an interview with Yoginder Sikand.[4] As a result, Iran's arch enemies Israel and the US have not (yet) been able to encroach upon its territory. This is a great lesson for Pakistan or any other nation with self-respect.

Addressing the UN General Assembly in late 2011, Turkish Prime Minister Recep Erdogan urged the international body that 'more effective efforts have to be exerted to resolve the Kashmir issue'.[5] This dispute continues to haunt South Asia. 'India has paid a heavy price in loss of security for having allowed the Bharatiya Janata Party [...] to conduct the nuclear tests of 1998. Here's the plain truth. Nuclear weapons have made India and Pakistan *more*, not less, insecure. Millions of unarmed civilians in both countries are vulnerable to attacks by nuclear-capable missiles, against which there is no defence. Both are stockpiling large quantities of bomb fuel. Pakistan is building new plutonium production facilities even as it expands its uranium enrichment programme' (Praful Bidwai, *Rediff.com*, 27 April 2012).

Also, according to Praful Bidwai, 'India and Pakistan have raised their conventional arms spending fourfold since 1998. India became the world's largest importer of arms in 2007–2011.' An April 2012 report released in Chicago suggests that over a billion people aross the world would face starvation if India and Pakistan unleashed nuclear weapons. The study's author Dr. Ira Helfand of the International Physicians for the Prevention of Nuclear War said: 'even the relatively small nuclear arsenals of countries such as India and Pakistan could cause long-lasting global damage to the Earth's ecosystems and threaten hundreds of millions of already malnourished people.'[6]

The Stockholm International Peace Research Institute (SIPRI) in its 2012 yearbook noted: 'India and Pakistan are increasing the size and sophistication of their nuclear arsenals. Both countries are developing and deploying new types of nuclear-capable ballistic and cruise missiles and both are increasing their military fissile material production capabilities.' The SIPRI report also said that Pakistan's doctrine is based on the principle of minimum deterrence but does not specifically rule out the first use of nuclear weapons to offset India's superiority in conventional arms and manpower. In such a scenario, millions of innocent lives will be at stake. Australian historian Christopher Snedden believes 'Pakistan is ready for a plebiscite, but India will never go for it.'[7] India's leadership should ask themselves if they value millions of human lives more than a piece of disputed real estate?

As for India, recent estimates have put its GDP at INR 90 lakh crore (approximately US$1.8 trillion). Its debt in 2012 is around INR 40 lakh crore (about $0.9 trillion). The current budget estimates for revenue and expenditure translate into a deficit of around INR 2.07 lakh crore ($0.05 trillion). These numbers mean that India has borrowed an amount equivalent to forty-five per cent of its GDP, or, to put it differently, four times its annual income. Despite living off debt, India is the biggest importer of arms in the world (*Time*, 1 April 2013)!

More than 40% of India's 61 million children are malnourished, prompting the Prime Minister Manmohan Singh to declare the problem a 'national shame'. But no one talks about 'government terrorism' when close to one million children die each year due to hunger-related factors. 25 million Indian children suffer from starvation, more than the whole of sub-Saharan Africa! However, the same Prime Minister is writing multi-billion dollar cheques to develop nuclear weapons and intercontinental ballistic missiles!

The BJP is the biggest proponent of nuclear arms in India. The BJP-ruled state of Madhya Pradesh, at 60%, has the highest percentage of malnourished children in the world – the worst figures in sub-Saharan Africa are much lower, at 24%. Delivering justice to its citizens is also not a priority for this 'largest democracy' and 'emerging super power'. 'We spend very little on the judicial system,' complained Satya Prakash in *Hindustan Times* (18 March 2013). He also warned of 'litigation explosion' in near term. His argument has strong merit: at the end of 2012, cases pending in the Supreme Court (59,816); and at the end of 2011 in twenty-one High Courts (4.3 million) and 17,000 Sub-courts (a staggering twenty-seven million)!

Equally startling, if not more, is this: 'Official statistic shows that some 60,000 children go missing every year.... According to Jitendra Singh, the federal minister of state for home affairs, about 22,000 of these missing children vanished without a trace in 2011.'[8] The Justice Verma commission found that a child goes missing in India every eight minutes, on average. Still, the *collective conscience of our nation* is not jolted!

The Arab uprisings of 2011 are great news for Kashmiris in general and Geelani in particular. Islamists like Geelani are receiving strong support at the ballot box, at the levels of the MUF before the rigged elections of 1987 in J&K. India needs to take serious note of this observation by Bobby Ghosh: 'The Arab Spring showed us what combination of circumstances can make a revolution: a corrupt and arrogant regime..., huge unemployment, soaring food prices, a small group of activists adept at using social networks and cell phones as organizing tools, plus a spark – a Tunisian fruit seller immolating himself in protest against corruption' (*Time*, 5 September 2011).

Newsweek (5 September 2011) also warned: 'If only a few people are better off as a result of economic growth, the strong GDP figures don't make a country stable. On the contrary, they can actually contribute to a revolutionary situation.' The National Human Rights Commission statistics show 14,231 custodial deaths from 2001 to 2010. In 2011 alone 132 persons died in Indian jails.[9] Unfortunately, despite vulnerable economic and social situation, India 'is constantly at war. And always against minorities – tribal people, Christians, Muslims, Sikhs, never against the middle class, upper-caste Hindus,' said Arundhati Roy in a July 2012 interview with *Outlook* magazine.

Geelani wrote in *The Oppressed Nation* (p. 3): 'Colonization, tyranny, violence, barbarism, expansionism and aggression are flourishing throughout the world. The vices have replaced human attributes of morality, kindness, honesty, trust, respect for rights, respect for freedom, justice, equality, and values of brotherhood.' He argues 'if Islam is given the opportunity to serve as a system of life for building the humanity, then rapid development and reformation of human society can be achieved. But it is tragic for the entire humanity that Islam is not being given the opportunity to work with its true and real features. The entire world is hostile to Islam and trying its best not to allow it a foothold anywhere in the world.' The animosity against Islam was confirmed by Philip Stephens in the *Financial Times* (1 June 2012): 'Democracy is all very well as long as it does not threaten Western interests. Elections are fine *except* when voters seem likely to embrace Islamists.' But there are also defenders of truth in the West. Concurring with Geelani's view historian William Dalrymple says: 'I don't believe Muslims are a problem and I don't think Islam is a threat.'[10]

The marriage ceremonies of Geelani's grandson and granddaughter were scheduled for 20 September 2011. But police maintained strict restrictions on his movements and denied him the opportunity to attend the ceremonies at his ancestral house in Sopore. On 6 April 2012, Geelani went to Baramulla, the north Kashmir district and, after offering Friday prayers, addressed a gathering. J&K Police later registered a case of attempted murder and stone pelting against the eighty-three-year-old Geelani in Baramulla Police Station! The FIR (No. 78/2012, dated 6 April 2012), states that Geelani was booked under sections 307/336/392/427/148/149/124-A153/332 of RPC, according to Station House Officer, Baramulla, Javaid Makhdoomi. Addressing a conference in New Delhi, Jamia Millia Islamia Vice Chancellor Najeeb Jung said the problem is: 'The loyalty of the state [J&K] was always suspected and, for the past six decades, no [Indian] government has sensitized mainstream India to the unique situation in there' (*Greater Kashmir*, 3 May 2012).

In the words of Martin Luther King Jr., 'Injustice anywhere is a threat to justice everywhere.' Geelani reminds Muslims of the well-known Prophetic hadith addressed to the Companion, Mu'adh ibn Jabal: 'In future there will be rulers who will decide your fate. If you obey them they will lead you astray. If you disobey them, they will put you to death. Mu'adh asked the Prophet: What should we do then? He replied: Do what the followers of Jesus Christ did. They were cleaved with saws and hanged. But they said: It is better to die while following the commands of God than to lead a life of disobedience to Him.'[11] Geelani's own advice to the emerging global Muslim leadership is:

1 Concrete and visibly effective steps should be taken to solve all regional, geographical and political disputes at global level – disputes like Palestine, Kashmir, Chechnya and others should be solved as a priority.

2 Muslim countries should strengthen their unity and increase their mutual cooperation so that they are able to exercise influence in the international arena to solve various problems. Their guiding principle on foreign affairs should be based on the Qur'anic teaching of 'cooperation for good and pious deeds and non-cooperation for crime and aggression'. They should not be guided or influenced by selfish national, economic or political interests.

3 In the light of the following verse: 'O Believers, stand out firmly for God as witnesses for fair dealing, and let not hatred of others make you swerve, do wrong and depart from justice. Be just; that is next to piety and fear of God. For God is well acquainted with all that you do' (al-Ma'idah 5: 8), enmity with any country or people should not prevent or deter Muslims from justice and fair dealing.[12]

While traitors are sooner or later identified and despised, due to his remarkable consistency, clarity and candor Geelani has earned respect of even his political foes. A top NC leader and current Member of Parliament Ghulam Nabi Ratanpuri confessed that his party's founder Sheikh Muhammad Abdullah was a 'man of flaws, failures and fallacies' and declared that 'Geelani is the tallest leader of 21st century' (*Greater Kashmir*, 1 March 2013).

APPENDIX

I CITE BELOW passages from official government commissions that, following investigation of communal riots between Muslims and Hindus, indicate conclusively the responsibility and role of militant Hindu groups in deliberately inciting such riots and atrocities against Muslims. The BJP is the political wing of RSS and has been leading the government in many provinces for the last two decades.

(1)   Here [there] was not only a failure of intelligence and culpable failure to suppress the outbreak of violence but (also) deliberate attempts to suppress the truth from the Commission, especially the active participation in the riots of some RSS and Jan Sangh leaders.

Report of the Justice Jagmohan Reddy Commission on the Ahmedabad riots of 1969

(2)   The organisation responsible for bringing communal tension in Bhiwandi to a pitch is the Rashtriya Utsav Mandal. The majority of the leaders and workers of the Rashtriya Utsav Mandal belonged to the Jan Sangh [the predecessor of the BJP] or were pro-Jan Sangh and the rest, apart from a few exceptions, belonged to the Shiv Sena.

Report of the Justice D. P. Madon Commission on the Bhiwandi, Jalgaon and Mahad riots of 1970

(3)   In Tellicherry the Hindus and Muslims were living as broth-
      ers for centuries. The 'Mopla riots' did not affect the cordial
      relationship that existed between the two communities in
      Tellicherry. It was only after the RSS and the Jan Sangh
      set up their units and began activities in Tellicherry that
      there came a change in the situation. Their anti-Muslim
      propaganda, its reaction on the Muslims who rallied round
      their communal organisation, the Muslim League which
      championed their cause, and the communal tension that
      followed prepared the background for their disturbances...
      That is what the rioters who attacked the house of Muham-
      mad asked him to do. 'If you want to save your life you
      should go round the house three times repeating the words,
      'Rama, Rama'. Muhammad did that. But you cannot expect
      the 70 million Muslims of India to do that as a condition
      for maintaining communal harmony in the country. This
      attitude of the RSS can only help to compel the Muslims to
      take shelter under their own communal organization.

      Report of the Justice Joseph Vithyathil Commission on the Tellicherry
      riots, 1971

(4)   The dispute on the route of the procession became sharp,
      and agitated reactions from a group of persons calling
      themselves the Sanyukt Bajrang Bali Akhara Samiti who
      systematically distributed pamphlets to heighten commu-
      nal feelings and had organisational links with the RSS. A
      call for the defiance of the authority and the administration
      when it refused permission for one of the routes led to a
      violent mob protesting and raising anti-Muslim slogans.
      Thereafter an incendiary leaflet doing the rounds of Jam-
      shedpur that is nothing short of an attempt to rouse the
      sentiments of Hindus to a high pitch and to distort events
      and show some actions as attacks on Hindus that appear
      to be part of a design. A survey had already established that
      all policemen, havaldars, home guards etc. were at heart
      ready to give support to them [the Hindu communalist
      organizations].

      Report of the Commission of Inquiry into the Communal Distur-
      bances at Jamshedpur, April 1979

(5) The RSS adopts a militant and aggressive attitude and sets itself up as the champion of what it considers to be the rights of Hindus against minorities. It has taken upon itself to teach the minorities their place and if they are not willing to learn their place, to teach them a lesson. The RSS methodology for provoking communal violence is: (a) rousing communal feelings in the majority community by the propaganda that Christians are not loyal citizens of this country; (b) deepening the fear in the majority community by a clever propaganda that the population of the minorities is increasing and that of the Hindus is decreasing; (c) infiltrating into the administration and inducing the members of the civil and police services by adopting and developing communal attitudes; (d) training young people of the majority community in the use of weapons like daggers, swords and spears; (e) spreading rumours to widen the communal cleavage and deepen communal feelings by giving a communal colour to any trivial incident.

Report of the Justice Venugopal Commission on Kanyakumari riots between Hindus and Christians, 1982

(6) Even after it became apparent that the leaders of the Shiv Sena were active in stoking the fire of the communal riots, the police dragged their feet on the facile and exaggerated assumption that if such leaders were arrested the communal situation would further flare up, or to put it in the words of then Chief Minister [of Congress], Sudhakarrao Naik, 'Bombay would burn'; not that Bombay did not burn otherwise.

Report of the Justice B. N. Srikrishna Commission on the Mumbai riots of 1992–3

ENDNOTES

PREFACE

1. Mandela, *Long Walk to Freedom* (1994), 567.
2. Ibid., 748.
3. http://www.washingtonpost.com/wp-srv/politics/daily/may98/goldwaterspeech.htm.
4. Siddhartha Vardarajan (ed.), *Gujarat: the Making of a Tragedy* (2002), 29.
5. http://sharmilasays.wordpress.com/2011/01/10/lets-not-use-the-s-word-by-pritish-nandy/.
6. Ram Puniyani, *Malegaon to Ajmer: the Trail of Terror* (2010).

1. THE DISPUTE

1. Source: http://www.google.com.sa/imgres?q=Geographical+map+of+Jammu+and+Kashmir&hl=en&safe=active&tbo=d&tbm=isch&tbnid=3F4xyT5FFIXGVM:&imgrefurl=http://newsletter.flatworldknowledge.com/bookhub/reader/10997%3Fe%3Dberglee_1.0-ch09_s02&docid=4CI89kYXiSQS5M&imgurl=http://images.flatworldknowledge.com/berglee/berglee-fig09_008.jpg&w=974&h=721&ei=Hy0bUd3rENC10QXCu4CYAQ&zoom=1&iact=hc&vpx=553&vpy=456&dur=9687&hovh=193&hovw=261&tx=154&ty=119&sig=105581309692700742125&page=1&tbnh=124&tbnw=151&start=0&ndsp=34&ved=1t:429,r:23,s:0,i:152&biw=1280&bih=823.
2. http://www.rediff.com/news/2007/jan/09inter.htm

3. Ravi Nanda, *Kashmir and Indo-Pak Relations* (2001), 21.
4. Tariq Ali, '*Bitter Chill of Winter*', *London Review of Books* (2011), 18-27.
5. R. Dossani and H.S. Rowan, *Prospects for Peace in South Asia* (2005), 113.
6. Interviewed by Yoginder Sikand, November, 2010.
7. http://tehelka.com/nehru-didnt-want-to-publicise-the-poonch-rebellion-because- it-would-have-strengthened-pakistans-case/.
8. http://www.rediff.com/news/2007/jan/09inter.htm
9. http://www.countercurrents.org/choudhry030510.htm
10. Geelani, S.A. (November, 2001; p. 27)
11. Ravi Nanda, *Kashmir and Indo-Pak Relations* (2001), 68.
12. Mandela, *Long Walk to Freedom*, 443.
13. Lee Kuan Yew, *From Third World to First* (2006), 541.
14. Alija Izetbegovic, *Inescapable Questions* (2003), 293, 370.
15. KAC E-newsletter, June 2011.
16. http://jkann.blogspot.com/2011/12/new-delhi-conspiring-to-alter-j.html
17. KAC E-newsletter, April 2012.
18. Ibid.
19. B. Howard Schaffer, *The Limits of Influence: America's Role in Kashmir* (2009), 153.
20. http://www.brookings.edu/~/media/press/books/2007/11/fourcrisesandapeaceprocess/four crisesandapeaceprocess_chapter.pdf
21. *The Hindu* (28 November 2010):http://www.thehindu.com/news/national/article918002.ece. A must read to fully grasp the promises and pledges of Indian leaders to Kashmiris
22. http://www.aljazeera.com/indepth/spotlight/kashmirtheforgottenconflict/2011/07/2011726122116677591.html.
23. See Surjit Singh, *From Punjab to New York: A Reflective Journey* (1999), 240.
24. *Economic & Political Weekly*, 31 March 1990.
25. See US government archive at: *foreignaffairs.house.gov/news/blog/?refine=subcommittee*.
26. Tavleen Singh, *Kashmir: A Tragedy of Errors* (1995), 196.
27. *Ibid.*, p.xi.
28. *Ibid.*, p. xii.
29. See his (8 April 2000) interview at: http://www.rediff.com/news/2000/apr/08inter.htm.
30. Tahir Amin, *Mass Resistance in Kashmir: Origin, Evolution and Options* (1995), 145.
31. http://www.aljazeera.com/indepth/features/2011/07/20117552852830932.html .
32. http://tehelka.com/nehru-didnt-want-to-publicise-the-poonch-rebellion-because- it-would-have-strengthened-pakistans-case/

2. A Lifeline of Resistance

1. *Greater Kashmir* (15 May 2012)
2. Greater Kashmir (15 May 2012)
3. Mandela, *Long Walk to Freedom*, 159.
4. The Constitution of Jama'at-i-Islami (www.jamaat.org)
5. *Tafheemat* (Urdu), Part III, MMI Publications, New Delhi, 363.
6. Geelani, *Oppressed Nation*, 14.
7. Tavleen Singh, *Kashmir*, 110.
8. Geelani, *Oppressed Nation*, 9.
9. Tavleen Singh, *Kashmir*, xvi-xvii.
10. Geelani, *Oppressed Nation*, 22.
11. Cited in an article by Rekha Choudhary, *The Economic and Political Weekly*, 22 July 2000.
12. Ravi Nanda, *Kashmir and Indo-Pak Relations*, 84-85.
13. Geelani, *Oppressed Nation*, 36.
14. http://www.scribd.com/doc/17779877/A-Historical-Survey-of-J-K .
15. Manoj Joshi, *The Lost Rebellion: Kashmir in the Nineties* (1999), 30.
16. Ravi Nanda, *Kashmir and Indo-Pak Relations* (2001), 165.
17. Addressing a seminar in Srinagar (December 2007).

3. Neighbouring Peoples

1. Geelani, *11 September 2001: What Should Be Done?* (2001), 27.
2. Geelani, *Oppressed Nation*, 71.
3. See rediff.com interview (6 May 2002): http://www.rediff.com/news/2002/may/06inter.htm. See also: *Rape and Molestation: A Weapon of War in Kashmir* (10 March 1998).
4. Geelani, *11 September 2001*, 19-54 summarized and edited. The length of this extract is justified as it illustrates how clearly (and Islamically) Geelani thinks.
5. See *ibid.*, 33-6.
6. In point of fact, the US focus and forces were moving to Iraq at this time.
7. Geelani, *11 September 2001*, 51.
8. Geelani, *Oppressed Nation*, 86.
9. *International Socialist Review*: http://www.isreview.org/issues/77/featint-arundhatiroy.shtml.
10. Geelani, *Oppressed Nation*, 87.
11. http://syedalishahgeelani.blogspot.com/ (29 September 2009)
12. Geelani, *11 September 2001*, 50.
13. Nanda, *Kashmir and Indo-Pak Relations*, 131.

14. Mandela, *Long Walk to Freedom*, 153.
15. http://www.rediff.com/news/slide-show/slide-show-1-is-it-the-end-of-the-road-for-kayani/20110618.htm
16. http://kashmirwantsfreedom.wordpress.com/geelani/
17. *Extremist Movements and their Threats to the United States* (2 November 1999).
18. See his interview at: http://www.cfr.org/pakistan/pakistans-road-disintegration/p23744.
19. Geelani, *11 September 2001*, 50.
20. Izetbegovic, *Inescapable Questions*, 25.
21. Geelani, *Oppressed Nation*, 87.
22. Ibid., 64.
23. Ibid., 55.
24. Ibid., 56.
25. Ibid.
26. *International Socialist Review*: http://www.isreview.org/issues/77/featint-arundhatiroy.shtml.
27. Ravi Nanda, *Kashmir and Indo-Pak Relations*, 106.
28. http://tehelka.com/muslims-they-dont-deserve-to-live - A must read to understand what happened in Gujarat under Narendra Modi.
29. Siddartha Vardharajan, *Gujarat: the Making of a Tragedy*, 8.
30. Ibid., 9.
31. Ibid., 14.
32. He is accused of leading a mob that set fire to the houses of some forty families in Ahmedabad's Muslim-dominated Shahpur area, was never charged. Even after a decade of leading that carnage, he is a free bird! (AFP Photo: http://www.hindustantimes.com/photos-news/Photos-India/decadesincegodhra/Article4.aspx).
33. Sarmila Bose, *Dead Reckoning: Memories of the 1971 Bangladesh War* (2011: 181).
34. http://tehelka.com/muslims-they-dont-deserve-to-live - A must read to understand what happened in Gujarat under Narendra Modi.
35. http://www.rediff.com/news/slide-show/slide-show-1-inside-story-modi-s-game-plan-for-the-top-post-in-2014/20130307.htm#3
36. http://www.project-syndicate.org/commentary/india-s-corruption-curse
37. http://tehelka.com/too-many-spooks-spoil-the-case-2/
38. For details on the state of indian Muslims, see http://tehelka.com/the-muslim-question-stories-of-false-terror/
39. I.e. liable to an 'encounter', the term usually applied in India to incidents (real or faked) when security forces kill those suspected of taking part in or assisting illegal activity.
40. See his 21 March 2011 article at: http://www.countercurrents.org/alam210311.htm

4. Imprisonment and Writings

1. Mandela, *Long Walk to Freedom*, 212.
2. Ibid., 463.
3. Ibid., 381.
4. *Economic and Political Weekly*, January 20, 2001.
5. Ibid.
6. Geelani, *Nava-i Hurriyat* (1992), 92–3.
7. Cited by Yoginder Sikand in his *Economic & Political Weekly* article, 20 January 2001.
8. Geelani, *Hijrat awr Shahadat* (July 1998), 3–4, Tulu Publications, Srinagar, J&K.
9. Geelani, *Maslay ka hal* (The Solution to the Dispute), (1992).
10. Geelani, *Oppressed Nation,* 41.
11. Geelani, *Maqtal say vaapsi,* Srinagar, n.d.
12. Mandela, *Long Walk to Freedom,* 420.
13. Ibid., 394.

5. Kashmir's Pandits And Its Integrity

1. Tavleen Singh, *Kashmir: A Tragedy of Errors,* 54.
2. Manoj Joshi, *The Lost Rebellion: Kashmir in the Nineties* (1999), 66.
3. Tavleen Singh, *Kashmir: A Tragedy of Errors,* 148.
4. Siddhartha Vardarajan, *Gujarat,* 33.
5. *Wounded Valley Shattered Souls.* 6th Indian Peoples' Tribunal Report (1997), Bombay. Also See Aparna Rao, *A Tortuous Search for Justice: Notes on the Kashmir Conflict, Himalayan Research Bulletin* XVIV (I) 1999.
6. http://news.rediff.com/slide-show/2010/aug/19/slide-show-1-yoginder-sikand-reads-the-kashmiri-sentiment.htm#7.
7. *Greater Kashmir*, 18 April 2011

6. Human Wrongs

1. Mandela, *Long Walk to Freedom*, 622.
2. http://www.canadafreepress.com/2007/mir010607.htm
3. Tavleen Singh, *Kashmir: A Tragedy of Errors*, 132.
4. Ibid.
5. Manoj Joshi, *The Lost Rebellion*, 116.
6. Ibid, 121.
7. Arjun Ray, *Psychology of Militancy* (1997), 83.
8. Manoj Joshi, *The Lost Rebellion*, 209–10.

9. Ibid., 416–17.
10. Mandela, *Long Walk to Freedom*, 644.
11. Manoj Joshi, *The Lost Rebellion*, 421.
12. Cited in *Military Intervention and Secession in South Asia* (2007), 84.
13. Tavleen Singh, *Kashmir: A Tragedy of Errors*, xii.
14. Arjun Ray, *Psychology of Militancy*, 150–2.
15. Izetbegovic, *Inescapable Questions*, 42.
16. Arjun Ray, *Psychology of Militancy*, 197–8.
17. http://www.satp.org/satporgtp/countries/india/states/jandk/terrorist_outfits/Hurriyat_tl.htm.
18. Arjun Ray, *Psychology of Militancy*, 20.
19. *Greater Kashmir*, 13 May 2001; also: http://hindu.com/2001/05/11/stories/01110003.htm.
20. Geelani, *11 September 2001*, 71.
21. Manoj Joshi, *The Lost Rebellion*, 235.
22. Arjun Ray, *Psychology of Militancy*, 148.
23. Geelani gave a full breakdown of land taken up by the occuping forces: 14,420 kanals in frontier district of Kupwara where there are 92 camps, in Varmul district 31,789 kanals and 121 camps, in district Islamabad 6,874 kanals and 32 camps, in district Kulgam 1,215 kanals and 24 camps, in district Shopain 3,108 kanals and 37 camps, in district Budgam 19,562 kanals and 56 camps, in district Pulwama 18,785 kanals and 52 camps, in district Srinagar 27,000 kanals and 51 camps, in district Ganderbal 14690 kanals and 56 camps, in district Doda 14,523 kanals and 40 camps, in district Rajouri Poonch 30,898 kanals and 60 camps, in district Jammu 1,30,074 kanals, in district Kathua 21,620 kanals, in district Udhampur 30,000 kanals and in district Leh 2,26,539 kanals.
24. Syed Ali Geelani, 'A Dream of Independent Kashmir', Facebook [website], 10 December 2010, https://m.facebook.com/story.php?story_fbid=177668112253051&id=135310683180621.
25. Izetbegovic, *Inescapable Questions*, 194.
26. Tavleen Singh, *Kashmir: A Tragedy of Errors*, 149.
27. Arjun Ray, *Psychology of Militancy*, 68.
28. Cited in *Hindustan Times*, 24 May 2011.

7. Terrorists or Freedom Fighters?

1. http://en.wikipedia.org/wiki/Reuters.
2. Cited in *Hindustan Times*, 5 September 2007.
3. Mandela, *Long Walk to Freedom*, 277.
4. www.chomsky.info/articles/199112--02.htm.

5. Ian S. Wood, *British History in Perspective: Churchill* (2000), 163-4.
6. Arjun Ray, *The Psychology of Militancy*, 27.
7. Geelani, *11 September 2001.*
8. See his article *Terrorized by 'War on Terror'* in *The Washington Post* (25 March 2007).
9. http://syedalishahgeelani.blogspot.com/2009/09/wiki-knowledge-bank-of-world-comments.html.
10. *International Socialist Review* (May–June 2011).
11. http://www.loonwatch.com/2010/01/terrorism-in-europe/
12. Source: *Times of India*, 15 September 2013.
13. Ibid.

8. Insurgency And Counter-Insurgency

1. Mandela, *Long Walk to Freedom*, 338.
2. *Canada Free Press* (6 January 2007): http://www.canadafreepress.com/2007/mir010607.htm.
3. Cited in Yoginder Sikand, *Kashmiri Muslim Perspective on Inter-Religious Dialogue* (2000), 16.
4. Tavleen Singh, *Kashmir: A Tragedy of Errors*, 38.
5. Mandela, *Long Walk to Freedom*, 322.
6. Manoj Joshi, *The Lost Rebellion*, 35.
7. Geelani, *Oppressed Nation*, 10.
8. Ibid., 72.
9. See his interview of 9 January 2007 at: http://www.rediff.com/news/2007/jan/09inter.htm.
10. See Rajya Sabha Speeches at: http://rajyasabha.nic.in/rsnew/publication_electronic.
11. See his interview of 9 January 2007 at: http://www.rediff.com/news/2007/jan/09inter.htm.
12. Manoj Joshi, *The Lost Rebellion*, 141.
13. Geelani, *Oppressed Nation*, 25. Also see *Wular Kinaray* I and II, Millat Publications, Srinagar, J&K.
14. See full report on: http://www.aljazeera.com/indepth/features/2011/04/201141710204769839.html
15. http://www.pvchr.net/2012/07/saga-of-torture-in-kashmir.html.
16. https://bloodiedrivers.wordpress.com/page/4/
17. http://www.jammu-kashmir.com/archives/archives1998/98december07b.html.
18. See full report on: http://www.aljazeera.com/indepth/opinion/2011/03/201132512818508559.html
19. Adil Salahi, *Muhammad: Man and Prophet* (1995), 362.

20. 9 January 2007: http://www.rediff.com/news/2007/jan/09inter.htm.
21. Geelani, *Oppressed Nation*, 12.
22. http://www.satp.org/satporgtp/countries/india/states/jandk/timeline/index.htm.
23. See his 8 April 2000 Rediff interview at: http://www.rediff.com/news/2000/apr/08inter.htm
24. Ravi Nanda, *Kashmir and Indo-Pak Relations*, 134.
25. Tavleen Singh, *Kashmir: A Tragedy of Errors*, 175.
26. 6 May 2002: http://www.rediff.com/news/2002/may/06inter.htm.
27. Arjun Ray, *Psychology of Militancy*, 167.

9. ELECTIONS AND THE PEACE PROCESS

1. Manoj Joshi, *The Lost Rebellion*, 32.
2. Manoj Joshi, *The Lost Rebellion*, 288.
3. United Jihad Council is an umbrella organization of armed militants headed by Salahuddin.
4. Geelani, *11 September 2001*, 68.
5. Geelani, *Oppressed Nation*, 38.
6. Izetbegovic, *Inescapable Questions*, 186.
7. Mandela, *Long Walk to Freedom*, 626.
8. Ibid., 641.
9. Ibid., 691, 694.
10. Geelani, *Kargil: A Short Review* (undated), 16.
11. *MidDay*, 22 January 2004; *The Age*, 24 January 2004.
12. Mandela, *Long Walk to Freedom*, 722.
13. In an interview with *The Newsline* (15 November 2004).
14. Ibid.
15. See Geelani's 8 April 2000 interview at: http://www.rediff.com/news/2000/apr/08inter.htm
16. See rediff.com interview (6 May 2002) at: http://www.rediff.com/news/2002/may/06inter.htm.
17. Geelani, *Kargil: A Short Review*, 30.
18. http://kashmirwantsfreedom.wordpress.com/geelani/.
19. Tavleen Singh, *Kashmir: A Tragedy of Errors*, 189.
20. See 'Kashmir's forgotten plebiscite' at: http://news.bbc.co.uk/2/hi/south_asia/1766582.stm.
21. In the 8 April 2000 interview with Rediff: http://www.rediff.com/news/2000/apr/08inter.htm.
22. Mandela, *Long Walk to Freedom*, 574.
23. http://ghazwathulhind.blogspot.com/2007/01/interview-with-hizb-chief-syed.html.

10. The Kargil Fiasco

1. Prem Mahadevan, (*No. 29, 2011*); KW Publications Pvt Ltd, New Delhi, 11.
2. Associated Press (26 April 2008): See full report at: http://www.ynetnews.com/articles/0,7340,L-3536087,00.html
3. Adil Salahi, *Muhammad: Man and Prophet*, 597.
4. Geelani, *Kargil: A Short Review*, 28–30.
5. Adil Salahi, *Muhammad: Man and Prophet*, 364.
6. 'A vast majority of militants are Kashmiris. Guest [foreign] militants constitute about 15 percent of the total militant population in J&K': Arjun Ray, *Psychology of Militancy*, 22.
7. Geelani, *Kargil: A Short Review*, 30–1.
8. http://forums.bharat-rakshak.com/viewtopic.php?f=1&t=6078&start=2760.

11. Ceasefire

1. Adil Salahi, *Muhammad: Man and Prophet*, 359.
2. Ibid., 358.
3. Ravi Nanda, *Kashmir and Indo-Pak Relations*, 177.
4. See the Indian newspaper *Daily News & Analysis (DNA)*, 11 June 2012.
5. Please read Shubh Mathur's brilliant article http://www.guernicamag.com/features/impunity-in-india/.

12. The Hurriyat Split and Efforts Towards Unity

1. Joshi, Manoj, *The Lost Rebellion*, 216.
2. Geelani, *Oppressed Nation*, 8.
3. Mandela, *Long Walk to Freedom*, 126.
4. Joshi, Manoj, *The Lost Rebellion*, 219.
5. See rediff.com interview (6 May 2002): http://www.rediff.com/news/2002/may/06inter.htm.
6. Mandela, *Long Walk to Freedom*, 464.
7. Adil Salahi, *Muhammad: Man and Prophet*, 408.

13. AILING BUT NOT CAVING IN

1. Izetbegovic, *Inescapable Questions*, 44.
2. Mandela, *Long Walk to Freedom*, 119.

14. A BILATERAL OR INTERNATIONAL ISSUE?

1. US Department of State, Office of the Historian. See full memo at: http://history.state.gov/historicaldocuments/frus1961-63v19/d190.
2. Manoj Joshi, *The Lost Rebellion*, 317.
3. Geelani, *Oppressed Nation*, 96.
4. Izetbegovic, *Inescapable Questions*, 437.
5. h t t p : / / w w w . a l j a z e e r a . c o m / i n d e p t h / o p i n i on/2012/02/20122241944465992.html.
6. Ravi Nanda, *Kashmir and Indo-Pak Relations*, 192.
7. Michael Shank, 'Chomsky on India-Pakistan Relations', *Foreign Policy in Focus* (22 May 2007, Washington DC).
8. For details see Zbigniew Brezinski, *The Grand Chessboard* (1997).
9. Geelani, *11 September 2001*, 34.
10. Izetbegovic, *Inescapable Questions*, 255.
11. See his 16 January 2013 interview at: http://www.rediff.com/news/slide-show/slide-show-1-i-dont-believe-muslims-are-problem-and-islam-a-threat/20130116.htm.
12. Samuel P. Huntington, *The Clash of Civilizations and the Remaking of World Order* (1996), 51.
13. http://www.goodreads.com/quotes/142210-the-west-won-the-world-not-by-the-superiority-
14. Izetbegovic, *Inescapable Questions*, 442.
15. On 12 October 2004 in the New Zealand Parliament. See: http://www.parliament.nz/en-NZ/PB/Debates/Debates/Daily/6/a/7/47HansD_20041012-Volume-620-Week-70-Tuesday-12-October-2004.htm.
16. Geelani, *11 September 2001*, 52.
17. Manoj Joshi, *The Lost Rebellion*, 330.
18. In a 2010 interview to Aljazeera.
19. *Indian Express*, 16 May 2011; *Greater Kashmir*, 17 May 2011.
20. Ravi Nanda, *Kashmir and Indo-Pak Relations*, 196.
21. *Avoiding Water Wars: Water Scarcity and Central Asia's Growing Importance for Stability in Afghanistan and Pakistan* (22 February 2011). It is available at: http://www.fdsys.gpo.gov.
22. http://www.biyokulule.com/view_content.php?articleid=4178.

23. Bharat Verma and Manvendra Singh (eds.), *KASHMIR: The Troubled Frontiers* (1994).
24. Geelani, *11 September 2001*, 33–7.
25. *International Socialist Review* (May–June 2011): http://www.isreview. org/issues/77/featint-arundhatiroy.shtml.

15. THE BOTTOM LINE

1. Tavleen Singh, *Kashmir: A Tragedy of Errors*, 7.
2. Izetbegovic, *Inescapable Questions*, 278.
3. Tahir Amin, *Mass Resistance in Kashmir: Origin, Evolution & Options* (1995), 16.
4. Ravi Nanda, *Kashmir and Indo-Pak Relations*, 216.
5. Izetbegovic, *Inescapable Questions*, 346, 357.
6. *Times of India*, 17 August 2008; and http://archives.dawn.com/ archives/1793.
7. *Caught gambling in the Washington casino* (27 July 2011); http://www. aljazeera.com/indepth/opinion/2011/07/201172672822527671. html.

16. NOT THE END

1. http://wikileaks.org/gifiles/docs/5237164_-ct-ct-morning-sweep-290711-.html.
2. http://news.oneindia.in/2012/05/09/terror-war-us-prohibits-aid-to-pak-till-it-cooperates-997760.html.
3. http://www.rediff.com/news/special/special-jihadist-pakistan-is-indias-worst-nightmare-says-bruce-riedel/20110119.htm.
4. http://www.rediff.com/news/slide-show/slide-show-1-interview-hindus-muslims-are-separate-nations-geelani/20101101.htm.
5. http://forums.bharat-rakshak.com/viewtopic.php?f=1&t=5419&start=240.
6. *India Today*, 25 April 2012. See full report at: http://indiatoday. intoday.in/story/india-pak-war-may-cause-nuclear-famine/1/185953. html.
7. http://www.tehelka.com/nehru-didnt-want-to-publicise-the-poonch-rebellion-because-   it-would-have-strengthened-pakistans-case/.
8. http://www.aljazeera.com/indepth/features/2013/02/ 2013219121326666148.html

9. http://www.aljazeera.com/indepth/features/2013/03/20133121268301751.html
10. See his 16 January 2013 interview on Rediff.com.
11. Geelani, *Oppressed Nation*, 69.
12. Geelani, *11 September 2001*, 33–4.

REFERENCES

Amin, Tahir (1995), *Mass Resistance in Kashmir: Origin, Evolution & Options* (Leicester, UK: The Islamic Foundation).

Bose, Sarmila (2011), *Dead Reckoning: Memories of the 1971 Bangladesh War* (London: Hurst & Company).

Brezinski, Zbignew (1997), *The Grant Chessboard* (New York: Basic Books).

Geelani, S. A. (1992), *Maslay ka hal* (Sringar: Tulu Publications).

Geelani, S. A. (1993), *Rudad-e Qafas* (Urdu) (Srinagar: Al Huda Publishing House).

Geelani, S. A. (July, 1998), *Hijrat aur Shahadat* Tulu Publications, Srinagar, J&K).

Geelani, S. A. (Nov. 2001), *The Oppressed Nation: People of Jammu & Kashmir* (Sringar: Tulu Publications).

Geelani, S. A. (n.d.), *Maqtal say vaapsi* (Srinagar).

Geelani, S. A.; (Dec. 2001), *11 September 2001: What Should be Done?* (Sringar: Tulu Publications).

Geelani, S. A. (Undated), *Kargil: A Short Review* (Srinagar: Tulu Publications).

International Commission of Jurists, Geneva (1995), *Mission Report on Human Rights.*

Izetbegovic, Alija (2003), *Inescapable Questions* (Leicester, UK: The Islamic Foundation).

Joshi, Manoj (1999), *The Lost Rebellion: Kashmir in the Nineties* (Penguine Books, India).

Kashmir Calling, 1 (Sep.–Oct. 2001) (Srinagar: Human Rights Wing of Islamic Students League).

Lee Kuan Yew (2006), *From Third World to First: The Singapore Story: 1965–2000* (PLACE: Marshall Cavendish Editions).

Mahadevan, Prem (2011), (New Delhi: K.W. Publications Ltd.).

Mandela, Nelson (1994), *Long Walk to Freedom* (New York: Little Brown and Company).

Nanda, Ravi Col. (2001), *Kashmir and Indo-Pak relations* (New Delhi: Lancer's Books).

Puniyami, Ram (2010), *Malegaon to Ajmer: the Trail of Terror* (Mumbai: Institue for Peace Studies and Conflict Resolution).

Rape and Molestation: A Weapon of War in Kashmir (10 March 1998). (Srinagar Institute of Kashmir Studies.)

Ray, Arjun Maj.-Gen. (1997), *Psychology of Militancy* (New Delhi: Manas Publications).

Salahi, Adil (1995), *Muhammad: Man and Prophet* (Leicester, UK: The Islamic Foundation).

Sawhney, Karan R. (ed.) (2001), *How Far Can Vajpayee and Musharraf Go?* (New Delhi: Peace Publications).

Schofield, Victoria (2000), *Kashmir in Conflict* (London: I.B. Tauris).

Sikand, Yoginder (2000), *The Islamic Movement and Political Challenge* (Bangalore).

Sikand, Yoginder (May 2000), *Kashmiri Muslim Perspective on Inter-Religious Dialogue* (Bangalore).

Sikand, Yoginder (July 2000), *Islam and the Kashmiri Struggle – The Writings of Syed Ali Shah Geelani* (Bangalore).

Singh, Tavleen (1996), *Kashmir: A Tragedy of Errors* (Penguin: India).

Vardarajan, Siddhartha (ed.) (2002), *Gujarat: The Making of a Tragedy* (Penguin Books, India).

Verma, Bharat and Manvendra Singh, (eds.), *KASHMIR: The Troubled Frontiers* (New Delhi: Lancer Publications Ltd., 1994)

Wood, Ian (2000); *British History in Perspective: Churchill*; MacMillan Press Ltd, UK.

ALSO MENTIONED IN THE BOOK.

Avoiding Water Wars: Water Scarcity and Central Asia's Growing Importance for Stability in Afghanistan and Pakistan (22 February 2011)

Extremist Movements and their Threats to the United States (2 November 1999) (Washington, DC: US Government Printing Office)

Military Intervention and Secession in South Asia, Praeger Security International (2007).

IMAGE CREDITS

INDEX